Paul Johnson, former editor of the *New Statesman,* is among Britain's foremost writers on politics and current affairs. His considerable reputation as an historian has been established through such highly acclaimed works as his biography of Elizabeth I, *A History of Christianity,* and *The Offshore Islanders.* A frequent TV and radio broadcaster, Paul Johnson is also a regular contributor to newspapers and journals on a wide range of subjects.

S0-AYW-521

Paul Johnson

Ireland

A History from the Twelfth Century to the Present Day

A PANTHER BOOK

GRANADA
London Toronto Sydney New York

Published by Granada Publishing Limited in 1981

ISBN 0 586 05453 7

First published in Great Britain by
Eyre Methuen Ltd 1980 under the title *Ireland: Land of Troubles*
Copyright © Paul Johnson 1980

Granada Publishing Limited
Frogmore, St Albans, Herts AL2 2NF
and
36 Golden Square, London W1R 4AH
866 United Nations Plaza, New York, NY 10017, USA
117 York Street, Sydney, NSW 2000, Australia
100 Skyway Avenue, Rexdale, Ontario, M9W 3A6, Canada
61 Beach Road, Auckland, New Zealand

Printed and bound in Great Britain
by Cox and Wyman Ltd, Reading
Phototypesetting by Grainger Typesetters Ltd, Southend
Set in Baskerville

Granada ®
Granada Publishing ®

Contents

Illustrations

MAPS

Acknowledgement and thanks for permission to reproduce the illustrations are due to Aerofilms Ltd for plates 1 and 2; to the Irish Tourist Board for plate 11; to the British Library for plate 3; to the National Portrait Gallery for plates 4a, 4b and 5b; to the National Gallery of Ireland for plate 5a; to the National Library of Ireland for plates 6, 8, 14a, 14b and 14c; to the Mansell Collection for plates 9a, 9b, 10a, 10b and 12; to Punch Publications Ltd for plates 13a and 13b; to the BBC Hulton Picture Library for plates 15, 16b, 17b, 18a and 18b; to Gael-Linn for plate 16a; and to J. Cashman, Dublin, for plate 17a; plates 19–20b were taken from David Barzilay's *The British Army in Ulster*, Vols 1, 2 and 3 (Century Books). The maps were drawn by Neil Hyslop. Map 2 was taken from Thomas Pakenham's *The Year of Liberty* (Hodder and Stoughton) and map 3 from *Report of the Irish Boundary Commission* 1925 (Irish University Press).

Too long a sacrifice
Can make a stone of the heart.
O when may it suffice?
William Butler Yeats

TO

TOM CASSIDY

Entrepreneur and Master of Hounds

CHAPTER 1

Gaelic Ireland and the English Pale

The English presence in Ireland arose from the failure of Irish society to develop the institution of monarchy. The Irish, of course, had kingship; too much of it, indeed. The chief kings were those who held Meath and Leinster, Munster, Connaught and Ulster; but between the fifth and twelfth centuries, with a population which never exceeded 500,000, Ireland had about 150 kings at any given date, each ruling over a *tuath* or tribal kingdom. A *chanson de geste* describing the Anglo-Norman invasion of the twelfth century says

> En yrland event reis plusur
> Cum alures erent les cunturs

('In Ireland there were as many kings as counts elsewhere').[1] The twelfth-century English chronicler William of Newburgh, in his *Historia Rerum Anglicanum*, says that Ireland at the time of the invasion was like Britain in times of old.[2] By this he meant that the Irish, like the Saxons with their *bretwalda*, had the notion of an over-king, which they called a high king. But whereas the Bretwalda was developed by the royal house of Wessex into a national monarchy, which the Norman kings of England inherited, the Irish high kingship at no stage implied monarchy. Even Brian Boru, who destroyed the Norse tyranny of the ninth and tenth centuries, and was acknowledged as high king by his peers between 1002 and his death in battle in 1014, never exercised governmental authority over the whole of Ireland. In Ireland, the high king reigned but did not rule. The concept of monarchy required a radical revolution which in highly conservative Irish society could only be brought about by foreign intervention.[3] Such intervention was inspired by the modernizing and reforming spirit of the Church of Rome. The Hildebrandine reforms, called after their progenitor Archdeaçon Hildebrand, later Pope Gregory VII, spread over Western Europe in the closing decades of the eleventh century. Pope Gregory sanctioned the Norman conquest of England by William I, who carried with him the credentials of a crusader and a papal command to reform the English church, regarded by Rome as corrupt, heretical and schismatic. This William did, under his great Archbishop of Canterbury Lanfranc; and Norman barons also took the Hildebrandine programme to Scotland (under Queen Margaret) and to Wales. In every case these ecclesiastical reforms were accompanied by conquest and settlement. It was almost inevitable that the same pattern should be repeated in Ireland.

The essence of the papal reform was the establishment of strong bishoprics in the principal towns and cities, linked to Rome by a regular chain of command underwritten by canon law. In practice such reforms could only be achieved with the cooperation of powerful, centralizing monarchs. There was no possibility of such a monarchy evolving in native Ireland. There, kings were not merely myriad but limited in sovereignty by customary law guarded by a class of professional law-minders or *brehons*. The kings could not change the law: they could only interpret it. The bishops were mere functionaries of rural monasteries, under abbots drawn from the ranks of local ruling families. In practice, then, the many Irish communities were ruled not as monarchies but as triarchies, the law giving equal status to kings, chief *brehons* and abbots.[4] Canon law was received only in so far as the abbots permitted it, and there were innumerable irregularities. Irish laws, for instance, accepted eight forms of marriage and permitted divorce and concubinage.[5]

There were, however, modern-minded Irish churchmen who favoured reforms, chiefly in the Norse trading settlements established at Dublin, Waterford, Wexford, Cork and Limerick. These were the only towns in Ireland, largely inhabited by people of Norse descent – Ostmen, as the Irish called them. Their bishops sought to regularize themselves with Rome and to promote the reforms. Thus Patrick, chosen Bishop of Dublin in 1075, travelled to Canterbury, was consecrated by Lanfranc and swore obedience to him as Primate, and brought back with him a letter to the high king, Turloch O'Brien, asking him to reform abuses in the church. Thereafter, bishops from the Ostmen towns usually slipped over to England for consecration, and wrote letters to Rome complaining bitterly of the state of the church in the rest of Ireland: the absence of a single, proper ritual, and of canonical marriage, the non-observance of clerical celibacy, the failure to pay tithes, and the secular control of church appointments. Church reform and strong government went together, and it is notable that reforming bishops were supported by those Irish kings who sought to make the high kingship a reality. Thus Turloch More O'Connor, king of Connaught and high king in 1119–56, tried to centralize the reform, and place it firmly in an Irish national context, by cutting the links with Canterbury and holding a synod at Kells in 1152.[6]

The synod, however, seems to have been a failure, and the death of Turloch in 1156 led to a period of secular confusion, of marching and countermarching until all Ireland, as the annalist put it, became 'a trembling sod'.[7] In 1154 an English monk from St Albans, Nicholas Brakespear, became Pope as Adrian IV, and revived the Hildebrandine programme. The same year Henry II was universally acknowledged King of England, thus ending the anarchy of King Stephen's reign, and immediately set about a vigorous process of centralization. It was natural, then, that Pope Adrian should turn to Henry, the strongest monarch in Western Europe, to carry through the reforming programme in Ireland, though it is likely that the initiative came in the first place from Archbishop Theodore of Canterbury, who had lost his authority over the bishops in the Ostmen towns.[8] Probably in

1155, Adrian issued a Bull, *Laudabiliter*, giving Henry authority to enter Ireland:

> Laudably and profitably does Your Majesty contemplate spreading the glory of your name on earth . . . [whereas] you have expressed to us your desire to enter the island of Ireland in order to subject its people to law and to root out from them the weeds of vice. . . . We, therefore, meeting your pious and laudable desire with due favour and according a gracious assent to your petition, do hereby declare our will and pleasure that, with a view to enlarging the boundaries of the church, restraining the downward course of vice, correcting evil customs and planting virtue, and for the increase of the Christian religion, you shall enter that island and execute whatever may tend to the honour of God and the welfare of the land; and also that the people of that land shall receive you with honour and revere you as their lord. . . .[9]

The text of *Laudabiliter* does not survive in the papal archives and we have it only through the twelfth-century *Expugnatio Hibernica (The Conquest of Ireland)* written by the Welsh cleric Giraldus Cambrensis, and which is anti-Irish in tone.[10] At one time Irish nationalist historians questioned its authenticity, but modern scholarship has resolved any reasonable doubts.[11] The Bull was probably brought to England by the great clerical scholar John of Salisbury, who (writing in 1159) says that Adrian 'sent by me to the King a golden ring, adorned with a fine emerald, in token of his investiture with the government of Ireland'.[12] According to one authority, the issue was debated at Henry's council in 1155, but the King declined to take on any more responsibilities at present.[13]

What prompted Henry's intervention, fifteen years later, was the need to control his own feudatories. Dermot MacMorrough, King of Leinster, was a modernizer (and for that reason has been portrayed as a bad man by the Celtic monks who wrote the Irish annals). He wished to combine his own secular ambitions with the introduction of church reforms. In 1166 Dermot travelled to Bristol to recruit Norman mercenaries and subsequently saw Henry II in Acquitaine to get his permission.[14] This was granted and Dermot (who lacked an heir) sealed the arrangement by marrying his daughter Eva to Richard Fitzgilbert, Earl of Clare, known to history as 'Strongbow'. Giraldus says of Strongbow that his 'his pedigree was longer than his purse', and he evidently seized on the opportunity to carve out for himself a kingdom in Ireland. The first Normans landed in the summer of 1167, and they were strongly reinforced in May 1169 when Robert Fitzstephen and Maurice Prendergast landed at Bannow Bay in Wexford with '30 knights, 60 men-at-arms wearing breastplates, and 300 archers'. At the Baginbun headland they built their first motte-and-bailey castle of timber and earth. Most of the archers were from the Flemish community which had settled in Pembrokeshire, and the Irish annals say: 'The fleet of the Flemings came to Erin: there were 90 heroes dressed in mail, and the Gaels set no store by them.'[15] Giraldus recounts that after Fitzstephen had helped Dermot to beat his enemies, the severed heads of some 200 of them were laid at the King's feet. Then, to the disgust of Fitzstephen, 'he lifted up to his mouth the head of one he particularly loathed, and taking it by the ears and hair, gnawed at the nose and cheeks, a cruel and most inhuman act'.

Strongbow himself came in August 1170, with 1,000 men, took Waterford and married Eva in its cathedral. Then he occupied Dublin. When Dermot died the following year, Strongbow asserted his claim to the kingdom of Leinster and made it good by winning a pitched battle on the banks of the Liffey outside Dublin. It was this event which provoked the intervention of Henry II. No doubt he was anxious to divert attention from the atrocious murder of Archbishop Becket in December 1170, by belatedly carrying out the *Laudabiliter* programme. But his chief motive was to stop Strongbow creating a position of private, quasi-regal power beyond his own authority.[16] He ordered Strongbow to surrender all ports and castles, and when he landed on 18 October 1171 he took with him no less than 500 knights, mounted- and foot-archers and a large quantity of siege equipment: this was plainly aimed at Strongbow's castles, not the Irish.[17]

In fact there was no fighting, and Henry was immediately acknowledged as lord by all concerned, Norman and Irish, lay and ecclesiastical. He called a council of kings and bishops at Cashel and, according to Giraldus, 'There the monstrous excesses and vile practices of that land and people were investigated, recounted at a public hearing and put into writings under the seal of the Bishop of Lismore, the papal legate, who on that occasion presided over all the others by virtue of his seniority'.[18] Giraldus says the King then issued constitutions for the church based upon English practice, 'For it is proper and most fitting that, just as by God's grace Ireland has received her Lord and King from England, so too she should receive a better pattern of living from that quarter'.[19]

Henry's proceedings were endorsed in September 1172 by Pope Alexander III, who wrote three letters, to Henry himself, to the kings and princes of Ireland, and to the Irish bishops. That to the bishops says he has heard from several of them

> how great are the enormities of vice with which the people of Ireland are infected, and how they have departed from the fear of God and the established practice of the Christian faith, so that souls have been placed in peril. We have further learnt from your letters that Henry, the noble king of the English, our dearest son in Christ, moved by inspiration from God and summoning all his strength, has subjugated this barbarous and uncouth race, which is ignorant of divine law; and through his power those forbidden things which used to be practised in your lands,

now begin to diminish ... we earnestly pray that through
the vigilance and care of the King, and by your
cooperation with him, this undisciplined and untamed
people may in every way be led to respect the Divine law
and the practice of the Christian faith.[20]

In fact Henry II never carried out the papal programme in
full; nor did he conquer Ireland. Irish history would have
been very different, and perhaps happier, had he done so.
Henry never returned to Ireland, thus inaugurating the tragic
English tradition of benign (some would say malign) neglect.
In 1175 he signed the Treaty of Windsor with Rory
O'Connor, the high king, in which Rory did him homage.[21]
He sent over Hugh de Lacy as Constable of Dublin, and
effectively viceroy, to balance Strongbow, and Hugh, says
Giraldus, 'won the confidence of the Irish by the leniency of
his government and his strict regard for treaties'.[22] With the
analogies of Scotland and Brittany in mind, Henry made his
youngest son, John, *Dominus Hiberniae* or Lord of Ireland, in
1185. Of course John was not expected to become King of
England too; thus when he did so in 1199, the lordship of
Ireland then became accidentally attached to the English
crown. But Henry II was never prepared to devote either time
or money to the conquest and unification of Ireland.

Instead, the process of subjugation and settlement was
undertaken by individual great lords. Strongbow, and his
famous son-in-law, William Marshall Earl of Pembroke, who
inherited his claims, feudalized an area covering the five
modern counties of Wexford, Carlow, Leix, Kilkenny and
Kildare. The vassals of this great liberty included the
founders of famous Irish names: the Fitzgeralds in Naas, the
Berminghams in Carbery, the Carews in Carlow and the
Prendergasts in Wexford.[23] The de Lacys created a palatine
empire of 500,000 acres in Meath, divided into eighteen
baronies, some of which lasted until the Battle of the Boyne,
and gave to Ireland such names as Tyrel, Fleming, Nugent,

Nangle and Petit.[24] The de Courcys conquered eastern Ulster, and enfeoffed baronies owned by the Hackets, Russells, Savages, Whites and Logans. From 1235 the de Burghs moved into Connaught, planting Welsh settlers who provided Ireland with another string of famous names: the Barrets, Lynnets, Merricks and Walshes in Mayo, with the Joyces in the mountains between Mayo and Galway.[25]

This conquest was underwritten by wooden motte-and-bailey castles, replaced in stone as quickly as time and money allowed. The first real Irish castle was Carrickfergus, 1180–1204, built by John de Courcy on Belfast Loch, with a great square four-storey keep, ninety feet high and big enough to stand comparison with Rochester, Dover, Newcastle or the White Tower in London. The de Lacys put up Trim, in Meath, the largest Anglo-Norman fortification in Ireland, covering three acres and with a wall perimeter of 1,500 feet. Of the great Fitzgerald castle at Maynooth in Kildare, only the fine gate-tower and massive keep remain. At Athenry in Galway, built by the Berminghams, only the three-storey keep remains also, but it is exceptionally well-preserved and for its date (1238) has unusually elaborate decorations on doorways and windows. There were also royal castles: Dublin and Kilkenny, Limerick, built by King John around 1200, Athlone, built in 1210 by his justiciar, John de Grey, and the magnificent castle at Roscommon, built by the justiciar Robert de Ufford around 1280.[26]

But despite this considerable military and settlement effort, the installation by John, William Marshall and Hubert de Burgh of an Irish Exchequer, Treasury and Chancery (in Dublin Castle), and of Irish justices of Assize, only a small part of Ireland was administered on English lines during the thirteenth century. In 1217 Magna Carta was published in an Irish version, directing that English Common Law was to apply there, and that Common Law writs were valid in the King's courts. But the process of 'shiring', that is creating counties as administrative units, each with a sheriff and coroner, proceeded very slowly. By 1260 there were only seven: Cork, Limerick, Waterford, Kerry, Tipperary, Connaught and Louth. The justiciar, the King's viceroy in Dublin, did not control the great feudal liberties of the interior. Thus Ireland was divided into three: an area of direct English administration, radiating from Dublin, the feudal territories of the Anglo-Norman barons, and 'Irish' Ireland, where there was virtually no English presence. This last was itself divided into two, for though such kings as the O'Connors and the O'Briens held their land in the north by royal grant and under royal suzerainty, west of the River Bann, there were Gaelic kings who who had not admitted English overlordship at all. Irish kings such as Brian O'Neill of Ulster assumed the title of High King as late as 1260. The most independent were the O'Donnells of Tirconnel in Ulster, who claimed 'every man should have his own world'.[27]

It was to the advantage of the Irish generally to get access to English law, and of course it was to the King's financial advantage to give it to them. But Henry III never visited Ireland; nor did Edward I, that great jurist and legislator, who was too busy settling Gascony, Wales and Scotland. In 1277 the Archbishop of Cashel and his suffragans petitioned Edward to make English law compulsory over the Irish. Edward was willing, and in 1292 he decreed in council that any Irishman who demanded the right to be taken under the protection of Common Law should have it.[28] The task of turning this policy into a reality was entrusted to Edward's great justiciar, John de Wogan, in 1295. Two years later Wogan held the first real Irish parliament, which included barons, bishops and abbots and two knights summoned from each of nine counties and five liberties. But the most the parliament could do was to shire two new areas, Kildare and Meath. It drew attention, on the other hand, to a growing problem – the tendency of the English to 'degenerate' by the adoption of Irish customs, speech and clothes.

We come here to a phenomenon still little understood: the

'Celtic revival' of the late-thirteenth and fourteenth centuries. The Irish Gaels had never worn mail or armour, simply their native linen. Hence the annalist's lament for the death of Brian O'Neill in 1260 at the Battle of Downpatrick:

> Unequal they came to the battle,
> The foreigners and the race of Tara;
> Fine linen shirts on the race of Conn,
> The foreigners one mass of Iron.

From about this date, however, the Irish kings began to engage the services of gallowglasses from the Western Isles of Scotland, men of Norse descent (the word means foreign soldier), who fought with six-foot battleaxes, helmets and coats of mail. These Scottish bands not only fought in Ireland (they were still a significant factor in the sixteenth century) but settled there and became important northern clans – MacSweeneys, MacDowells, MacDonalds, Macruaries.[29] They helped the Irish to win battles at Callan, in 1261, and at Athankipp in 1270.

It was, however, in Scotland itself that the Gaelic revival achieved its most spectacular success, with the crushing victory over Edward II's forces at Bannockburn in 1314, followed by the invasion and occupation of parts of northern England. It is significant that, immediately afterwards, Donal O'Neill, who claimed the high kingship, offered it to Robert Bruce's brother, Edward, who arrived in Ireland with 6,000 veterans the following year. Two years later the Irish princes sent a long collective petition to the Pope, John XXII, explaining that they had thrown off their English overlordship as a result of innumerable injustices. This is a very dramatic document, couched in the most colourful Latin – the progenitor of many similar anti-English declarations right up to 1916 – which details a number of specific atrocities committed by the English. It draws attention to the racial discrimination of the English courts, which refuse to consider the killing of an Irishman murder, and decline to allow

Irishmen (bishops excepted) to bring actions. But its main animus is against 'the men of the middle nation' – that is, the great Anglo-Irish lords of the liberties.[30]

The Pope passed on the remonstrance to Edward II in 1318, advising him to investigate the grievances; but his only reply to the Irish was to excommunicate Bruce and his clerical adherents. This made it easier for the English to restore order. For the first time the crown sent to Ireland a Lord Lieutenant, Mortimer of Wigmore. He landed with an army and broke the back of the invasion; and in October 1318 Bruce was defeated and killed by an Anglo-Irish force under John de Bermingham. The Scots seem to have made themselves even more unpopular than the English barons, for in the *O'Madden Tract*, the annalist says of the slaying of Bruce: 'There was not done from the beginning of the world a deed that was better for the Men of Ireland than that deed. For there came dearth and loss of people during his time in all Ireland for the space of three years and a half, and people undoubtedly used to eat each other throughout Ireland.'[31]

But if English lordship was reestablished, it remained on the defensive. The increase in English population which had made possible the twelfth- and thirteenth-century settlements tapered off. The English economy was in decline in the early fourteenth century, and after the plague epidemics of the 1340s, 1350s and 1360s, the population fell sharply. The Black Death hit Ireland too, especially the towns, killing many more English settlers than natives. Virtually no new castles were built in the fourteenth century. Edward III and his knights looked to France for profitable military expeditions. Ireland was ruled by a succession of knightly justiciars of comparatively lowly birth who carried little weight with the Anglo-Irish grandees; and they themselves survived by turning native or, in legal terms, becoming 'degenerate'. A recent study of Ireland at this time describes it as 'a collection of pockets of land separated by natural features and areas of Irish supremacy'.[32] Outside the few towns it was a marcher society. Anglo-Irish lords survived by balancing local factions and 'Irishing' themselves; the more vulnerable their lordships, the more need they had to cut a figure in Irish eyes and acquire native clients. Such magnates had to develop an additional Gaelic personality. Often they had Irish mothers who taught them Irish lore. Thus John de Bermingham, Earl of Louth, took an Irish harper with him everywhere. The de Mandevilles changed their name to MacQuillian. The third Earl of Desmond, though justiciar, was known as 'Gerald the Poet' because he composed Irish verse.[33] Great Anglo-Irish lords, ignoring the crown, made private treaties with Irish clans.[34]

The crown retaliated in 1366 by getting the Irish parliament to pass the Statutes of Kilkenny. Its preamble states:

> Now many English of the said land, forsaking the English language, fashion, mode of riding, law and usages, live and govern themselves according to the manners, fashion and language of the Irish enemies; and also having made divers marriages and alliances between themselves and the Irish enemies aforesaid ... the English language, the allegiance due to our Lord the King and the English laws there are put in subjection and decayed, and the Irish enemies exalted and raised up, contrary to right.

Hence it ordained that 'no alliance by marriage, gossipred, fostering of children, concubinage or amour' be made between English and Irish. The English were forbidden to sell Irishmen horses, armour or 'any manner of victuals in time of war'. They were commanded to use only English law for settling disputes, English-type saddles, on pain of forfeiture of their horse, and the English language, on pain of forfeiture of estate or gaoling. They were not to call each other 'Englishhobbe' or 'Irishdogge', or to play hurling, 'with great clubs at ball upon the ground, from which great evils and maims have arisen' or 'that other game which men call coitings'. No Irish were to receive benefices; and, since Irish minstrels 'spy out the secret customs and policies of the English', it was forbidden for 'tympanours, pipers, story-tellers, babblers, rhymers, harpers or any other Irish minstrel, to come among the English', who were likewise, 'on pain of life and limb', forbidden to 'keep kernes, hobelers or idlemen' (i.e., private armies of Irish).[35]

These statutes legalized the concept of an English-speaking Pale. The term 'Irish Enemies' became the official designation of Irish living outside the Pale, which was defined in Richard II's reign as running from Dundalk to the Boyne and down the Barrow to Waterford. The Kilkenny Statutes were often broken or suspended; on the other hand, between 1366 and 1495 they were confirmed many times, and they were not repealed until 1613. Their aim, to bolster up the English presence, was reinforced by an Act of Absentees (1368), ordering all Irish landowners to return to their estates.[36] But the biggest absentee landlord was the English royal family (Edward III's son, the Duke of Clarence, was Earl of Ulster and Connaught by virtue of his heiress wife, Elizabeth de Burgh), and above all the Lord of Ireland himself, the King. The Irish had a saying: 'A land without a lord is a dead land.' The central weakness of English policy in Ireland was the unwillingness of the monarch to go there. Sir John Davies, the Jacobean attorney-general of Ireland, in his book surveying the course of Anglo-Irish history, summed it up in a phrase: 'The lion himself came not to the hunt and left the prey to the inferior beasts.'[37]

A royal visit to Ireland always brought dividends. Richard II was there between September 1394 and May 1395, and his offer to admit Irish kings and chiefs to full legal status under the crown brought about the most general recognition of English overlordship throughout the medieval period. The O'Neills, the O'Briens, the O'Connors and the MacCarthys made personal submission and were knighted by Richard. They dropped the title of 'king' (for example, MacCarthy became 'MacCarthy More' instead of 'King of Desmond'), though the conservative annalists continued to use the term 'ri' of great princes, and one potentate, MacMurrough Kavanagh, had a seal calling himself *Rex Lagenie* until the reign of Henry VIII.[38] In a letter from Ireland, Richard divided the population into 'the wild Irish, our enemies, English rebels and obedient English'; he says of the 'rebels' that 'they have become disobedient through injustice practised upon them by our officers, and if they are not won over they will join our Irish enemies'. True enough; and Richard returned to Ireland in 1399 to put down unrest. But the news from England of Bolingbroke's rebellion cut short the royal visit, and that was the last Ireland saw of a reigning monarch until the arrival of William III 300 years later.

The 'obedient English' thus had to look to their own defences, though some government support was provided. A statute of Henry VI (1429) states:

> It is agreed and asserted that every liege-man of our Lord the King of the said counties (Dublin, Meath, Kildare and Louth) who chooses to build a castle or tower sufficiently embattled or fortified, within the next ten years, to wit 20 feet in length, 16 feet in width and 14 feet in height or more, that the Commons of the said counties shall find the said person to build the said castle £10 by way of subsidy.

This produced the famous 'Ten Pound Castles' of Ireland, the mass of fourteenth-century tower-houses which constitute the most evident ancient feature of the Irish countryside. Limerick alone had over 400, Cork 325, Tipperary at least 253 and Clare 120.[39] They have something of the North-Country pele tower, something of the Scottish tower-house, but with very characteristic Irish-style machicolation. Two splendid examples are Clara and Burnchurch, both in Kilkenny. The fifteenth century also saw the erection of more elaborate castles, of which the MacCarthy stronghold at Blarney (Cork) and the O'Briens' at Bunratty (Clare) are outstanding examples. But it is indicative of the relatively slight English impress that Ireland never developed the great concentric castles of thirteenth–fourteenth-century England, nor the elaborate fortified gateway-towers which succeeded them.

It is the same story in church architecture. Before the Normans came, Ireland had its own form of Romanesque, as is illustrated by the superbly strange west door of Clonfert Cathedral in Galway. Thereafter, Ireland got its Gothic through England, St Patrick's Cathedral, Dublin, being the first true example. But Ireland never accepted Perpendicular, the English national style of the fourteenth and fifteenth centuries, clinging on to a form of Decorated which has more in common with Scottish or even French modes than English ones.

The decline of the English monarchy under Henry VI and the subsequent Wars of the Roses inevitably led to a feudal revival in Ireland, Irish 'bastard feudalism' taking the form of what the statutes passed against it called 'coigny, livery, Kernety, bonnaught and cuddies', denounced collectively as 'abominable Irish customs' and 'Irish cuttings and spendings'. Richard Duke of York was heir to the Ulster lordship, and eventually, through his mother, united it to the lordships of Trim, Leix and Connaught, together with his vast holdings in Wales and England. Appointed Lord Lieutenant of Ireland in 1447, he made it a great Yorkist stronghold for half a century, only the Butlers of Ormonde being staunch Lancastrians.

While in Ireland, Richard 'got him such love and favour of that country and its inhabitants that their sincere and lovely affection could never be separated from him and his lineage'. The Duke used Ireland as a jumping-off ground in his bid for the English crown; and when beaten at Ludlow in 1459, he returned to Ireland, summoned a parliament at Drogheda, and got it to pass, in 1460, a unilateral declaration of independence:

The land of Ireland is, and at all times hath been, corporate of itself by the ancient laws and customs used in the same, freed of the burden of any special law of the realm of England, save only such laws as by the Lords Spiritual and Temporal and the Commons of the said land have been in Great Council of Parliament held there admitted, accepted, affirmed and proclaimed.[40]

Hence, when Henry VII ascended the English throne he found that Ireland enjoyed a form of home rule, exercised through the great marcher lords, chief of whom were the Fitzgerald Earls of Kildare. They had held the Lord Lieutenancy under the Yorkist kings and remained Yorkist even after the Tudor triumph in England. Garret More, the great Earl of Kildare, virtually ruled Ireland, in or out of office, from 1477 until his death in 1513. He was described as a 'mighty man of stature, full of honour and courage, open and plain, hardly able to rule himself when he was moved to anger, easily displeased and soon appeased, of the English well beloved, a good justiciar, a suppressor of rebels and a warrior incomparable'. Henry VII would not tolerate such a personage in England, but in Ireland he felt obliged to do so, even when Kildare recognized the pretender Lambert Simnel and crowned him in Dublin.

When Henry felt strong enough, he asserted his authority. Thus in 1494 he made his own son, Prince Henry, Lord Lieutenant, and sent out a reliable knight, Sir Edward Poynings, as Deputy. Poynings held a parliament at Drogheda in the winter of 1494–5, and passed forty-nine statutes, the ninth of which became famous as Poynings' Law:

... no parliament be holden hereafter in the said land of Ireland but at such season as the King's lieutenant and council there first do certify to the King, under the Great Seal of that land, the causes and considerations and all such acts them seemeth should pass in the said parliament, and such causes, considerations and acts affirmed by the

King and his council to be good and expedient for that
land and his license thereupon, as well as affirming of the
said causes and acts as to summoning the said parliament
. . . and if any parliament be holden in that land hereafter
contrary to the form and provision aforesaid, it is deemed
void and of none effect in law.

What this meant in practice was that any legislation in the
Irish parliament had to receive prior approval by the English
privy council, and as such Poynings' Law, repeatedly
affirmed, made the Irish parliament wholly subordinate to
the English government.[41]

Nevertheless, it is significant that Henry VII reappointed
Kildare Deputy for the rest of the reign, thus signifying that,
whatever his theoretical claims, he could not in practice hold
Ireland without the cooperation of the magnates. Indeed by
the year 1500 three of them, the Fitzgerald Earls of Desmond
and Kildare and the Butler Earls of Ormonde, owned all of
Ireland south of the Upper Boyne and Limerick.[42] The home-
rule lords continued to dominate Ireland for the first twenty-
five years of Henry VIII's reign, though the 'obedient
English' of the Pale periodically complained about 'the old
English Irelandised', and said of the Irish themselves, 'there
be no more industrious people under the sun than the churls
and husbandmen, if their lords do not eat them out'. But in
the 1530s the Reformation introduced a new dimension to
Irish politics. In 1534 the greatest lord of all, 'Silken Thomas'
of the Kildare Fitzgeralds, threw off his allegiance to Henry
VIII on the grounds that the King, now excommunicated,
had thereby forfeited the Lordship of Ireland, which was still
seen there as the gift of the Pope.

At this point Thomas Cromwell decided to break the home
rule party, and sent out Sir Thomas Skeffington as Deputy
with a large English army. Skeffington took the massive
Kildare stronghold at Maynooth after a two-week siege, and
Silken Thomas and his chief relatives were sent to the Tower

in chains. Whilst they were there, the Treasurer-at-War in Dublin wrote to Cromwell begging him to wipe out the Geraldines: 'for the poor commonalty be very true people, and conformable to all good order, and the destruction of the land is wholly by the extortions of the lords and gentlemen of the country'. Cromwell accepted this advice and hanged Silken Thomas and five of his uncles at Tyburn in 1537. The Irish parliament then passed the Reformation legislation without apparent protest. To ram the point home, at a parliament in 1541, Henry VIII was declared 'King of this land of Ireland, as united, annexed and knit forever to the imperial crown of the realm of England'.[43] The way was now at last open for the effective conquest of Ireland.

CHAPTER 2

Conquest and Plantation

It was of the essence of Tudor policy in Ireland that all estates should be held or reconfirmed under English law, a policy followed with great success in Wales. But in Ireland it was more easily proclaimed than done until the whole country was effectively 'shired'. Under Philip and Mary, two new counties, King's and Queen's, were created, and parts of Leix, Offaly, Clanmalier and Slievemargy were thrown open to settlement. 'Planters' had to be English or 'English born in Ireland', to build stone houses, serve the Deputy with a given number of troops, pay quit-rent and employ only English servants. With the English population again expanding fast, the human means were available for the Anglicization of the country. But at Queen Elizabeth's first Irish parliament, early in 1560, only ten counties and twenty-eight towns were represented. That marked the extent of true English sovereignty. English statesmen were baffled by the failure of Ireland to yield any revenue. It was, said Sir William Cecil, 'a strange example and not to be found again in any place'.[1] Sir Nicholas Wotton considered it 'a great shame to us, that the crown of England having been conquerors in Ireland these four hundred years well near, could not all this while bring that realm to a good civility and obedience, nor take some honest commodity or profit of that country so good and so fruitful'.[2]

Ireland, it was agreed, had to be held for reasons of national security. The Earl of Sussex, Elizabeth's first Deputy, wrote in 1560: 'I am forced by duty to give advice ... not so much for the care I have of Ireland, which I have often wished to be sunk in the sea, as if the French should set fast therein, they should not only have such an entry into Scotland as her

Majesty could not resist...but should take utterly from
England all kind of peaceable traffic by sea.'³ There was
always a risk that a foreign power, first France, later Spain
and the Papacy, might exploit an Irish rising for its
geopolitical purposes.

Elizabeth herself liked some of the Irish grandees. A
particular favourite was James Butler, Earl of Ormonde; she
also took a fancy to Shane O'Neill, who came to court with his
gallowglasses in 1562. The Irish government took a different
view. Sir Henry Sidney, Deputy from 1566-71, wrote:
'Lucifer was never puffed up with more pride or ambition
than O'Neill is. He continually keepeth 600 armed men about
him and is able to bring into the field 1,000 horsemen and
4,000 foot... he armeth and weaponeth all the peasants of his
country.'⁴ The O'Neills rose in 1559-66, the Fitzmaurices in
1569-72, the Desmonds in 1579-83; and when not 'out'
against the government, the Old Irish and Old English often
fought amongst themselves. The English authorities viewed
such in-fighting with cynical approval. Sir Nicholas Arnold,
Lord Justice of Ireland, wrote to Cecil in 1565: 'I am with all
the wild Irish at the same point I am with bears and mad dogs
when I see them fight: so that they fight earnestly indeed, and
tug each other well, I care not who have the worse.'⁵

Indeed, cynicism tinged all England's dealings with
Ireland. Elizabeth herself 'grew weary with reading the Irish
dispatches'.⁶ Her Secretary, Sir Thomas Smith, noted that
her tendency to put off decisions was most marked when
Ireland was discussed.⁷ Most English people knew nothing of
Ireland. Even the people of Dublin knew little of the interior.
As late as 1609 Sir John Davies admitted that Ulster was
'heretofore as unknown to the English here as the most inland
part of Virginia as yet unknown to our English colony there'.⁸
Ireland, wrote Francis Bacon, was 'the last of the daughters of
Europe', waiting 'to be reclaimed from desolation and a
desert (in many parts) to population and plantation; and from
savage and barbarous customs to humanity and civility'.⁹

Edmund Spenser, who knew Ireland well and wrote a book about it in 1596, compared Ireland to Britain in the Dark Ages. He found something mysterious and baffling about the failure to solve the Irish problem:

> Marry, so there have been divers good plots devised, and wise counsels cast already about reformation of that realm; but they say, it is the fatal destiny of that land, that no purposes, whatsoever are meant for her good, will prosper or take effect which, whether it proceed from the very genius of the soil or influence of the stars, or that Almighty God hath not yet appointed the time of her reformation, or that he reserveth her in this unquiet state still for some secret scourge, which shall by her come into England, it is hard to be known, yet much to be feared.[10]

The English found Irish behaviour horrifying. Spenser said he had seen an old woman, after the execution of a rebel at Limerick, 'take up his head while he was quartered and suck up all the blood that ran thereout, saying that the earth was not worthy to drink it, and therewith also steeped her face and breast'. The Queen was disgusted in 1597 to receive a present of the severed head of a leading Irish rebel, Fiach McHugh, and angrily ordered the Council to 'send the head back again by the same messenger'.[11] Elizabeth was tired of hearing from loyal servants how many rebels they had killed, the Earl of Connaught boasting in the 1570s that 'I did within one twelve-month hang my own son, my brother's son, and one of the captains of my gallowglass, besides 50 of my own followers'.[12]

Dublin parliaments repeatedly attempted to enforce legislation on the lines of the Kilkenny Statutes, particularly over dress. The Irish mantle, Spenser said in his book, 'is a fit house for an outlaw, a meet bed for a rebel, and an apt cloak for a thief'. Sir John Perrot, Deputy in 1571, laid down:

> The inhabitants of cities and corporate towns shall wear no

mantles, shorts, Irish coats or great shorts, nor suffer their hair to grow long . . . but to wear gowns, jerkins and some civil garments; and no maid or single woman shall put on any great roll or kirchen of linen cloths upon their heads, neither any great smock with great sleeves, but to put on hats, caps, French hoods, tippets or some other civil attire . . . All carroughs, bards, rhymers and common idle men and women within this province making rhymes . . . to be spoiled of all their goods and chattels and to be put in the next stocks, there to remain till they shall find sufficient surety to leave that wicked 'thrade' of life.[13]

The ablest of Elizabeth's Deputies, Sir Henry Sidney, who had been highly successful in Wales, wanted the whole of Ireland ruled directly by the crown: that is, divided into 'presidencies', each with a governing council (like the presidencies of the North and of Wales), and subdivided into counties. That, he told Elizabeth, was what the Irish wanted:

The gentlemen of Cork was begging for it, with open mouth and held up hands to heaven, crying out for justice, and that it might please your Majesty to cause your name to be known among them, with reverence, and your laws obeyed, offering to submit themselves, life, lands and good, to the same.[14]

The great difficulty, as Sidney admitted, was the deplorable poverty and ignorance of the people. Both Reformation and Counter-Reformation had passed them by:

Surely there was never people that lived in more misery than they do, nor as it should seem of worse minds, for matrimony among them is no more regarded in effect than conjunction between unreasonable beasts. Perjury, robbery and murder counted allowable. Finally, I cannot find that they make any conscience of sin; for neither find I a place where it should be done, nor any person able to instruct them in the rules of a Christian.[15]

But direct rule cost money. That was why Elizabeth regarded Sidney as 'a very expensive servant', always clamouring for cash. Presidencies were created in Connaught and Munster, and settlement followed. But the military presence was inadequate and its soldiers of poor quality – 'the men are such poor and miserable creatures,' wrote Sir Walter Raleigh, one of the settlers, 'as their captains dare not lead them to serve'.[16] The settlements under Mary had almost vanished by the time Elizabeth came to the throne. It was true, as the 'undertakers' (colony-planners) boasted, 'You may keep a better house in Ireland for £50 a year than in England for £200 a year'; but that house often had to be defended by force. In 1572, a colony was set up by Thomas Smith, son of the Secretary of State, on the borders of Ulster; next spring, Smith was murdered by his Irish household servants, and the colonists dispersed. The 1st Earl of Essex organized another plantation in Antrim; this failed through disease and shortage of supplies. After the suppression of the Desmond rebellion there was a major plantation in Munster in 1583–5. Among the undertakers were Raleigh, who got 12,000 acres near Youghal – the nucleus of the later territorial empire of the Boyles, Earls of Cork – and Spenser, who paid £8 13s 9d a year for 3,000 acres near Cork. But this too was largely a failure, most of the settlers, Spenser included, being driven out by the 'wild Irish'. In the *Faerie Queene* he conjured up the terror of an Irish 'rising':

> ... with outrageous cry
> A thousand villeins round about them swarmed
> Out of the rocks and caves adjoining nye;
> Vile caitive wretches, ragged, rude, deformed,
> All threatening death, all in straunge manner
>   armed;
> Some with unwieldy clubs, some with long speares,
> Some rusty knives, some staves in fier warmed ...

The area of settlement slowly expanded all the same. Perrot's parliament of April 1585 contained 118 deputies from 31 towns, and no less than 27 shires. But the panoply of constitutional rule was not enough. Ralph Rokeby, one of Sidney's legal assistants, wrote of Connaught: 'It is not the mace nor the name of a Lord President and Council that will frame them to obedience, it must be fire and sword, the rod of God's vengeance that must make these cankered sorts and stubborn minds to yield for fear. . . . It must be valiant and courageous captains and hardy soldiers that must make a way for law and justice in these remote parts or else, farewell Ireland.'[17]

Meanwhile, from 1580 the Jesuits were active in Ireland. For the first time religion became a serious factor in the struggle for mastery, not least because it was known that Philip of Spain was anxious to open up a second front there. On average there were less than 5,000 English soldiers to keep order; even in the suppression of the Desmond rebellion they had not numbered more than 9,000.[18] In the 1580s and 1590s, Hugh O'Neill, Earl of Tyrone, began to organize a military force on modern lines, with firearms, redcoats, disciplined drilling, even cavalry. His men worked the land in winter and campaigned with him in summer. In 1595 he felt strong enough to take the forbidden title of 'The O'Neill', and enter into contact with the Spanish, who got money and supplies to him the next year. In 1598 he made open war against the state by blockading the key fort on the Blackwater which penned him into Ulster.

The Marshal of the Army, Sir Henry Bagenal, marched north in a hurry to deliver the fort, taking with him only 300 cavalry, the most he could gather in the time. At the Yellow Ford on the Blackwater he found Tyrone's army, backed by the troops of the O'Donnells, the other leading Ulster family, and made a frontal assault, relying on his superior firepower. He was in fact walking into a carefully prepared trap, for the Irish had firearms and knew how to use them. The van, caught by fire from both sides, broke and fell back on the main body; the Irish mercenaries in the English army deserted, as did many of the raw English recruits. With the English army in disorder, the O'Neills and the O'Donnells charged. This was the moment for the English to deploy cavalry, the one arm the Irish really feared. But none was available. The two regiments of the English rearguard were not enough to prevent a general retreat and the inevitable heavy losses which followed. Bagenal was killed and 1,300 of his men reported lost or missing, with a further 700 deserters. Camden wrote: 'Since the time the English first set foot in Ireland they never received a greater overthrow.'[19] The authorities in Dublin panicked and the Lords Justice wrote to Tyrone in grovelling terms, pleading with him for an armistice.

This disaster at least had the effect of forcing Elizabeth to take the Irish problem seriously and to commit to its solution the necessary quantities of men and money. Though she failed with her first general, the 2nd Earl of Essex, she found in his successor, Charles Blount, 1st Lord Mountjoy, a warrior of the Wellington cast, slow, sure and steady.[20] He began, wrote his secretary, Fynes Moryson, by rebuilding morale: 'The hearts of the English common soldiers, broken with a current of disastrous successes, he heartened and encouraged by leading them warily, especially in his first action: he was more careful that our men should not be foiled, than that the rebels should be attempted with boldness.'[21] His strategy was to hold down pacified areas with blockhouses, thus limiting Tyrone's mobility, and he destroyed the rebels' food supplies by campaigning through the winter. This cost vast sums – £300,000 a year according to Robert Cecil.[22] It was also hard on the troops, who cursed the incessant Irish rain which destroyed their food supplies too, rusted arms and equipment and rotted their clothes. The whole island, Moryson wrote, was 'uneven, mountainous, soft, watery, woody and open to wind and floods of rain, and so fenned that it hath bogs on the very tops of mountains, bearing nor man nor beast but very dangerous to pass'.[23] Mountjoy scrapped his campaign finery and concentrated on keeping warm and dry: he wore an extra pair of woollen stockings, three waistcoats and a special thick ruff, and wound a 'russet scarf' three times round his neck.[24]

The war came to a climax in September 1601 when the Spaniards, long awaited, finally eluded the English fleet and landed 5,300 men, plus some artillery, at Kinsale, which they fortified. Tyrone marched south to join them and Mountjoy leapt at the chance to destroy the rebels in open battle. He wrote to the Council in London: 'If we beat them, let it not trouble you though you hear all Ireland doth revolt, for (by the grace of God) you shall have them all return presently with halters round their necks: if we do not, all providence bestowed on any other place is vain.'[25] On Christmas Eve 1601 the Irish army deployed itself in open country and Mountjoy at last had the opportunity to use his cavalry, which made short work of Tyrone, taking less than an hour. The Spanish in Kinsale promptly asked for terms. Their commander said he found the Irish 'not only weak and barbarous but (as he feared) perfidious friends'. Reporting this, Mountjoy noted: 'The contempt and scorn in which the Spaniards hold the Irish, and the distaste which the Irish have of them . . . [mean] it will be a difficult thing for the Irish hereafter to procure aids out of Spain.'[26]

Tyrone remained at large for over a year, hunted by Mountjoy's men. He was anxious to submit but fearful of Elizabeth's determination to hang him. In fact, shortly before her death in March 1603, she relented and authorized Mountjoy to accept his submission.[27] King James I, anxious to make a fresh start, began his reign with an Act of Oblivion in February 1604. Indeed, Ireland was not included in the draconian Penal Laws, passed in 1606 in the aftermath of the Catholic Gunpowder Plot. James was anxious that Catholic Irishmen should be able to take an oath of loyalty to him, provided they repudiated the doctrine that a prince excommunicated by the Pope might be lawfully deposed or murdered. This they were willing to do; but any such oath

1.   Copy of a manuscript map of Ireland, about 1609, in the library
of Trinity College, Dublin. The original is inscribed on the back: 'To
the moste honorable... Earl of Salsburye... John Norden'.

was condemned by the Papacy as sinful, and from 1606 a series of state proclamations in Ireland led to the expulsion of the Jesuits and mass-priests, and growing economic pressure on the Catholic gentry. In 1607, Tyrone and the O'Connell Earl of Tyrconnell, fearful of arrest, fled to Rome with nearly a hundred of their followers. It was the end of the old Gaelic order; and the forfeiture of the earls' estates presented James's government with an irresistible temptation to 'plant' backward Ulster.

Men like Sir John Davies, Attorney-General of Ireland and one of the main architects of the Jacobean policy, were not anti-Irish; far from it. Davies's book was a serious attempt to discover why English policy in Ireland had failed over 400 years and why 'the manners of the mere Irish had so little altered since the days of Henry II'. His conclusion, after travelling in every part of the country, was that the English had failed to give the Irish the benefit of English law, particularly of land-tenure. In 1606 and 1608, as a result of his urging, the judges condemned the two outstanding characteristics of Irish land-law, gavelkind and tanistry, both of which militated against the English principles of primogeniture and entailment, and tended to split lands up into minute parcels, besides producing all the anti-social features of bastard feudalism.[28] These and other changes in the law would effectively break the power of the old lords, in Davies's opinion. 'The common people,' he wrote, 'were taught by the justices of assize that they were free subjects to the kings of England, and not slaves and vassals of their pretended lords, that the cuttings, costeries, fessing and other extortions of their lords were unlawful ... they gave a willing ear to these lessons and thereupon the greatness and power of these Irish lords over the people suddenly fell and vanished.'[29] Davies had complete confidence in Irish acceptance of English law in these circumstances: 'For the truth is, that in time of peace the Irish are more fearful to offend the law than the English, or any other nation whatever.' Hence, he triumphantly concluded, 'the clock of civil government is now well set, and all the wheels thereof do move in order; the strings of the Irish harp, which the civil magistrate doth finger, are all in tune and make a good harmony in the commonwealth; so as we may well conceive a hope that Ireland...will, from henceforth, prove a land of peace and harmony.'[30]

Yet the plantation of Ulster in 1610, the biggest of the new settlements, went against the principles Davies applauded, since it did discriminate between 'loyal' settlers (those able to take the oath in good conscience) and the Catholic 'mere Irish'.[31] Under the Articles of Plantation, 500,000 acres of good land were thrown open to settlers. English and Scottish undertakers were invited to assume estates of 1,000, 1,500 or 2,000 acres to hold of the crown in socage. They had to be 'English or inland Scots' (i.e., lowlands) and 'civil men well affected in religion'. A second rank of Servitors (mostly Scots) held land on less favourable terms. Both these groups had to take the Protestant Oath of Supremacy. A third rank, of natives, were not required to take the Oath. Some Irish had already been confirmed in their estates, and 58,000 acres went to 280 native freeholders. But all the best land went to the settlers, and they were forbidden to sell land to the Irish. Even if they merely took native tenants they had to pay a heavier rent.

It is true that nobody was expelled – orders of expulsion, issued in 1612, remained a dead letter. But Sir Arthur Chichester, the Lord Deputy, claimed that half the land should have gone to the Irish; instead, they became a minority in their own province. In 1614, Sir George Carew, a former President of Munster, sent James a paper arguing that the Old English among the Irish Catholics would now be pushed into the hands of the native Irish and would rebel 'under the veil of religion and liberty than which nothing is more precious in the hearts of men'.[32] By the end of the 1630s, in six Ulster counties, Protestants owned 3,000,000 out of 3,500,000 acres. But the native Irish were sufficiently numerous to make a rebellion formidable, and there were enough Catholic gentry left to lead it: thus Sir Henry Oge O'Neill retained a big estate, and his grandson, Felim of Kinard, was to lead the 1641 rising.

In the rest of Ireland further Protestant plantations were made, especially in areas where 'Irish titles' could be overthrown in the new English-style courts in favour of dormant crown-titles: North Wexford, South Carlow, parts of Wicklow, Longford, Leitrim and South Offaly. The natives were obliged to surrender a third or a quarter of their land, but given secure possession of the rest. The effect of this planting was to reduce the number of freeholders and increase dependent tenures, which became leaseholds, cottageholds or tenancies-at-will. It also abolished the 'names' of chiefs, bards and other survivals of English law and custom.

Yet it must be borne in mind that, up to the 1640s, Catholics (chiefly Old English) still held more than two-thirds of the land of Ireland as a whole. Moreover, the plantations were confirmed by the Irish parliament of 1613–15, in which the Old English formed a majority of the peers, and Catholics sat in the Commons. There was, however, a small Protestant majority, set up by election-management by the sheriffs and by the creation of thirty-nine new boroughs. The Catholics of the Pale, with names like Talbot, Roche, Barry, Butler and Nugent, protested against the transformation of 'miserable villages, by whose votes extreme penal laws shall be imposed on the King's subjects' into parliamentary seats; and six Catholic lords wrote a formal letter to James.[33] He answered cynically: 'What if I created 40 noblemen and 400 boroughs? The more the merrier!' As for religion, he added, they were but half-subjects and deserved only half-privileges.

In practice, however, James was more lenient. The 1613 parliament passed no penal statutes and forced attendance at church was scrapped. Recusancy fines (which should have brought in £20,000 a year) were not always enforced, and nor were oaths for office-holders, or the Supremacy Oath which, in theory, was obligatory when a tenant-in-chief sued for possession of his lands. Indeed, some peers, such as the Bagenals and the Brownes, Earls of Kenmare, even became Catholics under James I. But the Court of Castle Chamber, the Irish equivalent of Star Chamber, nearly always threw its weight behind Protestant interests; and the Irish Court of Wards, which administered the estates of tenants-in-chief who were minors, always had them brought up as Protestants. Thus James Butler, Earl (and later Duke) of Ormonde, was educated at Lambeth Palace, and by 1640 four other peers, the Earls of Thomond, Kildare, Barrymore and Inchiquin, were Protestants.[34]

Moreover, the climate of government tended to favour Protestants, especially English Protestants. One such Jacobean success story was the tale of Richard Boyle. He came to Ireland in 1588 with (according to one Irish historian) '£27, a stolen ring and a forged letter of introduction'.[35] After a dubious career in the Escheator General's office, he acquired the great Raleigh estate in south-east Ireland for a mere £1,000; and thereafter (according to John Aubrey) 'by his diligent and wise Industry, raised such an Honour and Estate, and left such a Familie, as never any subject of these three Kingdomes did'.[36] He developed the linen industry and set up iron-smelting works, using for charcoal the immense primeval forests of Ireland, which from this date were rapidly demolished. He built towns and villages, controlled eight seats in the Irish House of Commons, and in 1620 was made Earl of Cork. Of his fourteen children, one was the great chemist Robert Boyle, and four won themselves peerages.[37] Boyle was a prime example of a new, modern-minded aristocracy which, under the cover of Protestantism, was replacing the old Anglo-Irish ruling class.

With the accession of Charles I, the thrust of British policy shifted to finance. Always desperate for money, Charles and his council, like the Elizabethans before them, could not understand why Ireland did not yield more cash to the crown, and they set about tapping its resources. One milch-cow, obviously, was recusancy: in 1627 Charles made a bargain with the Catholic peers. In return for £120,000, spread over three years, all land-titles going back sixty years were to be declared valid, and (a very important point) Catholics would be allowed to practise law by a simple oath of allegiance to the crown. The money was paid over but Charles could not keep his side of the bargain, since the Dublin parliament, now definitely Protestant, would not pass the necessary legislation, and Charles could only continue his policy of toleration by the exercise of his prerogative.

In 1632 he sent over Sir Thomas Wentworth as Deputy, with a wide-ranging mandate to enforce royal authority, and to turn Ireland from a source of weakness into a pillar of strength to the crown. This was what contemporaries called 'the policy of thorough', and Wentworth (who became Lord Lieutenant and Earl of Strafford in 1639) undoubtedly made it work. His view was that Ireland, with its powerful nobles and weak crown, was like England during the Wars of the Roses. Now, he said, 'Ireland was a conquered country and the King could do as he liked'. He was a formidable figure, 'clad in black armour, with a black horse and a black plume of feathers'.[38] He turned the Court of Castle Chamber into an effective prerogative instrument, and in the 1634–5 parliament he skilfully balanced Catholic against Protestant MPs to get his way. If anything, he thought the new Protestant magnates more dangerous to the crown than the Old English. Hence his Defective Titles Act, which he pushed through parliament, was used as fiercely against the Protestants as against the Papists. This Act set up an examining commission, controlled by Strafford, and through it he forced the Earl of Cork to surrender the College of Youghal, obtained from the Fitzgerald Earls of Desmond, and fined him £15,000. He discovered that the London merchant companies who had planted a settlement in Ulster under a royal charter had not fulfilled its conditions, and fined them £70,000. He examined

ancient rights of the crown under town-charters and customs
farms all over the country, and wherever he discovered a
usurpation of royal profit, he acted mercilessly. In many
respects, with his promotion of industry and his creation of an
Irish mercantile marine, he was merely doing what Boyle had
done, only on a national scale and in the name of the crown.
But he also raised an army, paid for out of the Irish royal
revenues.[39] This had never been done before, and the
rebellious Commons of England suspected it might be used
against them.

Fear of the Irish army was the basis of the parliamentary
case against Strafford. But he had also aroused religious
enmities. As the foundation of the Protestant faith in the
country, the 1615 Convocation of the Church of Ireland
passed 104 Articles of Religion, giving doctrine a pronounced
Calvinist flavour. In 1634 Strafford replaced them with the 39
Articles of the Church of England, highly objectionable to
many Irish Protestants, especially in the north. At Trinity
College in Dublin, Ireland's only university, he imposed a set
of statutes approved by Archbishop Laud of Canterbury,
including an Oath of Supremacy, which made it impossible
for practising Catholics to obtain degrees or hold scholarships
or fellowships. His regime was thus inimical to most religious
groups in Ireland.

When the Scots rebelled against Laudian episcopacy in
1638, Strafford immediately imposed an Oath of Non-
resistance in Ulster. His system held together so long as he,
and his army, were there to give it backbone. But in
November 1639 'Black Tom' was summoned back to
England, leaving the Earl of Ormonde in charge. As soon as
the Long Parliament met in 1640, it began to dismantle the
Strafford machine, starting by disbanding his army and
soliciting complaints against his rule. Charles I abandoned his
great proconsul, who was executed in 1641, withdrew the
Defective Titles commission, curbed the powers of the Court
of Castle Chamber, and transferred power in Dublin from

Ormonde, a loyalist, to two Lord Justices, both Parliament men. In a few months all Strafford's work was in ruins.

All previous English experience suggested that the only solution to Ireland was strong crown rule. Strafford had supplied it. But the great disadvantage of strong rule was that, the moment it was relaxed, rebellion was certain. And in the autumn of 1641 it came. The Irish had watched the Scots Presbyterians rebel successfully against English episcopacy. They asked: 'If the Scots may fight for their religion, why not we?' There was a Catholic plot to seize Dublin Castle on 23 October 1641. This failed, but it acted as a detonator to a general rising of Catholics in Ulster, under Sir Phelim O'Neill.

During this rising, directed mainly against Protestant settlers, Scots and English, many were killed outright and others died of exposure during the winter. Yet others fled to Dublin, carrying terrible tales of massacre and cruelty by the papists. The rising thus immediately acquired a political and religious folklore. It was a time when the presses had just been freed from royal censorship, and a violent war of propaganda was being waged in the cause of parliamentary politics and religious freedom of conscience. As early as 23 December 1641 a commission was set up in Dublin to take statements from British refugees, and a second one on 18 January 1642. These eye-witness accounts eventually filled thirty-three huge manuscript volumes, known as 'the Depositions', now in the library of Trinity College, Dublin.[40] As early as the winter of 1641–2, an official pamphlet appeared entitled *A brief declaration of the barbarous and inhumaine dealings of the northern Irish rebels . . . written to excite the English nation to relieve our poor wives and children, that have escaped the rebels' savage crueltie, and that shall arrive safe among them in England; And in exchange to send aid of men, and means forthwith to quell their boundless insolencies, with certain encouragements to the work*. This was issued, according to the title page, 'by direction of the State of Ireland'. It was the first of many propaganda tracts,

culminating in Sir John Temple's *The Irish Rebellion* (1646),
which conjured up the spectre of a general massacre.

It has since been argued that no such massacre took place,
and that the depositions reflect more the threat of a massacre
than its actuality.[41] That the leaders of the rebellion planned
no general killing is true. They were, in fact, particularly
anxious to have the Scots on their side, and the Scots were told
they had only to indicate their nationality on the doors of
their houses to be left alone. But this distinction, though clear
and important to the Catholic gentry, had no meaning for the
Irish peasants, who themselves feared a massacre by the
Puritans, who were often Scots. In the first week of November
1641, a group of 300 to 400 Scots who surrendered near
Augher were all killed. Sir Phelim's brother, Turlough
O'Neill, wrote to a Scots relation, Sir Robert Knight, on 22
November 1641: 'But for that ill-favoured massacre near
Augher, of those that were first taken to mercy, which did
since cost much blood, and it were better that both the nations
(Scottish and Irish) being formerly one should still so
continue, and like brethren than to be at variance together.'[42]
The savagery began at the bottom of the social scale and
spread upwards; in some cases Irish officers took part in the
killing, and in others they stopped it. The combination of an
ill-disciplined army and angry peasants was to blame. The
latest historical examination of the evidence concludes: 'For
all the exaggeration and repetition of rumour in the
depositions, there are enough eye-witness accounts of robbery
and murders, sometimes by several deponents describing the
same event, to satisfy the most sceptical critic of the
depositions.'[43]

The importance of these events in the long perspective of
Irish history is that they led the English parliament to pass the
'Adventurers' Act', which declared forfeit the property of all
who had taken part in the rebellion. The property thus seized
by the crown was then sold to subscribers to the parliamentary cause; and the Act further forbade any subsequent

government to pardon the rebels or restore their property. As such, it remained in force until the statutes enacted after the restoration of Charles II.

In the meantime, Ireland underwent the so-called 'War of the Three Kingdoms'. The complexities and confusions of this period are almost infinite. In April 1642, General Munroe landed at Carrickfergus with a Scots Presbyterian army, soon joined by the Ulster Scots and many Protestant leaders. When Charles I appointed the Earl of Ormonde his Lord Lieutenant, and set up his royalist standard at Nottingham, in the summer of 1642, a second Protestant, but royalist, army formed in Ireland. A third group, which included many Protestant leaders, like the Earl of Inchiquin, President of Munster, and Roger Boyle Earl of Broghill, plus the ruling Lord Justices in Dublin, sided with the English parliament. In October 1642 the Catholic Confederacy of Kilkenny assembled, with its own parliament and a Catholic army for each province. This was pro-royalist, although it was never regarded as legitimate in the eyes of Charles I's government. Both Catholic and Protestant royalists presented their rival demands to the King at Oxford.[44]

The Catholics had two different forces, one under General Owen Roe O'Neill, nephew of the last Earl of Tyrone, representing the Old Irish, and one under General Preston, representing the Old English Catholics. The position of the Catholics was further complicated by the arrival, in October 1645, of the papal nuncio, Runucini, with papal money. In August 1646 Charles instructed his Lord Lieutenant, Ormonde, to make an alliance with the Catholics, on the basis of a repeal of all religious penalties (including oaths) and the confirmation of land-titles. Though most Catholics wanted to accept, the nuncio rejected the offer, and his verdict was upheld by Owen Roe O'Neill and the Catholic Assembly in February 1647. By this time King Charles's cause was lost in England, and Ormonde duly handed over Dublin to the parliamentarians, saying he preferred 'English rebels to Irish rebels'.[45] Thereafter, the parliamentarians never lost it, and it was at Dublin that Oliver Cromwell landed, with 20,000 men, on 15 August 1649, as 'Lord Lieutenant and General for the Parliament of England'.

CHAPTER 3

From Cromwell to the Boyne

Oliver Cromwell arrived in Ireland in a mood of religious exaltation. Before embarking at Bristol he told his troops they were Israelites about to enter Canaan and extirpate its idolatrous inhabitants. In the forefront of his mind were three considerations: the need to avenge the massacres of 1641; the desire to establish Protestant freedom of conscience; and, most of all, the prime English consideration throughout the ages, the determination that Ireland should not become a foreign base hostile to England. He had told his colleagues on the Council:

> If our interest is rooted out there, they will in a very short time be able to land forces in England, and put us to trouble here. . . . If they shall be able to carry on their work they will make this the most miserable people in the earth, for everyone knows their barbarism.

To Cromwell, the Irish menace, with its papal links, was the most to be feared:

> I had rather be overrun with a Cavalierish interest than a Scotch interest; I had rather be overrun with a Scotch interest than an Irish interest; and I think, of all, this is the most dangerous. [1]

On his arrival he told the leading citizens of Dublin that 'as God had brought [him] thither in safety', so he did not doubt that, 'by His divine providence', he and his troops would 'restore them all to their just liberty and property' and 'carry on the great work against the barbarous and bloodthirsty Irish, and their adherents and confederates' and so restore 'that bleeding nation to its former happiness and prosperity'. [2]

No royalist or Irish army was capable of taking the field against Cromwell's Ironsides. But some towns were strongly held: that was why Cromwell brought a heavy siege-train with him. He made first for Drogheda, on the mouth of the Boyne, guarding the route to Ulster. Since the 'massacre of Drogheda' has passed into Irish demonology, it is important to be clear what happened there. Cromwell had nothing but contempt for the casual slaughter, on both sides, which was such a feature of Irish campaigning. He had his men under firm control, hanging two of them for daring to steal hens from the Irish.[3] He hoped that with his reputation, his siege-train and his formidable army he could induce the royalist towns to surrender peacefully. The rules of war were quite clear. Since a besieging army risked more, from what the Earl of Ormonde called 'Colonel Hunger and Major Sickness', quite apart from the assault itself, a besieged town risked massacre if it rejected terms of surrender before investment. Defiant garrisons were ruthlessly put to the sword to avoid costly sieges elsewhere; as Wellington was later to put it, 'The practice of refusing quarter to a garrison which stands on assault is not a useless effusion of blood'.[4] The rule was that, once the besiegers had gone to the bloody expense of breaching the wall, quarter could not be demanded. Nor did the rules of war exempt civilians in a town.[5]

After Cromwell had deployed his eleven siege guns in front of Drogheda, he expected Sir Arthur Aston, its governor (an Englishman and a Catholic), to surrender. He sent terms under a white flag, adding, 'If this be refused, you will have no cause to blame me'. Aston, confident he could hold the town – he boasted: 'He who could take Drogheda could take Hell' – did refuse, whereupon Cromwell replaced his white flag with a red one, signifying blood. That Aston knew what to expect is indicated by his message to Ormonde, which declared that he and his men were 'unanimous in their resolution to perish rather than give up the place'. In the event, though the bombardment was successful, two costly assaults were needed

before the town was effectively taken and Cromwell ordered
all those who had borne arms to be killed. Among them was
Aston, beaten to death with his own wooden leg, which the
soldiers wrongly believed was stuffed with gold pieces.
Cromwell wrote to the Speaker of the English parliament:
'... our men getting up to them, were ordered by me to put
them all to the sword; and indeed being in the heat of action, I
forbade them to spare any that were in arms in the town, and I
think that night they put to the sword about two thousand
men'.[6]

Cromwell gave no orders for the killing of the town's
civilians. It was the parliamentary printer, preparing his
dispatch as a pamphlet, who added to the last sentence 'and
many inhabitants'.[7] We have, however, a remarkable
eyewitness to events, for the antiquary Anthony Wood's
brother, Thomas, was one of Cromwell's officers. According
to Thomas's account, recorded by Anthony Wood,

> ... when they were to make their way up to the lofts and
> galleries of the church, and up to the tower where the
> enemy had fled, each of the assailants would take up a child
> and use it as a buckler of defence, when they ascended the
> steps, to keep themselves from being shot or brain'd. After
> they had killed all in the church, they went into the vaults
> underneath, where all the flower and choicest of the
> women and ladies had hid themselves. One of these, a most
> handsome virgin and array'd in costly and gorgeous
> apparel, kneel'd down to Tho. Wood with tears and
> prayers to save her life: and being strucken with a profound
> pity, he took her under his arm, went with her out of the
> church, with intention to put her over the works and let her
> shift for herself; but then a soldier perceiving his intentions,
> ran a sword up her belly or fundament. Whereupon Mr
> Wood, seeing her gasping, took away her money, jewels,
> etc., and flung her down over the works.[8]

Cromwell argued that the killings were 'a righteous judgment of God upon these barbarous wretches... it will tend to prevent the effusion of blood for the future, which are satisfactory grounds to such actions, which otherwise cannot but work remorse or regret'.[9] On this last point he was certainly correct, Dundalk and other royalist garrisons promptly surrendering. Ormonde complained they were 'stupefied' with fear.[10] At Wexford, however, there was some dithering on the part of the garrison, and in the event the castle was betrayed without any terms being negotiated. Cromwell's men broke into the town. He reported to parliament:

> And when they were come into the market-place, the enemy making stiff resistance, our forces brake them, and then put all to the sword that came in their way.... I believe, in all, there was lost to the enemy not many less than two thousand; and I believe not twenty of yours killed from first to last of the siege.[11]

Cromwell seems, for once, to have lost control of his men, who may have been inflamed by Wexford's reputation for piracy. On the Catholic side there were many reports of atrocities, especially to priests.[12]

The next few months saw Ireland effectively conquered. Owen Roe O'Neill died in November 1649. Ulster and Munster were pacified. In March 1650 Kilkenny surrendered and the Irish Confederacy dissolved. The only rebuff inflicted on Cromwell was at Clonmel, where Hugh O'Neill, having defied the besiegers, slipped away during the night. By the end of the month Cromwell felt his work was done and returned to England, leaving his son-in-law General Ireton as commander-in-chief. As for the subsequent pacification, Cromwell himself did not favour severe measures. The Council of Officers of the New Model Army had already pledged that the army in Ireland should not be used 'to eradicate the natives or divest them of their estates'. Cromwell had hoped that 'the people of Ireland... may equally participate in all benefits, to use liberty and fortune equally with Englishmen, if they keep out of arms'. In December 1649, asking John Sadler to become Chief Justice of Munster, he wrote:

> We have a great opportunity to set up, until the Parliament shall otherwise determine, a way of doing justice among these poor people, which, for the uprightness and cheapness of it, may exceedingly gain upon them, who have been accustomed to as much injustice, tyranny and oppression from their landlords, the great men, and those that should have done them right, as, I believe, any people in that which we call Christendom.[13]

In this respect he echoed the view of Sir John Davies, and many other well-meaning Englishmen since, who believed that English rule could be acceptable to the Irish if only it brought justice. But Cromwell was not prepared to compromise on religion, as he made clear to the governor of New Ross when negotiating terms of surrender:

> For that which you mention concerning liberty of conscience, I meddle not with any man's conscience. But if by liberty of conscience you mean the liberty of exercising the mass, I judge it best to use plain dealing, and to let you know, where the Parliament of England have power, that will not be allowed of.[14]

The difference the Cromwellian conquest of Ireland made was that, for the first time, vigorous steps were taken to enforce the law against the mass.

Even more fundamental was the fact that Ireland, as Clarendon put it, was treated as 'the great capital out of which the Cromwellian army paid all debts, rewarded all services and performed all acts of bounty'.[15] It was an irresistible temptation to pay off the army by settling its men on land confiscated from the Irish rebels. The 30,000 royalist and Catholic soldiers who surrendered in 1651-2 were, on the whole, treated leniently, being allowed to go to France, Spain and other European countries, though a number of Irish were sent to the plantations in the West Indies, as slaves. Dr Henry Jones, Bishop of Clougher, drew up a report on the 1641 massacres, and a special court was set up in Dublin to try those responsible, though it executed only fifty-two of them (including Sir Phelim O'Neill). But the net was cast wide for those with land to be forfeited.

In August 1652, the English parliament passed An Act for the Settling of Ireland, one of the most radical measures in our constitutional history. The preamble states that the 'suppression of the horrid rebellion' in Ireland had cost so 'much blood and treasure' that a 'total reducement and settlement of that nation' was required. However, it continued, 'it is not the intention of parliament to extirpate that whole nation'. Instead, the Act listed ten categories of Irishmen. The first five categories, including active rebels, to the number of about 100,000, were to be hanged; the second five categories were to have their lives spared but lose all their property, though parliament would assign lands elsewhere to some of these groups in due course. A second Act provided for officers and soldiers who were owed back pay to be granted property 'out of rebel lands, houses, tenements and hereditaments in Ireland'.[16] Broadly speaking, the intention of these two acts was to move the Irish Catholic gentry and landowners into the west of the country, resettling their lands with New Model soldiers. By ordinances of June–July 1653 and a final Act of Satisfaction of September 1653, Ireland was divided into two: Clare and Connaught left to Irish gentry and landowners, and the rest of Ireland settled by the troops and the 'adventurers' who had subscribed under the Act of 1642. This was the notorious 'Hell or Connaught' policy.[17]

It is difficult to determine to what extent the intentions of parliament were carried out. Certainly, in conjunction with the warfare and expulsions which had taken place in Ireland since 1641, the new transplantations and settlements were the

culmination of a gigantic social upheaval, which transformed
the country's demographic and economic structure. Parliament employed the economist William Petty to make the first
accurate land survey of Ireland (called the *down* survey,
because it was put down on paper). According to Aubrey, he
performed his task

> with that exactness, that there is no Estate there to the
> value of three-score pounds but he can show, to the value;
> and those that he employed for the Geometrical part were
> ordinary fellows, some (perhaps) foot-soldiers, that circum-
> ambulated with their *box and needles*, not knowing what
> they did, which Sir William knew right well how to make
> use of.[18]

Petty calculated that the population of Ireland in 1641 had
been 1,448,000, of which 616,000 had perished (504,000
natives, 112,000 settlers and troops). Some 40,000 more,
mainly Catholics, had gone into overseas service and 100,000
had been transported to the Americas. The loss of livestock
had been so severe that Ireland, traditionally a cattle-
exporter, had had to import cattle from Wales.[19] The fighting
had also accelerated the destruction of Ireland's forests and
woods.[20] While the population had declined by nearly half,
wolves had multiplied, so that the export of wolfhounds was
forbidden, and in December 1652 a public wolf-hunt was held
at Castleknock, with a bounty of £6 paid for a dead wolf-
bitch.[21]

Of the settlement itself, Petty says that out of a total of
twenty million acres, eleven million were confiscated. Some
19,000 soldiers were eligible for land-debentures, but many of
them sold their allocation to officers, land-speculators and
companies, and it is calculated that only about 25 per cent of
them remained after the Restoration. Nevertheless, a new
landlord class had been created; from this point onwards the
Catholic landowners were in a small minority, and in the
towns, too, Protestants became dominant.

Moreover, the Restoration of Charles II in 1660 did not put the clock back. The King was proclaimed in Ireland, following the *coup* of General Monck, by Lord Broghill and Sir Charles Coote, both parliamentarians, who were promptly created Earl of Montrath and Earl of Orrery for their change of allegiance. So it was the old Cromwellian leadership which restored the monarchy in Ireland, not the royalists, whether Catholic or Protestant. Charles II made Ormonde a Duke and restored him to the Lord Lieutenancy, but in public policy the distinction was made not between parliamentarians and royalists but between Catholics and Protestants. Theoretically, the whole land of Ireland was put at the crown's disposal. But as Charles II put it: 'My justice I must afford to you all, but my favour must be given to my Protestant subjects.'[22] The second Act of Settlement, in 1662, treated Catholic Irish in arms up to 1646 as rebels, and the crown remained pledged to the Adventurers' Acts of 1642. Irish Catholics who had not taken arms against the crown at any time had their lands restored, and some eighteen peers and other named proprietors were put back in possession at once.[23] The net effect of all these changes and restorations is that, between 1640 and the 1660s, the Protestant share of the land in Ireland increased from 41 per cent to 78 per cent.[24]

Ormonde had some sympathy with dispossessed Irish landlords, and his 1663 Act of Explanation forced Cromwellians to disgorge to 'unreprised' Catholics a third of the estates they held in 1659, the Court of Claims determining the transfers. But after 1667 Protestant influence was too strong to permit any further transfers. With the Oath of Supremacy imposed, Irish parliaments were overwhelmingly Protestant, and there was no sympathy for Irish papists in Westminster. Charles himself, a Catholic *in peto*, could do little to help them, as is revealed by a remarkable piece of paper, passed to and fro between him and the Earl of Clarendon while they attended a tedious Privy Council meeting in 1661:

Charles: When will it be fit to call in the Irish as they desired last night?

Clarendon: Whenever you have a mind to spoil the business.

Charles: Had we not promised to hear the Irish?

Clarendon: Have you not heard them? If you do call them, the other side must be called too, and then we are in till morning. If you are too tender-hearted on their behalf, I pray you leave them to the House of Commons and their work is done: they are mad, and do not understand their own interest.

Charles: For my part, rebel for rebel, I had rather trust a papist rebel than a Presbyterian one.

Clarendon: The difference is, that you have wiped out the memory of the rebellion of the one, whilst the other is liable to all reproaches.

(Clarendon, unlike Charles, remembered the impact of the 1641 rebellion on Westminster.)[25]

In general, the Restoration was not a happy time in Ireland. The new settlement acts angered the Protestants but completely failed to satisfy the Catholics. It was a source of particular resentment that ancient estates had gone to grasping officials, 'a generation of mechanic bagmen, strangers to all principles of religion and loyalty', as Richard Bellings, secretary to the Catholic Confederacy, wrote to Ormonde. The latter was hated by the Irish, as born and educated in England, and often heard to say that he was an Englishman by birth, extraction and choice. In fact Ormonde, who was Lord Lieutenant from 1661–69 and again from 1677–85, was liberal-minded for his age. But the religious settlement was not of his making. The Church of Ireland was restored, as the state church in 1661, with regular archbishops and bishops. It had the support of most of the Protestant gentry, but probably less than half of Ireland's 300,000 Protestants, let alone its 800,000 Catholics (Petty's figures).[26] Parliament was predominantly Anglican, though

Nonconformists and even Catholics still had the vote and the right to sit.

If the Protestants were divided, so were the Catholics. The crown made a major error in failing to make any state provision for the Catholic clergy; as a result, the priests relied entirely on parish collections and foreign aid. This tipped the scales in favour of the Ultramontane party within the Catholic church. In 1661 Richard Bellings drew up a document stating that no foreign power (i.e., the Pope) could release Irish Catholics from their allegiance. He hoped to get legal toleration in return. It was signed by 21 Catholic peers and 164 prominent laymen, but only about 70 out of 2,000 priests dared put their name to it. In 1665 the Catholic bishops also refused to condemn the deposing power and Bellings's document was angrily repudiated by the Papacy.

The failure of this scheme not only meant that legal discrimination against Catholics continued, but also implied that Catholics were under orders from their priests to be disloyal in certain circumstances. Though Ormonde might extend toleration in practice, he was powerless to stem the wave of anti-Catholicism which engulfed Britain during the Titus Oates Popish Plot. Archbishop Oliver Plunkett, the Catholic Archbishop of Armagh, was arrested, dragged to England, imprisoned, finally charged with high treason, convicted and executed in 1681, although even by Protestants he was 'generally pitied and believed to die very innocent of what he was condemned'.[27] Thus the ditch between the two communities was widened and deepened.

The reaction from the Popish Plot naturally benefited Irish Catholics. In the last year of his reign, Charles II began 'remodelling' town and city corporations in Ireland, as in England, and this had the effect of placing some of them back in Catholic hands. But James II, who succeeded Charles in 1685, rushed in where Charles had trod gingerly. He made Richard Talbot, the Catholic Earl of Tyrconnell, Lieutenant-General in command of the Irish Army. Though he was balanced by James's brother-in-law, the Earl of Clarendon (a Protestant), as Lord Lieutenant, such a combination was unworkable.

Tyrconnell wanted to turn Ireland into a Catholic kingdom, which meant repealing the Oath of Supremacy acts, so that Catholics could hold civil and military offices. He hastily commissioned Catholic officers and appointed them to key garrisons. The writ of *Quo Warranto* was used to make Catholics judges and sheriffs (who controlled elections). Since Tyrconnell's ultimate object was to recreate the Catholic ruling class, he had to have a Catholic parliament which would repeal not only the anti-Catholic penal acts but all the land settlement acts. When Clarendon objected, he was recalled, and Tyrconnell became Lord Lieutenant too. He announced that 'Ireland is in a better way of thriving under the influence of a native governor than under a stranger to us and to our country' and declared that his object was 'Reducing everything to that state that Ireland was in before Poynings' Law and before the Reformation of Henry VIII'.

This effectively united all Protestants against the regime. They had witnessed the fate of the Huguenots since Louis XIV revoked the Edict of Nantes in 1685, streaming to England as penniless refugees. Now, stripped of their offices, and with their land-titles in jeopardy, they had no alternative but to fight or flee. The two Acts of Indulgence towards Catholics of 1687–8 began a panic exodus of Protestants from Dublin. But the majority stayed and armed. There had been Protestant 'cities of refuge', such as Londonderry and Enniskillen, ever since 1641, and these were now refortified.

Up to this point the Catholic forces had not merely the bulk of the population but legality on their side. But William of Orange landed in England on 5 November 1688, and three months later, on 13 February 1689, the Westminster parliament voted for the joint rule of William and Mary. Under the Irish Restoration settlement, the law stated that 'the crown of Ireland was appendant and inseparably annexed to the imperial crown of England, and that whoever was King *de facto* in England was King *de jure* in Ireland'. When James II landed from France at Kinsale on 12 March he was no longer legally King of Ireland. He brought no French troops with him either, only officers; and Tyrconnell had fatally failed to rush the cities of refuge, Londonderry being saved in the nick of time by its 'Apprentice Boys'. Nevertheless, James held a parliament in May. Most Protestants refused to attend and, since it was overwhelmingly Catholic in composition, James soon lost control of it. It not only repealed Poynings' Law and the various Acts of Settlement and Explanation, but passed an Act of Attainder against over 2,400 Protestant landowners, stripping them of all their property. When James protested, he was told: 'If your Majesty will not fight for our rights, we will not fight for yours.'[28]

Meanwhile James had lost all England and Scotland, and he failed to secure all Ireland. Londonderry was relieved on 1 August 1689 and a fortnight later Marshal Schomberg, William III's commander, arrived in Bangor with 20,000 men. William himself followed in June 1690, and on 1 July he defeated James's army at the Battle of the Boyne. James could not even hold Dublin, and retired to France for good. He had made a disastrous impression on Irish opinion, and was unfavourably compared with William, who had fought gallantly at the Boyne, where he was wounded and coined the famous phrase 'Every bullet has its billet.'[29]

Fighting continued in Ireland for more than a year – the French succeeded in landing two small armies – but the Catholics had been divided even before the Boyne, and the death of Tyrconnell in August 1691 left the Stuart forces holding only Limerick. On 3 October, two peace treaties were signed there: one, a military capitulation, provided for the transport of the Irish Catholic army to France (11,000 sailed, but 2,000 remained in Ireland and 1,000 chose to serve William); the second was a civil treaty providing for the religious and civil liberties of Irish Catholics.[30]

The civil treaty was comparatively generous, in that it gave Catholics 'such privileges in the exercise of their religion, as are consistent with the laws of Ireland, or as they did enjoy in the reign of King Charles II' – that is, *de facto* toleration. It also provided some protection against the forfeiture of Catholic estates. But it required ratification by parliament. By an English parliament Act of 1691, extended to Ireland, Members of both Houses of Parliament had to take an oath of allegiance and, in addition, an oath abjuring the spiritual supremacy of the Pope, the Mass, Transubstantiation and other Catholic doctrines. It was framed specifically to exclude Catholics and did so effectively until the Catholic Emancipation Act of 1829. From henceforth, then, the Dublin parliament was wholly Protestant for the first time, and when it finally got round to ratifying the Treaty of Limerick in 1697 it did so only 'as may consist with the safety and welfare of your Majesty's subjects of this kingdom'.

As a result, about 1,700,000 acres of Catholic land was forfeited to the crown. These confiscations were eventually reduced by one-fourth, some 400,000 acres being restored to 'innocent papists' by an act of 1700. But over one million acres were sold in the market, Irish Catholics being debarred by law from buying more than two acres each. By 1700 Catholics held only one-eighth of the land in Ireland, and this proportion fell further over the next half-century as Catholic proprietors conformed to escape the rigours of the penal code.[31]

The code was built up by a series of statutes passed between 1695 and 1727. Some of its provisions were aimed as much at Dissenters as at Catholics: thus, the Tory 1704 Act required office-holders under the crown to take the sacrament according to the Anglican rite. This excluded Dissenters from state offices and corporations, so they lost control of Belfast and other towns, and disappeared from parliament. From 1710 their ministers no longer received any state stipend. But the most ferocious statutes were aimed at Catholics. They could not sit in parliament, bear arms (except for sport), own a horse worth more than £5, become apprentice to a gunsmith, hold an army or naval commission, keep a school at home, get education abroad, practise law, take more than two apprentices (except in the linen trade) and, from 1727, vote in a parliamentary election. Under a 1704 Act, land already held or hereditable by Protestants might not legally be transferred to papists, who could inherit only from each other and were forbidden to purchase land, lend on mortgage or take a lease over thirty-one years. A gavelkind act (reversing, for Catholics, Sir John Davies's beneficent work) forced Catholics to divide their estates between their sons, unless the eldest conformed. This provision was particularly hated because it blackmailed many landowners into changing their faith.

It is true that, as the eighteenth century progressed, many of the penal laws were not enforced. But the disabling acts were, because there was always constant pressure from Protestants to keep state jobs and the professions to themselves. So the Catholics were in practice confined to agriculture, the linen trade, medicine and brewing. Curiously enough, and perhaps deliberately, the penal code, while plainly designed to exclude Catholics from the ruling class and inhibit their opportunities among the middle class, did nothing to stop the peasants from retaining their faith. An Act of 1703 banished Catholic bishops, regular clergy and vicars-general; but a Registration Act permitted priests to say mass provided they took a simple oath of allegiance and registered themselves, which 1,000 did – being directed from afar by a 'shadow' hierarchy in Brussels.

The effect of this legislation and the manner in which it was enforced was to create the modern Irish problem, as it existed until the twentieth century: a landless Catholic peasantry governed by a legally exclusive Protestant ruling class, with a small predominantly Protestant middle class sandwiched in between, and a multi-class Protestant enclave in Ulster. The separate communities were divided not only by religion but by race and, not least, by culture: they learned different poetry, sang different songs, celebrated different victories, mourned different calamities and, above all, swore different oaths. Ireland became a country where privilege was upheld, and revenge planned, by the swearing of oaths. Catholic oaths were secret and furtive. Protestant oaths were public and assertive, indeed vainglorious and provocative, being turned into toasts. In the Victoria and Albert Museum there is a glass goblet with a toast which epitomizes the oath-taking folklore of Ascendancy Ireland:

> To the Glorious, Pious and Immortal memory of the Great and Good King William, who freed us from Pope and Popery, Knavery and Slavery, Brass Money and Wooden Shoes, and may he who refuses this toast be damned, crammed and rammed down the Great Gun of Athlone.[32]

CHAPTER 4

Rebellion and Union

The Ireland which emerged into the eighteenth century had its own parliament, composed overwhelmingly of descendants of Cromwellian and Williamite settlers, but in other respects was a British colony. The Act recognizing William and Mary as sovereign was passed by the Dublin parliament 'forasmuch as this kingdom of Ireland is annexed and united to the imperial crown of England, and by the laws and statutes of this kingdom (Ireland) is declared to be justly and rightfully belonging and ever united to the same'. A Declaratory Act of 1719 clarified and reinforced the subordinate position of Ireland.[1] After 1692 the principle of Poynings' Law was applied by a procedure known as the 'Heads of Bills'. Either Irish House of Parliament could propose a Bill, which had first to be accepted by the Irish Council, then passed by the Irish parliament. Thereupon it was passed to the English privy council, which could accept, alter or reject it. When it was returned, the Irish parliament had to accept or reject it as it stood. In addition, King and parliament in England had reserved power over foreign policy, defence, trade and navigation. The Irish parliament met every second year to vote supplies, but money Bills were jointly prepared by the Irish and English councils. While parliament actually met every two years its legal length was indefinite (George II's Irish parliament lasted thirty-three years, from 1727–60), for the Triennial and Septennial Acts did not apply to Ireland; nor did the Bill of Rights.

In any case, the English government appointed the Irish government and council. The Lord Lieutenant, nearly always English, was appointed by London and came under the British Secretary of State for Home Affairs, who directed him. The Lord Lieutenant appointed all the chief officers of the government. Until 1785, all the Irish Lord Chancellors were Englishmen, and the law was subordinate since the Declaratory Act abolished the appellate jurisdiction of the Irish House of Lords. If there was no Lord Lieutenant, rule was by the Lords Justices. An Englishman, Archbishop Boulter of Armagh (1724-42), ruled Ireland for nearly twenty years. Irish bishoprics served as prizes for ambitious English clergymen. Archbishop Hoadley of Dublin (1730-42) and Archbishop Stone of Armagh (1747-64) were both English.[2] In practice, all the important decisions on Ireland were taken in London or referred there. The Earl of Shrewsbury said in 1713 that the job of Lord Lieutenant was 'a place where a man had business enough to prevent him falling asleep but not enough to keep him awake'. Ireland was regarded as crushed. It is significant that it caused little anxiety even during the Forty-Five rising. When, on the morning prior to the Battle of Culloden, the Dublin Vice-Treasurer, Mr Gardiner, dashed into the bedchamber of Lord Chesterfield, the Lord Lieutenant, and shouted that the Irish were rising, Chesterfield consulted his watch and said: 'It is past nine o'clock – time for any honest man to rise – and I shall rise myself.'[3]

What the Protestants of the Ascendancy resented most, like their fellow-colonials in America, was the restrictive trade legislation passed by the British parliament for the benefit of English manufactures and other English economic interests. The original 1651 Navigation Act, passed under the Commonwealth, treated Irish ships as the same as English; but the Navigation Acts of 1663 and 1670 discriminated against the Irish mercantile marine and thus effectively excluded it from empire trade. The 1666 Irish Cattle Act was drawn up to exclude imports of cheap Irish beef into England, and there were other restrictive Acts against Irish agricultural produce.[4]

Irish anger was first effectively expressed by William

Molyneux's book, *The case of Ireland's being bound by Act of Parliament in England stated*, published in Dublin in 1697. As a Protestant he accepted the superior position of the English parliament, but he argued that the true alternatives were either a proper legislative union or greater economic freedom for Ireland. London's answer was the 1699 Act, which allowed the export of Irish manufactured woollen goods only to England, which had heavy duties, and so crushed the Irish woollen trade.[5]

Molyneux's arguments were taken up and enormously enlivened by the fiery pen of Jonathan Swift, Dean of St Patrick's Cathedral from 1713–45. Swift was an Ascendancy man first and last, and his sympathies were narrow-based. He hotly defended the over-privileged Church of Ireland against both Catholics and Presbyterians, though he was well aware how few of the common people supported it (in his first Irish benefice, greeted by a congregation of one, he began prayers: 'Dearly beloved Roger, the scripture moveth both you and me'). Yet Swift was the first Irishman (he was born in Dublin and educated at Trinity College there) to express in the English language the Irish consciousness of a separate identity, lit by a burning indignation at English injustice. He called his patriotism the 'perfect rage and resentment, at the mortifying sight of slavery, folly and baseness';[6] and he said he feared he would die in Dublin in a rage, 'like a poisoned rat in a hole.'[7] In 1720 he produced a *Proposal for the Universal Use of Irish Manufacturers*. It angered the Dublin Castle authorities – who could not get a jury to convict him – by virtually proposing a boycott of English goods. He quoted a former Archbishop of Tuam, 'that Ireland would never be happy until a law was made for burning everything that came from England except their people and their coals', adding: 'I must confess, as to the former, I should not be sorry if they would stay at home; and, for the latter, I hope in a little time we shall have no occasion for them.'

Swift carried on the campaign in his *Drapier's Letters* (1724)

by attacking the scandalous plan to give Ireland a copper
currency known as 'Wood's Halfpence'. An English iron-
master, William Wood, had been issued a patent to coin
£100,800 of halfpence and farthings; he had secured the
patent by agreeing to halve the profit – £40,000 – with George
I's ex-mistress, the Duchess of Kendal. Thanks to Swift, the
proposal was defeated; and when Dublin Castle tried to get a
jury to convict Swift's printer, it instead presented all those
who tried to impose the wretched coins as 'enemies of his
Majesty and the welfare of this kingdom'.

Swift touched a chord in the Irish nation, which was to
reverberate more and more. When he returned to Dublin in
1726, after the triumphant publication of *Gulliver's Travels* in
London, bonfires were lit, bells rung, the harbour was
crowded with boats, the mayor and corporation turned out
and he was carried in splendour to his Deanery.[8] Swift was
haunted by the notion that the real object of English policy
towards Ireland was depopulation. The first overseas
emigrations on a large scale began among the Ulster
Dissenters, in protest against their disabilities and the general
raising of rents in 1718. But Irish Catholics were leaving all
the time. It was said that in the forty years 1690–1730, some
120,000 'wild geese' as they were called had left to serve in
foreign armies. In his pamphlet *Answer to the Craftsmen* (1730),
Swift argued, with savage irony, that the Irish be encouraged
to join the French army, as this would produce depopulation,
the object of English policy. Ireland, he wrote, 'is the only
kingdom I have ever heard or read of, either in ancient or in
modern history which was denied the liberty of exporting
their native commodities wherever they pleased. Yet this
privilege, by the superiority of mere power, is refused to us in
the most momentous parts of commerce.'

No sensitive Irish intellectual – and Trinity College,
Dublin, was now producing more of them than Oxford and
Cambridge combined – could deny, whatever his faith, the
palpable misery of the great mass of Irish people. In 1729, in

an ironic comment on Irish poverty, Swift published his
*Modest Proposal for Preventing the Children of Poor People from
Being a Burden to their Parents*, suggesting that babies might be
boiled and eaten. His younger contemporary, George
Berkeley, Bishop of Cloyne, whose startling *Treatise Concerning
the Principles of Human Knowledge* (1710) had made him a
European figure while still in his twenties, published in the
1730s his *Querist*, asking awkward questions, such as:
'Whether there be upon earth any Christian or civilised
people so beggarly wretched and destitute, as the common
Irish?'[9] Ireland kept the Hearth Tax until the end of the
eighteenth century, though it was abolished in England in
1689 as too hard on the poor. Petty calculated that in Ireland,
out of 184,000 houses, only 24,000 had one or more chimneys.
The evidence of poverty was ubiquitous and overwhelming,
and though Catholic protest was mute, many Protestants had
Catholic mothers and felt the rage in their bones even when
availing themselves of Ascendancy privileges.

One such was Edmund Burke. Aged nineteen, while still at
Trinity College, Dublin, he produced a magazine, the
Reformer, in which he wrote on 10 March 1748:

> ... as you leave the Town, the Scene grows worse, and
> presents you with the Utmost Penury in the Midst of a rich
> Soil. Nothing perhaps shows it more clearly, than that
> though the People have but one small tax of Two Shillings
> a Year, yet when the Collector comes, for Default of
> Payment, he is obliged to carry off such of their poor
> Utensils, as their being forced to use denotes the utmost
> Misery; those he keeps, until by begging, or other Shifts
> more hard, they can redeem them. Indeed, Money is a
> stranger to them. ... As for their Food, it is notorious they
> seldom taste Bread or Meat; their diet, in Summer, is
> Potatoes and sour Milk; in Winter, when something is
> required Comfortable, they are still worse, living on the
> same Root, made palatable only by a little Salt, and

accompanied with Water: their Cloaths so ragged, that they rather publish than conceal the Wretchedness it was meant to hide; nay, it is no uncommon sight to see half a dozen Children run quite naked out of a Cabin, scarcely distinguishable from the Dunghill. . . . Let any one take a survey of their Cabins and then say, whether such a Residence be worthy anything that challenges the Title of a human Creature. You enter, or rather creep in, at a Door or Hurdles plastered with Dirt . . . within side you see (if the Smoke will permit you) the Men, Women, Children, Dogs and Swine lying promiscuously. . . . Their Furniture is much fitter to be lamented than described, such as a Pot, a Stool, a few wooden Vessels, and a broken bottle. In this manner all the Peasantry, to a Man, live: and I Appeal to any one, who knows the Country, for the Justness of the Picture.[10]

Burke was also honest enough to see the power-structure of Ireland for what it was: 'The Protestant Ascendancy is nothing more or less than the resolution of one set of people to consider themselves as the sole citizens of the Commonwealth and to keep a dominion over the rest by reducing them to slavery under a foreign power.' In the growing Age of Enlightenment, what struck disinterested English visitors was the huge gulf between rulers and ruled.[11] Arthur Young thought the penal laws 'better calculated for the meridian of Barbary' rather than civilized Europe. As for the relations between the classes:

A landlord in Ireland can scarcely invent an order which a servant, labourer or cottar dares to refuse to execute. Nothing satisfies him but an unlimited submission. Disrespect, or anything tending towards sauciness, he may punish with his cane or his horsewhip with the most perfect security: a poor man would have his bones broke if he offered to lift his hands in his own defence. Knocking-down is spoken of in this country in a manner which makes an

Englishman stare. . . . By what policy the government of England can for so many years have permitted such an absurd system to be matured in Ireland is beyond the power of plain sense to discover.[12]

Indeed, by the time Young made his tour of Ireland in the 1770s, many Englishmen, if they thought about Ireland at all, saw government policy there as indefensible. It is significant that Dr Samuel Johnson, though a vigorous defender of English rights in America, could not bring himself to defend them in Ireland. He had, says Boswell, 'great compassion for the miseries and distresses of the Irish nation, particularly the papists, and severely reprobated the barbarous, debilitating policies of the British government which, he said, was the most detestable form of persecution'. When it was suggested that the penal laws were needed to uphold English authority, he replied: 'Let the authority of the English government perish rather than be maintained by iniquity. . . . Better (said he) to hang or drown people at once, than by an unrelenting persecution to beggar or starve them.'[13]

In fact from the 1740s onwards (the same phenomenon was detectable in Scotland) Irish prosperity increased fairly steadily; and with it came a new self-assertiveness among Irish Protestants. In 1751 and again in 1753, the elements of a parliamentary opposition emerged in Dublin over the government's authoritarian use of Irish Exchequer surpluses. It was an axiom in London and in Dublin Castle that, *in extremis*, an Ascendancy opposition could always be bribed with titles and offices – indeed the entire Dublin parliament was managed by a system of rotten and pocket boroughs, owned by aristocrats squared by the crown, and government patronage. In this case a dukedom and an earldom did the trick; but the principle that future Exchequer surpluses be assigned to Irish needs was conceded.

Thereafter, Irish constitutional reformers sought steadily to widen this hole in colonial rule. Of course they were all

Protestants, mainly lawyers and Trinity College, Dublin, men; and some had wider aims than others. Henry Flood spoke only for 'the Protestant Nation'. Henry Grattan, who led a new Patriot party aligned with the English Rockingham Whigs, wanted to do something for Catholics also. But both agreed that the penal laws, as such, should be done away with, and on this point steady progress was made. Protestant reformers were helped by the emergence of an articulate, responsible Catholic middle class, who owed their prosperity to grazing and the food trade, and which in 1756 grouped itself round the Catholic Committee.

The first concessions to the Catholics arose from the government's need for Irish recruits in its imperial armies, the Augmentation of the Army Act. In return, Catholics were admitted to junior ranks. In 1771 the Bogland Act permitted Catholics to take up to fifty acres of 'unprofitable' land on long leases of sixty-one years. Negotiations conducted through Edmund Burke, now a British MP and London correspondent of the Catholic Committee, led to the framing of a new loyalty oath, which Catholics could take, embodied in statutory form in 1774; and this in turn produced the Relief Act of 1778 by which Catholics could take indefinite leases under the new oath.[14] The Gavelkind Act was also repealed, and in 1780 the Test Act, which barred Dissenters from office. Grattan wanted to give the vote to all Catholic freeholders, and to make Catholic landowners eligible for office and parliament. Flood would not go this far. But both pushed through the 1782 Second Relief Act which enabled Catholics, provided they took the new oath, to buy, sell, bequeath and mortgage freeholds on the same terms as Protestants. The penal acts on education, priests and arms were scrapped; by 1782, in fact, the penal system had gone, though 'disabilities' remained.[15]

Yet the main thrust of the Protestant reformers was to secure plenary powers for the parliament they dominated – Protestant Home Rule, in fact. The loss of the American colonies disposed London towards concessions. In 1778 the English parliament gave way over the Navigation Acts. Over the next few years the progress towards Irish nationhood seemed irresistible, as a wave of patriotic and romantic fervour swept over Protestant Dublin. When the Dublin parliament met in 1779, all MPs pledged themselves to wear clothes manufactured in Ireland. The processional route to parliament was lined by the new corps of Irish Volunteers, a citizen army, 80,000 strong at its peak – and virtually all Protestants – dressed in gaudy uniforms and armed by the government. They were, said Grattan, the 'armed property of the nation', and Flood argued that the Volunteers existed to secure Ireland's rights from England, and would remain in arms until those rights were conceded. When the Commons assembled they passed a motion declaring that 'only by a free trade could this nation be saved from impending ruin', and they declined to vote supplies for more than six months. At the end of the year, the enfeebled North government in London surrendered and passed laws giving Ireland freedom of trade with the colonies and the free export of wool, woollen cloth and glassware.

The floodtide of the 'Protestant Nation' came in 1782, when a Convention of the Volunteers at Dungannon passed a resolution, recalling the Yorkist Parliament of 1460 and the Jacobite Parliament of 1689, which stated that 'the claim of any other than the King, Lords and Commons of Ireland to make laws to bind this kingdom is unconstitutional, illegal and a grievance'; so were 'the powers exercised by the Privy Councils of both kingdoms under Poynings' Law'. By this time the Whigs were in power in London, and they yielded gracefully by repealing the Declaratory Act, thereby abolishing the rights of the English and Irish privy councils to alter or kill Bills passed in Dublin. This enabled the Dublin parliament to pass legislation establishing the independence of the Irish judiciary and Supreme Court, limiting the Mutiny Act to two years, and drawing the teeth of Poynings' Law.[16]

The following year the parliament in London conceded
that Ireland now had legislative independence, had a new
constitution in fact, by affirming 'that the right claimed by
the people of Ireland to be bound only by laws enacted by his
Majesty and the parliament of that kingdom, in all cases
whatever shall be, and is hereby, declared to be established
and ascertained for ever, and shall at no time hereafter be
questioned or questionable'. Delighted, the Irish gratefully
voted £100,000 for the Royal Navy and presented Grattan,
deemed to be the hero of the new deal, with £50,000. He made
a much-quoted speech, which ended: 'Ireland is now a
nation. In that character I hail her and, bowing in her august
presence, I say *Esto perpetua.*'

But in Irish history there is never a happy ending. The new
constitution (or 'Grattan's Parliament') lasted only eighteen
years. The truth is, it represented a halfway house, from
which either advance to full independence or retreat into
subservience were both possible. Equipoise was out of the
question. As Grattan realized, in an age when the United
States had just achieved independence under a non-
confessional constitution, the great majority of Irishmen
could not be excluded from power in a country with a quasi-
independent legislature merely on religious grounds. That
was why he wanted to open the franchise, parliament and all
offices (except the highest) to Catholics as rapidly as possible.
So did Burke.[17] Flood's determination to maintain the
Protestant Ascendancy was incompatible with his desire to
secure home rule because in the last resort the Protestant
ruling class would always have to look to British power to
maintain itself.

Moreover, there were many powerful Protestants who
grasped the grim logic of their position and who, asked to
choose between their privileges and independence, would
always choose the former. The Ascendancy was rotten at its
core: the 'new constitution' rested on an unreformed
parliament. The MPs from the thirty-two counties, elected on

a forty-shilling freehold qualification vote, and from some of the bigger towns, were reasonably independent, but of the 300 MPs, no less than 176 were nominated by aristocratic patrons (86 of them from rotten boroughs). As Grattan said, in 1790, two-thirds of the seats in the Irish House of Commons were private property. Some 18 aristocrats controlled 70 of the 235 borough seats, and only 13 boroughs were not under the control of a single interest. The electors were corrupt too. When the head of the Stewart clan was made Lord Londonderry in 1789, and his heir Lord Castlereagh, aged just twenty-one, had to fight a contested election for the family seat in County Down the following year, there was polling over sixty-nine days and his father had to provide over £60,000 – family properties in Dublin, books and paintings had to be sold, and work stopped on their grandiose new house at Mount Stewart.[18]

The system might have been reformed from within. But when he was asked to take office in 1782, Grattan refused. That left Dublin Castle to the hard men, led by John Fitzgibbon, later Earl of Clare, who was successively Attorney-General and Lord Chancellor for twenty years. Clare was a realist. He thought the effervescence of 1782–3 a 'fatal infatuation'. He believed that the British connection must have priority over everything else; a constitution which underpinned and maintained the Protestant Ascendancy came next – the two stood or fell together. He and his friends at Dublin Castle, whom Burke called the *click* (clique) or *junta*, thus had a common interest with the London government, which from 1783, when William Pitt the Younger took power, was to be Tory for the best part of half a century.[19]

Pitt began as a reformer, but his ardour progressively cooled, and it is notable that all English politicians in office (even the Whigs) were less keen on reform in Ireland than in England. Pitt and the junta had another thing in common: they believed radicalism could be killed by prosperity. Since the 1740s, Ireland's economy had improved steadily. In 1784

John Foster, the junta's Chancellor of the Exchequer, introduced a corn law which turned Ireland into a great grain-producing country. In 1793 the Hearth Tax was abolished, giving the peasants an incentive to build decent cottages for themselves. By 1799, Forster could claim that the population had increased from 1.5 million at the beginning of the century to 4.5 million, that linen exports had risen from half a million yards a year to 47 million, and that exports as a whole had multiplied nearly tenfold.[20]

In 1784 Pitt wanted to reinforce this rising prosperity with an Anglo-Irish trade treaty. It was negotiated in Ireland on a basis of near-equality and passed by the Irish Parliament in 1785. But Westminster amended it to bar direct Irish exports to Latin America and India, and when the treaty got back to Dublin it barely scraped through parliament and so was dropped. Grattan said the treaty, as amended, meant for Ireland 'a surrender of trade in the east and of freedom in the west'. That was one indication, to Pitt, that the new Irish constitution would not work. Another was disagreement over how to handle George III's incipient madness, for Pitt a matter of political life or death. The Dublin parliament, desiring the return of the Whigs to power, carried by a two-to-one majority a loyal address to the pro-Whig Prince of Wales, asking him 'to assume the government of this nation during his Majesty's indisposition, under the style of Prince Regent of Ireland, and to exercise the prerogative of the crown'. The King's recovery enabled Pitt to survive, but thereafter he distrusted the Irish parliament and his thoughts began to move towards a legislative union.

Pitt and Dublin Castle still disposed of the real power in Ireland: to that extent the new constitution was an illusion, for the only real check on the executive which the Dublin parliament possessed was the right to refuse supply or to reject the Mutiny Bill, leading to an automatic disbanding of the army – an unlikely course for a Protestant legislature. The cabinet in London could still advise the sovereign to veto Irish bills, and it controlled the Lord Lieutenant through the Home Secretary. Thus the junta was effectively kept in power by London, and the Irish parliament could not remove any of its members by a vote.

Underpinning the junta were the aristocratic borough-mongers led by the clan of the Beresfords, Earl of Tyrone. It was said that the Beresfords controlled a quarter of the jobs-for-the-boys in Ireland; and John Beresford, MP for Waterford, was Pitt's political manager in Dublin (as Boulter has been Walpole's).[21] Irish government pensions rose to £100,000 by 1790; the Speaker, a key man in drilling the parliament, got the enormous salary of £4,500 a year, plus £500 for each session. Efforts by Grattan and Flood to reform the Dublin Castle patronage system, kill corrupt boroughs and enlarge the franchise were voted down: half the Commons, it was claimed, were government pensioners or placemen.[22] While holding out the carrots, Pitt did not forget the stick: the introduction of a new militia, which government could control.

Pitt remained committed to Catholic Emancipation. There was a Catholic Relief Act in 1792 and another in 1793, which enabled Catholics to bear arms, take degrees at Trinity College, Dublin, hold most ranks in the army, sit on town and city corporations, act as grand jurors and vote as forty-shilling freeholders – everything except become an MP or hold government office.[23] In 1795 Pitt planned to go further. Under a deal with the Old Whigs, Earl Fitzwilliam was sent out as Lord Lieutenant with a mandate to push through Catholic Emancipation in full. He dismissed Beresford and planned to dispose of the rest of the junta. But Lord Chancellor Clare, as Keeper of the King's (Irish) Conscience, persuaded George III that the admission of Catholics to office and parliament would be a violation of his coronation oath. Fitzwilliam had to be recalled after only a month in Dublin and Emancipation was put off for more than thirty years.[24]

Thus the power to control or even influence events slipped out of the hands of the Protestant constitutional reformers. In Ireland there are always wilder men waiting in the wings. Throughout the eighteenth century there had been illegal peasant trade unions in Ireland – Whiteboys and Shanavests for the Catholics, Steelboys and Oakboys for the Ulster Presbyterians. The hated tithes, whereby poor Catholics and Dissenters were forced to support a church they despised, were the focus of anger. There were also tenants' associations, Defenders' Clubs for the Catholics, 'Peep O'Day Boys' for Dissenters. The coming of the French Revolution in 1789 did not create a mass movement in Ireland, but it gave it a focus and, more important, a middle-class leadership. Flood died in 1791, a back number, and the same year Grattan was elbowed aside by a young Kildare lawyer, Wolfe Tone, the son of a coachbuilder, who was neither Catholic nor Protestant but a Deist, and who denounced the 1782 constitution as a swindle. In 1791 he brought the ideas of the Revolution to Ireland with his Society of United Irishmen; it was to unite Catholics and Dissenters behind a non-denominational national parliament, and its first head-quarters, significantly, were in Belfast.[25] Under Tone's inspiration, democrats took over the Catholic Committee and purged it of its aristocratic constitutionalists.

While the nationalist movement was falling into the hands of revolutionaries, the Paris terror and the outbreak of war with France in 1793 pushed the London and Dublin governments towards repression. An Arms Act abolished the Volunteers and a Convention Act forbade any assemblies of representative bodies, thus making non-violent agitation for reform virtually impossible. Wolfe Tone went to Philadelphia and later to Paris to organize foreign support: after a century of introspection, Irish nationalism was again playing the foreign card. But to play the foreign card made it much more difficult to play the Ulster one. The United Irishmen now began to administer oaths and organize a military command structure. This brought the hidden religious conflict into the open again: in September 1795 in Armagh a pitched battle between Catholic and Presbyterian bands led to the creation of the Orange Order 'to maintain the laws and peace of the country and the Protestant Constitution, and to defend the King and his heirs as long as they shall maintain the Protestant Ascendancy'.

Thus the political logic which men like Lord Clare accepted was made public and given a popular basis.[26] The machinery of repression did the rest. An Insurrection Act in 1796 allowed the Lord Lieutenant to rule through martial law in 'proclaimed' districts, imposed the death penalty for administering an unlawful oath and transportation for life for taking it, and authorized magistrates to seize suspects and 'press' them into the Navy. The same year Habeas Corpus was suspended. The Presbyterian popular leader William Orr was hanged for using the United Irishmen oath, and in the summer of 1797 Ulster was partly disarmed by General Lake, a hard-liner, 50,000 muskets and 70,000 pikes being taken in. To tilt the military balance still further, yeomanry regiments were created of Protestant tenant-farmers commanded by Protestant gentry.

Yet the polarization of Catholics and Protestants was not complete. Among the United Irishmen was Lord Edward Fitzgerald, son of the Duke of Leinster. Some members of the Ascendancy favoured emancipation in full. When Lord Fitzwilliam left Dublin he was given a rousing send-off. Even Castlereagh, now Irish Secretary, wanted to end Catholic disabilities. Grattan did not give up hope of constitutional reform until 1797, when he left parliament in despair. But by this point fear of revolution and the attrition of war had driven most of the Protestant reformers, on both sides of the Irish Sea, into the repressive camp. As Burke put it in 1796, the year before he died, 'Ireland cannot be separated for one moment from England without losing every source of her present prosperity and every hope of her future'. He was a

universe apart from Tone, who said: 'The truth is. I hate the
very name of England. I hated her before my exile and I will
hate her always.' In Paris, Carnot made him a general in the
revolutionary army, and successive plans were made for a
French seaborne invasion.

Dublin Castle knew that both a French invasion and a
popular uprising were coming: their policy was to prevent
both occurring simultaneously. Here, they were lucky. In
December 1796 a great French expedition of 35 ships and
12,000 soldiers, with Tone aboard and General Hoche in
command, slipped past the English blockade off Brest and
made for Bantry Bay. On 21 December the fleet stood by in
the bay in calm weather, waiting for Hoche's ship to appear
before landing. That night, however, the wind changed,
storm followed, and the frustrated expedition eventually
sailed back to France. The following summer, a Franco-
Dutch fleet, with a 14,000-man expeditionary force, was
assembled in the Texel; but Admiral Duncan's successful
action at Camperdown led to its dispersal.

The general assumption in Ireland was that the rising
would come in 1798. A popular prophecy went:

> A wet winter, a dry spring,
> A bloody summer, and no King.

In fact by the beginning of 1798 the government had, in
theory at least, huge forces at their disposal: 15,000 regulars,
18,000 militia and up to 50,000 yeomanry. But it was a rabid
and ill-disciplined army, more fit for a pogrom than a
campaign. General Sir Ralph Abercrombie, who took over
command at the end of 1797, was disgusted by what he found
and by the intolerance and cruelty of the Ascendancy. He
issued a famous General Order on 26 February 1798 that the
army was 'in such a state of licentiousness as must render it
formidable to every one but the enemy'. This ill-advised
message merely played into the hands of the Dublin Castle
junta, who promptly had Abercrombie replaced by Lake, a

man more to their taste.

The rebellion was timed for 23 May, but an informer, Thomas Reynolds, a Catholic silk-merchant, provided the government with advance warning and a copy of a paper of the Supreme Executive of the United Irishmen, showing that no less than 279,896 men were sworn and armed to rise. Preventative arrests followed. Lord Edward Fitzgerald, who had provided himself with a revolutionary uniform consisting of a bottle-green braided suit with crimson cape, cuffs, silk, lace and a Cap of Liberty two feet long, was surprised at a secret lodging. He put up a ferocious resistance, stabbing a yeomanry officer fourteen times, using his special 'revolutionary dagger' with a zig-zag design (both the officer and Lord Edward died of their wounds). As a result of the arrests there was no general rising and very little trouble in Dublin. Lord Clare was hissed, and 'Some forty or fifty blackguards did follow me down Castle Hill. But, as I never go out unarmed, on my facing them suddenly with a pistol in my hand, they retreated with precipitation.'[27]

In Dublin and all over the country the yeomanry made desperate efforts to get nationalists to disgorge their arms supplies. Peasants were flogged until they betrayed the hiding places, and houses where arms were found were burnt to the ground. Beresford, not a squeamish man, reported:

> Numbers have been flogged who have been caught with pikes, and all but one peached and discovered. I have seen none of these floggings, but it is terrible to hear the perseverence of these madmen. Some have received three hundred lashes before they would discover where the pikes were concealed. . . . Many people, on being terrified by the appearance of triangles and cat o' nails, have discovered and peached their brother committee men. All the gaols are full.[28]

On 25 May Sir Jonah Barrington saw the bodies of rebel dead piled in the Lower Yard of Dublin Castle, an ancient Irish

2.   Ireland in 1798 at the time of the Great Rebellion.

custom which antedated even the days of Strongbow; he
termed it 'the most frightful spectacle that ever disgraced a
royal residence, save the seraglio'.[29] It was a hot day. During
the afternoon, one of the 'bodies' came to life, was taken into
the guardroom, made a full confession and in due course was
pardoned by the Lord Lieutenant.[30] In country districts, the
militia and yeomanry, using the threat of the lash, forced
Catholics to pray on their knees for the King and to curse all
United Irishmen. To obtain information, a militia sergeant,
called Tom the Devil, invented the 'pitch cap' – a mixture of
pitch and gunpowder which was rubbed into the victim's
head and set alight. At Dunlavin the yeomanry shot in cold
blood twenty-eight 'suspects' lodged in the gaol, and
murdered another score at Carnew. At Gorey it was said that
the amputated finger of a nationalist had been used to stir the
punch at an Orange feast.[31]

The new Lord Lieutenant, General Cornwallis, complained that the talk at his dinner table in the Castle ran on
nothing but 'hanging and shooting'. 'The violence of our
friends,' he wrote in a private letter, 'and their folly in making
it a religious war, added to the ferocity of our troops who
delight in murder, most powerfully counteract all plans for
conciliation.'[32] The plain object of the Ascendancy was to
strike mortal terror in the heart of every Catholic, a campaign
epitomized by the jeering song of the yeomanry, *Croppies lie
down*:

> In Dublin the traitors were ready to rise
> And murder was seen in their lowering eyes.
> With poison, the cowards, they aimed to
>   succeed,
> And thousands were doomed by Assassin to bleed.
> But the Yeomen advanced, of Rebels the dread
> And each Croppy soon hid his dastardly head.
> *Chorus:* Down, down, Croppies lie down![33]

The rising itself, at the end of May, was provoked as much by government arrests as by any plan. The stopping of the mail-coaches out of Dublin was the signal for action. There was trouble almost everywhere, but chiefly in Meath, Leinster and Ulster, the worst affected being two traditionally peaceful areas – Wexford, where the Old English Catholics spoke a curious Saxon dialect, and among the Presbyterians of Antrim and Down. There, three small battles were fought before the rebels were crushed, and after the last of them, at Ballynahinch, two beautiful women, dressed in green silk, were found dead on the field: they were known as the Goddesses of Liberty and Reason and had carried the rebel standard, though in civil life they were the town prostitutes.[34] Further south, however, the rising was plainly sectarian, led often enough by priests. Protestant men, women and children were piked to death; not even Protestant dogs were spared. In Wexford town, which the rebels seized and held, Catholic mobs under the incitement of a man called Captain Dixon held trials of prisoners – charges ranged from burning Catholic houses to keeping a wife away from Mass – who were later 'piked' on the bridge. News of Catholic atrocities took the heart out of the Presbyterian rebels in the North, while the yeomanry were rushed south to deal with the papists. The end came on 21 June when General Lake and 13,000 men stormed the rebel headquarters on Vinegar Hill, eighty miles south of Dublin.

Thereafter the rebellion lost its Protestant element and degenerated into an orange-and-green affair, though most of the leaders and planners were Deists or freethinkers, as their forty-page 'confession' makes clear. The only born Catholic among them, McNevin, said: 'For my part I would as soon establish Mahommedanism as the Popish religion.'[35] Castle-reagh called the rising 'a Jacobin conspiracy with Popish instruments', Cornwallis 'a deep-laid conspiracy to revolutionise Ireland on the principles of France by men who had no thought of religion but to destroy it'. General John Moore, ablest and most chivalrous of the government commanders, blamed the yeomanry for the scale of the rising: 'I cannot but think,' he wrote in his diary in June, 'that it was their harshness and ill-treatment that drove the peasants to revolt.' Even Clare favoured a general amnesty to appease the Catholics, and pardons were quickly issued. Only when it was all over, on 23 August, did the French, under General Humbert, succeed in landing about 1,100 men at Killala, thirty miles west of Sligo. They were quickly rounded up. Tone was arrested wearing the uniform of a French colonel, with blue coat and pantaloons, heavy gold epaulettes and a tricolour cockade.

The crown refused to accept Tone's plea that he was a combatant soldier, and sentenced him to be hanged. He asked only to be shot by firing-squad. He said: 'What I have done has been clearly from principle and in the fullest conviction of its rectitude. I wish not for mercy. I hope I am not an object of pity. I anticipated the consequence of my capture and I am prepared for the event. The favourite object of my life has been the independence of my country and to that object I have made every sacrifice.' His request for a firing-squad was refused, so he cut his throat with a razor, severing his windpipe by mistake for the artery and lingering on for a week, to the disgust of the Ascendancy hard-liners. 'I would have sewn up his neck and finished the business,' said Sir George Hill. They had learnt nothing. 'I should look upon a [new] rising,' said Lord Roben, 'as a fortunate event, as by that means we should have an opportunity of annihilating one or two millions of inhabitants who are a disgrace to humanity.' Two years later, Irishmen made up 25 per cent of the convicts in the Botany Bay settlement.[36]

The 1798 rising convinced Pitt that the Protestants could not hold Ireland without help; he feared that Catholics and Presbyterians would win a majority in the Dublin parliament, sooner or later, and then make common cause with France. The only alternative was a union, on the lines of the 1707 union with Scotland, which had proved a resounding success. Cornwallis and Castlereagh agreed, as did Clare, having long regarded union as the least of several evils. Pitt also wanted to get rid of Irish governmental and parliamentary corruption, which he loathed. He had no difficulty in persuading the British parliament that union was inevitable. He argued that the new constitution of 1782–3 had not worked. The Catholics of Ireland had to be given emancipation but this could only be done within the framework of the British Isles, where they could never have a majority; otherwise, they would carry Ireland into the arms of France, which could not be beaten without the unity of the empire. He carried his case by a huge majority at Westminster.

In Dublin, Grattan's campaign against the union plan was joined by many supporters of government and he carried a hostile motion by 109 to 104. The response of Cornwallis was to dismiss the government rebels from office and form a ministry consisting of Clare, Castlereagh and himself. To rid Ireland of corruption and achieve the union, one last, final and gigantic spasm of corruption was required. As Castlereagh put it, it was necessary 'to buy out and secure for the Crown for ever, the fee simple of Irish corruption, which has so long enfeebled the powers of government and endangered the connection with England'.[37] In fact there was corruption on both sides. Cornwallis complained: 'The enemy to my certain knowledge offer £50,000 for a vote; if we had the means and were disposed to make such vile use of them, we dare not trust the credit of government in the hands of such vile rascals.'[38] On the government side, the bargaining took three forms. Some £50,000 was paid out directly, mainly in bribes to the press, pamphlets and pensions.[39] Secondly, there was direct compensation for parliamentary seats and suppressed offices: peers, nearly all anti-union, received three-fifths of the compensation granted in suppressing 200 seats, at a total of £1,260,000. Finally, there were a large number of promotions or creations in the peerage. Sir Jonah Barrington, in a work published in 1833, supplied some of the details of the operation:

J. Bingham Esq.: Created a peer; got £8,000 for two seats; and £16,000 compensation for Tuam. This gentleman first offered himself for sale to the anti-unionists; now Lord Clanmorris.

Sir Richard Butler: Purchased and changed sides; voted against the union in 1799 and for it in 1800; cash.

Charles H. Coote Esq.: Obtained a regiment (which was taken from Colonel Warburton), patronage of Queen's County, a peerage (Lord Castlecoote), and £7,500 for his interest in the Borough of Maryborough.

A. Fergusson Esq.: Got a place at the Barrack Board, £500 a year and a baronetcy.

William Fortescue Esq.: Got a secret pension out of a fund entrusted by parliament to the Irish Government solely to reward those who informed against rebels.

William Handcock Esq.: An extraordinary instance. He made and sang songs against the union in 1799, at a public dinner of the opposition; and made and sang songs *for* it in 1800: got a peerage.

Hon. G. Jocelyn: Promotion in the army, and his brother consecrated Bishop of Lismore.

Lord Loftus: Son to Lord Ely, Postmaster-General; got £30,000 for their boroughs; created an English Marquess.

Charles Osborne Esq.: A barrister; appointed a Judge of the King's Bench.

Rt. Hon. J. Toler: Attorney-General; his wife, an old woman, created a peeress; himself made Chief Justice and a peer.

Hon. J. Stafford: Paymaster of Foreign Forces, £1,300 a year; £7,500 for Baltinglass.

J. O. Vandaleur Esq.: Made Commissioner of the Revenue; his brother a judge.[40]

The Union Bill, introduced by Castlereagh, gave Ireland one hundred MPs and thirty-two Peers at Westminster. Ireland was to get all the benefits of free trade, but to retain its bounties on linen, the viceregal office, and its courts. On 7 June 1800 it passed its Third Reading by 153 votes to 88, and received the royal assent in August. Corruption brought the government's theoretical strength up to 180, though its highest actual vote was 162. It may have tried too hard, and spent too much, but Castlereagh was unrepentant: 'The Irish government,' he wrote, 'is certainly now liable to the charge of having gone too far in complying with the demands of individuals; but had the union miscarried and the failure been traceable to a reluctance on the part of government to interest a sufficient number of supporters in its success ... we should have met with and in fact deserved less mercy.'[41] He repented nothing: 'With respect to Ireland, I know I shall never be forgiven. I have with many others incurred the inexpiable guilt of preserving that main branch of the British Empire from that separation which the traitors of Ireland, in conjunction with a foreign power, had meditated.'[42]

There were, however, two fatal drawbacks to the manner in which the union was secured, which rendered any valid comparison with Scotland impossible. The Orange Order was anti-union, but with 100,000 troops in the country any significant popular demonstrations were impossible under the Insurrection Act. The Catholics, on the other hand, were duped into supporting union. Their bishops and priests had been horrified by the revolutionary and atheistic ideas of the 1798 rising leaderships. In January 1799, the assembled Catholic bishops accepted a government offer of state provision for the Catholic clergy, in return for allowing the state to confirm episcopal elections and the appointment of parish priests, a form of concordat. Some of the Catholic lay leadership, like Lords Kenmare and Fingall, were also pro-union. Most were hostile, but were given to understand that the Catholic gentry would be admitted to the new union parliament. But the Catholics got virtually nothing in the form of firm guarantees.

No doubt Pitt intended to keep his promises to the

Catholics. But he was certainly warned he might be prevented from doing so. A minute in Canning's hand records a meeting in London on 23 October 1798 between Pitt and Clare when union was first discussed, in which Clare 'confesses he fears nothing himself from the Catholics having *everything*, but it is impossible to carry that point in Ireland'. The minute ends: 'Conclusion: drunkenness at Bellamy's.' [43] Moreover, Pitt never pledged his whole cabinet on the Catholic issue and he did not keep George III informed. In the event, the King refused to stomach emancipation, as before, and was supported by Pitt's Lord Chancellor, Loughborough. Pitt feared he would bring back the King's madness if he pressed the issue; so he reneged on his bargain and the Catholics got nothing.

What made matters worse was the spectacular collapse of the Protestant opposition to union, once it became a *fait accompli*, and the eagerness with which the Ascendancy rushed to get their snouts in the new trough. One of the most vociferous opponents, William Plunkett, had said of the union in parliament: 'I will resist it to the last gasp of my existence and with the last drop of my blood, and when I feel the hour of my dissolution approaching I will, like the father of Hannibal, take my children to the altar and swear them to hostility against the invaders of their country's freedom.' In fact he did nothing of the sort, but took office as Solicitor-General for Ireland. When he was promoted to Attorney-General in 1805, his successor was another anti-unionist, Charles Kendal Bushe, known as 'The Incorruptible'. John Foster, the anti-unionist Speaker, had said he would refuse to surrender the mace; in fact he quickly transferred himself to the Westminster parliament, and in 1804 took office under Pitt. [44] In 1800, after the union was through, Grattan had said: 'Yet I do not give up my country. I see her in a swoon but she is not dead: though in her tomb she lies helpless and motionless, still on her lips is the spirit of life and on her cheeks the glow of beauty.' Yet Grattan too, even Grattan, transferred himself to the Westminster parliament in 1805.

This rapid reconciliation of the Protestant ruling class to the fact of union reminded the great mass of Irishmen that the 'English garrison' had another country to go to and serve; in the last resort they could do without independence and still flourish. By accepting the union they necessarily relinquished the leadership of the nationalist movement to the Catholics and in a few years they found themselves transformed into a colonial ruling class. Thereafter, it was the Catholics who stood for an independent parliament, and the Protestants for union. The idea of a Protestant nation was dead.

CHAPTER 5

Famine and Diaspora

By tamely accepting the union, the Protestant Ascendancy effectively forfeited its right to lead the Irish nation. By reneging on its bargain, and by delaying Catholic emancipation for nearly thirty years, the British government turned Catholics away from union and made the Catholic Church the central depository of Irish nationalism. These were irremediable errors, which set in motion the tragic but logical process of modern Irish history. Before the union, government could certainly have done a deal with the Catholic Church: acceptance and political control in return for establishment and stipends. Such a deal was done with the Presbyterians: their ministers had for long been receiving small sums called the *Regium Donum*; in 1802 these were increased to from £50 to £100 a year for each minister, in return for loyalty. Certainly, the Catholic peers favoured a deal. The bishops were less keen: in 1808 and again in 1810 they turned down Grattan's schemes to get official recognition and finance in return for a government veto over episcopal appointments. In 1814 the Vatican was persuaded to consent to the veto. But by then it was too late. The new priests coming out of the Maynooth seminary, set up in 1795, were far more hostile to the English connection than their well-born predecessors, educated on the Continent.

Even more important was the loss by the Catholic aristocracy of their leadership over the nationalist movement. In 1807 it was reorganized as the Catholic Association, with Daniel O'Connell, the son of a minor landlord, in control. He was the first Irishman to see that nationalist objectives were more likely to be achieved not through the Protestant elite, nor through a revolutionary mob, but by the legal and

organized use of Catholic power, based on professional
political agents and the parish priests. A deal between the
church and the government would thus be fatal to his
methods, and he rejected it absolutely, brushing aside the
papal permission. 'How dismal the prospect of liberty would
be,' he said, 'if in every Catholic diocese there were an active
partisan of the government, and in every Catholic parish a
priest as an active informer.'

O'Connell's programme was simple. First, he would
organize a legal mass campaign to secure Catholic emancipation and the vote. Then, on the basis of the political power
thus secured, he would campaign for repeal of the union. He
tried to keep within the law: no easy matter, for with the
Convention Act, various Coercion Acts and the periodic
suspension of Habeas Corpus, there were only four or five
years of normal government in the whole period from 1796 to
1823. Twice O'Connell had to dissolve and refound his
organization in order to comply with the law. To remain legal
was essential to him, for his power rested on his superb ability
to enthuse and control great mass meetings. He had no time
for the secret oath and the arms cache: Irish freedom, he said,
was not worth the shedding of a single drop of English blood.
He repudiated Wolfe Tone and his colleagues as 'criminals'.
'As to '98,' he said, 'we leave the weak and wicked men who
considered force and sanguinary violence as part of their
resources for ameliorating our institutions, and the equally
wicked and designing wretches who fomented the Rebellion
and made it explode.... We leave both these classes of
miscreants to the contempt and indignation of mankind.'[1]

Instead, O'Connell invented the 'Catholic rent', which
enlisted mass support of the nationalist cause by collecting a
penny a month from every family. Thus financed, he set
about organizing the Catholic forty-shilling freeholders, who
now numbered over 100,000. They had the vote even though
they could not legally send a Catholic to Westminster. In
1826, in the Waterford by-election, in the heart of Beresford

country, the landlords' candidate, Lord George Beresford, was defeated by a liberal Protestant by the huge margin of 2,057 to 982, thanks largely to O'Connell's organization. In 1828 he went a stage further, getting himself elected for County Clare by a similar margin. Of course he could not legally take his seat. The Clare victory finally persuaded the Duke of Wellington, the Prime Minister, that the only alternative to conceding Catholic Emancipation was coercion leading to civil war. He told the House of Lords that he did not think the Catholic Association could be put down by force, and added:

> even if I had been certain of such means of putting it down, I should have considered it my duty to avoid those means. I am one of those who have probably passed a longer period of my life engaged in war than most men, and principally in civil war; and I must say this, that if I could avoid by any sacrifice whatever even one month of civil war in the country to which I was attached, I would sacrifice my life in order to do it.[2]

The Emancipation Act of 1829 for the first time brought into existence the 'Catholic Nation' as a legal and constitutional force. (Of course, the removal of the sacramental test also opened parliament to the Ulster Dissenters.) It was now possible for Irish Catholics to go to Westminster and, under the leadership of O'Connell, to bargain with their votes in return for further concessions. And, in a growing number of fields, Irish aspirations coincided with the great wave of reform now sweeping over Britain after a half-century of Tory resistance. In 1831 came the first national scheme for Irish education. The 1832 Reform Act for Ireland did not democratize the vote by any means – restricting it to £10-householders in towns and £10-freeholders and £20-lease-holders in counties – but it enfranchised the Catholic middle class in the towns, and prepared the way for the 1840 Municipal Reform Act which abolished the corrupt old

Protestant corporations in favour of a mass suffrage. The
Catholics now began to take over the towns and cities,
O'Connell himself becoming Mayor of Dublin. A new police
force eventually called, the Royal Irish Constabulary, was
organized on a non-sectarian basis, and for the first time the
normal processes of law enforcement ceased to be a discrimina-
tory Protestant weapon.[3]

From his position in Westminster, O'Connell organized the
campaign for repeal through his National Repeal Association.[4] As he put it, he was *against* national separation, *for*
national independence, blithely ignoring the inherent contra-
diction in this formula. He also drew a distinction between the
Orangemen, 'our enemies', and 'the Liberal Protestant',
whom he called 'the object of great affection and regard from
the entire Catholic population'. He appealed to ingrained
Irish conservatism with his demand for the restoration of 'the
old house on College Green' (i.e., an Irish parliament), and
though he used the new technique of the mass meeting,
speaking to 250,000 people on the sacred Hill of Tara, he tried
– not always successfully – to conduct a constitutional
campaign. His speech at Mullingar on 14 May 1843
epitomizes the O'Connell approach:

> They say we want separation from England, but what I
> want is to prevent separation taking place. There is not a
> man in existence more loyally attached than I am to the
> Queen – God bless her. The present state of Ireland is
> nearly unendurable, and if the people of Ireland had not
> some person like me to lead them in the paths of peace and
> constitutional exertion, I am afraid of the result (*hear!*).
> While I live I will stand by the throne (*hear, hear!*). But what
> motive could we have to separate if we obtain all those
> blessings and advantages I have been enumerating? They
> would all serve as solid, golden links of connection with
> England. But I would be glad to know what good did the
> Union do (*hear, hear!*)? What I want you to do is, for every

one of you to join me in looking for repeal. As many of you as are willing to do so, let them hold up their hands (*here every person in the immense assemblage raised his hand aloft amidst loud and continued cheers*). I see you have ready hands, and I know you have stout hearts too. But what do I want you to do? Is it to turn out into battle or war (*cries of 'No, no'*)? Is it to commit riot or crime (*cries of 'No, no'*)? Remember: 'Whoever commits a crime gives strength to the enemy' (*hear, hear and cheers*) .... I want you to do nothing that is not open and legal, but if the people unite with me and follow my advice it is impossible not to get the repeal (*loud cheers and cries of 'we will'*).[5]

Even in the early 1840s, however, there were indications that O'Connell's constitutionalism was being undermined by a new generation of nationalists, who looked back to the events of 1798 not with horror but with pride. The 'Young Ireland' movement was mainly Protestant middle class, from Trinity College, but it also included Catholics like Gavan Duffy and intellectual idealists from the new 'Queen's Colleges', founded in Dublin, Cork and Galway, open to Catholics. Some of them did not repudiate force. They objected to the posture of Ireland suing on her knees for English concessions grudgingly awarded, and talked in terms of 'national independence'.[6]

In any event, the age of O'Connell was swept away in the catastrophe of the Great Famine, which transformed Ireland demographically, economically, socially, politically and in terms of the outside world. Of course Ireland had always known periodic famine. Spenser's *View of the State of Ireland* gives a harrowing description of Munster after the Desmond wars:

Out of every corner of the woods and glens they came, creeping forth upon their hands, for their legs would not bear them: they looked like anatomies of death, they spoke like ghosts crying out of their graves; they did eat the dead carrions, happy where they could find them, yea, and one another soon after, in so much as the very carcasses they spared not to scrape out of their graves; and if they found a plot of watercress or shamrocks, there they flocked for a feast for the time . . . sure in all that war there perished not many by the sword but all by the extremity of famine.[7]

Such scenes were repeated many times in the seventeenth century. In its last quarter, however, the people of many of the poorer parts (as in Scotland and other areas) went over to an all-potato diet. This eased the pressure on existing sources of food, especially among the labourers and smallholders of the south and west, but it also made practicable further subdivisions of small plots. Thus (it was later argued) it led to earlier marriages and an increase in population.[8] In fact during the eighteenth century it was the fall in the death rate, through the reduction in epidemic disease, which was the main cause of population increase, in Ireland as elsewhere in Europe.

In the half-century 1735–85, the population of Ireland rose by one-third, to 4 million. In the next fifty years it doubled, reaching 8.2 million by 1841. The huge rise in agricultural productivity in the British Isles, and not least in Ireland – where three-quarters of the land went over to grain-production – enabled the new millions to be fed. As a result, during the eighteenth century Irish famines became much less frequent: the last *general* famine in Ireland was in 1740–1. Thereafter there was no general shortage of grain in the British Isles.[9] But the risk of partial famines, afflicting certain classes in certain areas, remained, indeed increased, for the potato was a high-risk crop and the classes which depended on it often had no regular source of cash to buy alternatives. Partial famines caused by potato failure occurred in 1799–1800, 1816, 1817, 1822 and 1836, but they were confined to the poorest regions and the single class of farm labourers, who gave their services unpaid in return for potato-patches.

Unfortunately there was another factor which caused increasing concern in Ireland: the decline of the domestic textile industry, especially in the poorer regions (County Mayo, for example). In the 1830s and 1840s, Ireland was becoming more rural and more dependent on agriculture. The towns were not siphoning off the surplus rural population, which was therefore driven back upon an already strained agricultural sector. Towns like Dingle, Cobh, Kinsale, Mountrath, Portarlington, Kilbeggan, Trim, Kells, Athboy, Westport and Castlebar were actually declining. The census of 1841 showed how important jobs in textiles, or domestic textile work, were in supplementing exiguous or non-existent rural cash incomes. As one Irish economic historian has put it, 'the background to the famine, through the crisis in domestic industry, is as much an industrial as an agrarian one'.[10] As population and unemployment grew, the diet in the south-west deteriorated. Milk became a luxury for the poor, who had no cash savings, or even any assets which could be sold; and in many of the western regions there was no retail food system. The poor did not know how to prepare meal or bake bread, and lacked the utensils to do it.

By the 1830s it was generally believed that the Irish peasantry was the poorest in Western Europe. Englishmen, and foreigners like de Tocqueville, went over to study it and write books. Gustave de Beaumont wrote in 1839 that, though he had seen the Red Indian in his forests and the American Negro in his chains, in Ireland he had come across 'the very extreme of human wretchedness'.[11] But hard facts were difficult to come by and opinions varied on whether conditions were getting better or worse. Anthony Trollope, who knew rural Ireland well both before and during the famine through his work as an inspector of postal services, castigated the idleness of the rural male. He said he was astonished, when he first arrived, to find able-bodied men standing around the streets talking, their knee-breeches unbuttoned, their stockings rolled down over their brogues:

'Nor, though thus idle, did they seem to suffer any of the distress of poverty. There were plenty of beggars, no doubt... but it never struck me there was much distress in those days. The earth gave forth its potatoes freely and neither man nor pig wanted more.'[12]

Thackeray, who visited Ireland in 1842 and wrote an excellent and fair-minded book about it, was frank about his difficulty in making an assessment. He wrote to his mother: 'I wonder who *does* understand the place? Not the natives, certainly, for the two parties so hate each other that neither can view the simplest proceedings of the other without distrusting, falsifying and abusing it.'[13] He told his readers: 'To have an opinion about Ireland one must begin by getting at the truth; and where is it to be had in this country? Or rather, there are two truths, the Catholic truth and the Protestant truth.... I shall never forget the glee with which a gentleman in Munster told me he had sent off Messieurs de Tocqueville and de Beaumont "with such a set of stories".'[14]

All the same, Thackeray vividly conveys the sense of a hopelessly overpopulated country, swarming with beggars. Since 1838 Ireland had come under the English poor law, and Thackeray saw the North Dublin Union House, 'an orderly establishment which accommodates 2,000 beggars... wherein the prisoners are better clothed, better fed and better housed than they can hope to be when at liberty'. But in the west he noted that 'many of the potato gardens were half dug-up, and it is only the first week in August, near three months before the potato is ripe and at full growth; and the winter still six months away'. He found

> throughout the south and west of Ireland the traveller is haunted by the face of popular starvation. It is not the exception, it is the condition of the people. In this fairest and richest of countries, men are suffering and starving by millions.... The epicurean and traveller for pleasure had better travel anywhere than here: where there are miseries

that one does not dare think of.[15]

English political opinion, too, was thoroughly pessimistic about Ireland, and well aware of the risk of a catastrophe. Sir Robert Peel, Prime Minister from 1841-6, said his views on Ireland 'had long been very gloomy'. It was in a state which 'seemed to preclude honest and impartial government'. His Home Secretary, Sir James Graham, agreed: 'Affairs are rapidly verging to a crisis.' He 'saw no cure for the evils which rendered impartial government...almost impossible'.[16] In 1845 the Devon Commission reported gloomily on the poverty of the people and the debts of the landlords.[17] At Westminster, the 'Irish Question' was never far from men's thoughts. In 1844 the young Benjamin Disraeli had electrified the House of Commons with a striking diagnosis:

> I want to see a public man come forward and say what the Irish question is. One says it is a physical question; another, a spiritual. Now it is the absence of the aristocracy, then the absence of railroads. It is the Pope one day, potatoes the next. Consider Ireland as you would any other country, similarly situated, in your closets. You will see a teeming population which, with reference to the cultivated soil, is denser to the square mile than that of China; created solely by agriculture, with none of those sources of wealth which develop with civilisation; and sustained, consequently, on the lowest conceivable diet, so that in case of failure they have no other means of subsistence upon which they can fall back. That dense population in extreme distress inhabits an island where there is an Established Church which is not their church (*loud Opposition cheers*) and a territorial aristocracy the richest of whom live in distant capitals. Thus you have a starving population, an absentee aristocracy and an alien church, and in addition the weakest executive in the world. That is the Irish question.[18]

The fungus *Phylophthora infestans*, which attacked the potato, was first noted in gardens near Cork in the second week of September 1845.[19] Only a fifth of the crop was lost, but in consequence the poorer cultivator (who got his patch in return for unpaid work) could not plant for the next season. In any case, the whole of the 1846 crop was seen to be a total loss by the second half of July. This led to an even worse disaster in 1847. Once the whole crop had been blighted in 1846 the labourers had to repudiate their agreements with the farmers, since only money wages seemed to offer any escape from starvation. So they cried out for payment in cash, instead of patches. The farmers generally refused to give it, so the labourers abandoned their plots for the workhouse, or public works if there were any.[20] In Cork, for instance, the potato acreage, already one-fifth down on 1845 levels, fell from 321,000 acres in 1846 to less than 40,000 in 1847. As it happened, there was no blight in 1847, and yields were average. Then, when more was sown in 1848, the blight returned, and the years 1849–51 were all bad.

Potatoes fed beasts as well as men – out of an average crop of 15 million tons, over 5 million went to livestock, chiefly pigs. So there was a general slaughter of livestock, and since the remaining herds and many humans switched to grain, Irish exports of grain fell from over 515,000 tons in 1845 to less than 150,000 in 1847.[21] Farm incomes collapsed, labourers, farmers and landlords blamed each other, and all three turned to government for relief.

The highly professional government of Peel and Graham were not caught unprepared. Ministers, wrote Graham, 'were driven to study the barometer with so much anxiety' and kept a particularly anxious eye on the Irish potato crop. When the worst was known, in October 1845, and Graham reported 'we have a nation to carry, as it were, in our arms', Peel decided to suspend the Corn Laws and open the ports. But for immediate purposes he authorized the expenditure of £600,000 on relief works, to provide cash wages, and he secretly purchased £160,000 worth of maize from the United

States, to be retailed to the Irish peasantry at 1d a pound. Hence, though Peel saw the famine as a final, clinching argument for free trade and the market system, he was not stupid enough to think he could dispense with emergency measures. As Graham put it, 'Ireland's distress could not be met by measures within the strict rules of economical science'.[22]

In fact Peel's policy of restraining speculation by the purchase and distribution of foreign grain in the early months of 1846 was very successful. The Irish poor did not like the look of the maize and initially christened it 'Peel's Brimstone'. Trollope, who was there, gives a graphic picture of its reception in his fine novel, *Castle Richmond*. But it made an adequate 'stirabout' and, mixed with rice, became the staple fare at soup-kitchens, public and private, throughout the famine years. Unfortunately, Peel's government resigned in 1846, and its Whig successor lacked both the authority to overrule doctrinaire officials, especially Sir C. E. Trevelyan, Assistant-Secretary to the Treasury, and the experience to temper economic dogma with common sense.[23] Peel's state purchases were discontinued on the grounds that they had 'paralysed the provision trade' and threatened to wreck the fragile retail system for food in the south and west. Under pressure from the Lord Lieutenant and the Irish landed gentry, Sir Charles Wood, the new Chancellor of the Exchequer, protested: 'It seems to me the misfortune of Ireland that every man looks to the government for everything.' How could government accept responsibility for a famine, he asked one critic; even 'Russian despotism never undertook such duties as you are imposing on the government of this country'. The new orthodoxy was summed up by Sir Randolph Routh of the Political Economy Club:

There is a general scarcity throughout all Western Europe, and we are almost wholly dependent on commerce for the means of relieving it. We must abstain from any attempt to tamper with prices. We must pay the true value for each article of food and encourage its importation on that principle. Any other line of conduct would expose us to the most fatal results.[24]

The Whig resolve was stiffened by a newspaper campaign in England, accusing the Irish landed classes, who were generally hated in England for their cruelty, extravagance, improvidence and meanness, of trying to free-load off the English taxpayer. The Whigs justified removing relief work from the Exchequer and putting it on the Irish rates with the cry 'Irish property must support Irish poverty'. Charles Greville, secretary to the Privy Council and diarist, summed up the prevailing view in the London clubs:

. . . the state of Ireland is to the last degree deplorable, and enough to induce despair: such general disorganisation and demoralisation, a people with rare exceptions besotted with obstinacy and indolence, reckless and savage – all from high to low intent on doing as little and getting as much as they can, unwilling to rouse and exert themselves, looking to this country for succour, and snarling at the succour which they get; the masses brutal, deceitful and idle, the whole state of things contradictory and paradoxi-all. While menaced with the continuance of famine next year, they will not cultivate the ground, and it lies unsown and untilled. There is no doubt that the people never were so well off on the whole as they have been this year of famine. Nobody will pay rent, and the savings banks are overflowing. With the money they get from our relief funds they buy arms instead of food, and then shoot the officers who are sent over to regulate the distribution of relief. While they crowd to the overseers with demands for employment, the landowners cannot produce hands, and sturdy beggars calling themselves destitute are appre-hended with large sums in their pockets – *28 November 1846.*[25]

By stopping direct intervention in the market, the Whigs made some starvation inevitable in 1846–7. Once the price of maize was freed, it rose from less than £10 a ton in early 1846 to £17 in December, many merchants making a huge profit at the expense of the poor. So did the government, which disposed of its own stocks for as much as £19 a ton.[26] In some areas wages on relief work were only 8d a day. Since even the local relief committees were now forced to charge 2d a pound for maize, and five to six pounds of meal a day were required to keep alive a labourer and his family of five, such wages were not enough to avert starvation.[27] We have a graphic description of the effects of this harsh arithmetic from the pen of Elihu Burritt, an American scholar and philanthropist, who visited County Cork in February 1847 (and was possibly the model for Elias Gotobed in Trollope's *The American Senator*). A doctor, Burritt was horrified to see men working on roads 'with their limbs swollen to almost twice their usual size'. The body of a twelve-year-old boy was 'swollen to nearly three times its usual size and had burst the ragged garments which covered him'. The arms of a two-year-old child were 'not much larger than pipe-stems', while its body 'was swollen to the size of a full grown person'. Near Skull,

we passed a crowd of 500 people, half naked and starving. They were waiting for soup to be distributed amongst them. They were pointed out to us, and as I stood looking with pity and wonder at so miserable a scene, my conductor, a gentleman residing at East Skull and a medical man, said to me: 'Not a single one of those you now see will be alive in three weeks: it is impossible.' . . . The deaths here average 40 to 50 daily. Twenty bodies were buried this morning, and they were fortunate in getting buried at all. The people build themselves up in their cabins, so that they may die together with their children and not be seen by passers-by.[28]

The government had recognized its errors by January 1847

and started soup-kitchens for destitute persons outside the workhouse. At their peak in July 1847 the kitchens were feeding 3,021,000. By then, the market system was beginning to work. In the first half of 1847, 2,850,000 tons of foreign grain converged on Ireland and maize had dropped to less than £7 10s a ton by the end of August. But outdoor relief was later withdrawn, and some people were still going hungry in 1851. What angered the Irish peasants was that wheat continued to be exported from Ireland throughout the very worst period. At Clonmel, where Trollope was stationed, laden barges filled up at the grain mills every week and set off for England protected by a British force of fifty cavalry, eighty infantry and two guns. The poor tried to set fire to the mills, and on one occasion in 1848 managed to hoist a red flag over them.[29] There were many cases of cattle-rustling and food-stealing, and of farmers arming themselves and firing at intruders. A starving labourer convicted of sheep- or cattle-stealing could expect seven to fifteen years' transportation for the first offence.[30]

In some places there were food riots, and shops were sacked. But most of the starving were too debilitated to show much fight. Police, troops and priests cooperated to avoid clashes, the priests preaching incessantly the virtues of patience. In fact there was more trouble from the flight from the stricken areas into the towns, Cork, for instance, being invaded by 20,000 paupers in April 1847 alone, with 5,400 crowded into one workhouse. The Mayor ordered magistrates to drive out of the city 'at once' all 'strolling beggars, vagabonds and idle persons seeking relief' and stationed armed constables at the city limits. Cholera, which broke out in 1849, and spread to other crammed cities and towns, may well have killed as many people as hunger.

What stayed longest and deepest in the collective memory of the Irish peasants was not so much the hunger itself as the way in which the landlords exploited the famine to disencumber their estates, actually emerging better off from the disaster. J. A. Froude, who visited the west of Ireland before and after the famine, noticed an enormous change. In 1845, he wrote, 'there was no visible ill-feeling between the serfs and their masters. The Orange lord was still the master whom they loved in their way, especially when he was out at elbows like themselves.' But in 1848 he found 'the most genuine hatred of the Irish landlords everywhere through the country'.[31]

As in Scotland during the 'Highland Clearances', the landlords hated the endless subdivision of plots and wanted to get most of the peasants off the land completely. In the long run the famine was a blessing to them, provided they could get the poor into the towns or onto the emigrant ships. One much-hated provision of the Whig Poor Law Amendment Act of June 1847 – inserted at the insistence of William Gregory, MP for Dublin, and known as the 'Gregory Clause' – stipulated that anyone occupying more than a quarter-acre of land was not to be considered destitute so long as he clung to his holding. The enforcement of this clause was entrusted to the Poor Law Guardians, who were usually, of course, landlords themselves, and reflected landlord interests. They insisted that the heads of starving families relinquish their holdings before being allowed to enter the workhouses, or kicked out those who were not technically destitute. Once a man relinquished his holding, his cabin was demolished or burnt. The landlords were just as hard on tenant-farmers, refusing to reduce rents and, if the farmers defaulted, raiding their crops under possession orders, protected by bailiffs and police.[32]

But the farmers could and did survive the famine; if anything they prospered. The number of farms over fifteen acres actually rose in the years 1845–51, and continued to rise slowly from 276,618 in 1845 to 303,529 in 1910. By contrast, the number of smallholders fell sharply, the group with holdings of only one to five acres being the hardest hit. The total of holdings not exceeding fifteen acres fell from 628,397 in 1845 to 317,665 in 1851 (and continued to fall, reaching 216,236 in 1910).[33] These were the real victims of the famine. As landlords had been liable for paupers' rates since 1843, and as Whig policy pushed the rates up sharply, they fell upon the Gregory Clause with enthusiasm, and 1847 was the year when the evictions began in earnest. They peaked in 1850, but were still numerous in 1852, thereafter declining. 'Crowbar Brigades' could be hired to do the demolition work at the rate of three shillings a house. There was practically no resistance from a despairing and demoralized people. Those who gave in without a fuss were allowed to carry away their timbers and thatch, and had their rent arrears cancelled. Some were given small sums of money. Modern-minded 'improving landlords' were the most systematic evictors, arguing that it was a case of rural 'slum clearance'. But even easy-going landlords evicted in these years. They defended themselves by asserting that the people they threw out would be better off in the poorhouse, or on the emigrant ships.

Indeed, it became the conventional wisdom of the more serious-minded Irish landlords and their agents that the famine was a kind of blessing in disguise. As one agent, John Smith, put it: 'The lands taken up were held by tenants who had neither skill nor energy to work them; and when it pleased Providence to afflict our country with the potato blight, it became evident that a new course of tillage was the only remedy'.[34] Already by 1851 landlords were beginning to grasp that there had been a marked improvement in their fortunes. One absentee, Sir John Benn-Walsh, after a visit in August to his Cork and Kerry estates, noted in his journal that he was leaving Ireland 'with far more hope and in better spirits' than on his last two visits, since his poor rates had fallen, the value of his farms had risen and his estates had been 'very much weeded both of paupers and of bad tenants'.[35]

One major beneficiary of the famine was the Foreign Secretary, Lord Palmerston. Throughout the international food crisis of 1846–7, he strongly urged foreign governments to export food as normal. In November 1847 he rebuked the Turkish government for suspending food exports from Lemnos during the famine there, giving them a lecture on the mechanism and economic merits of free trade. He himself, during the summer and autumn of 1847, got 2,000 people from his Sligo estates sent in nine ships to Quebec and St John in Canada. Always short of cash, he did not pay for the transport and merely contributed to the passage money, though he did arrange for them to be served with hot punch on board (following protests from priests and temperance societies, this was changed to coffee and biscuits). He had said he would provide each family with between £2 and £5 on arrival in Quebec. In fact there was nothing for them when they got there and they were left to beg in the snow, many barefoot and in rags, during their first winter in Canada. The Canadians were indignant at their condition on arrival. On one ship, which got to Quebec very late in the season, 107 of Palmerston's tenants had died on board of fever, and of 477 who survived, 174 were almost naked. The Canadians had to give them clothes before they could leave the ship. Another group of Palmerston's tenants arrived nine days later, one woman, completely naked, being carried ashore in a blanket.[36]

This pathetic series of incidents, for which Palmerston was fiercely criticized in the Canadian press, was merely one episode in a national diaspora which rivals that of the Jews. By the end of the century, the movement out of Ireland had embraced nearly 4 million people and reduced the population from over 8 million in 1846 to under 4,500,000 in 1901.[37] In the words of one American historian, 'Irish emigration thereby achieved the unenviable distinction of being the only migratory movement in modern history to have embraced a considerable proportion of a country's population and to have led directly to a definitive population decline'.[38]

The part played by the Great Famine in Irish population decline and in the emigration should not be exaggerated. Five

Irish counties of the south and west – Cork, Mayo, Galway,
Clare and Kerry – had an average excess mortality, during
the years 1846-50, of more than one-eighth of the total
population.[39] The impact of the famine reflected the regional
division of Ireland into three areas: the east and north,
generally prosperous; a region embracing much of the
midlands and the south, with a prosperous farming class and a
poor labouring class; and an area embracing part of the
counties of the western and southern seaboard, which was
desperately poor. There was very little famine in the north-
east; in the midlands and south it hit the poor elements, but no
one else; and in the special south-west region it was general.
Hence, in August 1847, when government soup kitchens were
providing food for 40 per cent of the population, this was
concentrated very heavily in the western and south-western
regions, where 70-80 per cent were on relief; in the midlands
and the south it was under 30 per cent; and in the east and
north below 20 or even 10 per cent. In the better off areas
deaths from undernourishment were rare, and high mortality
rates were caused by disease, especially in the towns. The
great famine, in short, was more a regional and a class
calamity than a national one.[40]

Between 1845 and 1851 the total population fell by about 2
million, of which half was accounted for by excess deaths and
half by emigration. (The cholera epidemic of 1849, which
contributed to the high death-rate, was not a consequence of
famine but spread outwards from Belfast; though it doubtless
killed more as a result of malnutrition.) The famine did not so
much cause the decline in population as contribute to it.
Emigration from Ireland was already rising sharply in the
decade before 1846; the effect of the famine years was to
accelerate the drift abroad, but emigration continued at a
heavy, though declining, rate for the rest of the century and
into the twentieth century (and was still causing concern as
recently as the 1950s), as the following figures indicate:

Year	Population	Emigration (total in decade)
1851	6,522,385	1851–60: 1,163,418
1861	5,798,967	1861–70: 849,836
1871	5,412,377	1871–80: 623,933
1881	5,174,836	1881–90: 770,706
1891	4,704,750	1891–1900: 433,526
1901	4,458,775	1901–1910: 346,024
1911	4,390,219	

There was no general correlation between the severity of the famine and areas of high emigration, or between poverty and emigration. On the whole, emigration was higher in the eastern and midland counties than in the west and south-west; and, since birth-rates were consistently higher in the poorer areas, population fell more sharply in the 'advanced' part of Ireland. In the east, emigration was much more steady, and people left more as individuals. In the poor areas it rose sharply after bad seasons (for example 1861), when whole families left. In the poor west, there was a curiously ambivalent attitude to emigration (and return), not easily explained or quantified, but captured in George Moore's haunting short story 'Home Sickness'.[41] In many of the poorest western districts, the population had recovered and passed its 1841 level by 1881, and in Mayo, the poorest of all, the population fell only 4 per cent in the 1860s and rose again in the 1870s.[42]

Nevertheless, in the century of emigration dating from the famine, almost every rural area in Ireland lost 50 per cent of its population, and in some parts the loss was as much as 70 per cent. Of course this phenomenon was not confined to Ireland. The history of the Highlands and Islands of the west and north of Scotland is very similar in a number of economic and demographic respects, and there too the population is lower today than it was in the first half of the nineteenth century. There are also parallels with Norway. What made

the loss of people so debilitating, psychologically and in real
terms, was its concentration on youth. Between 1850 and
1887, some 66 per cent of Irish emigrants were aged between
fifteen and thirty-five, and for the rest of the century it was
even higher, hardly ever dropping below 80 per cent.

Curiously enough, though the overwhelming majority of
emigrants were Catholics – to the concern not only of the
Catholic ecclesiastical authorities in Ireland but also of the
nationalist politicians – emigration seems to have had very
little effect on the Catholic–Protestant balance. Between 1861
and 1901, the proportion of Protestants in Ireland as a whole
rose only from 12 per cent to 13 per cent. The biggest decline
of the Catholic population took place in Ulster, but even there
it fell only 6 per cent in forty years. [43] It must be remembered
that during this period large numbers of Irishmen (including
a high proportion of Protestants) also moved eastward into
the English and Scottish cities, especially Liverpool and
Glasgow. Unlike Scottish emigrants, who favoured Canada,
Australia and New Zealand, Irish emigrants opted overwhelmingly for the United States. Though 15 per cent of the
Irish went to Canada, Australia and New Zealand, nearly 85
per cent of the 4 million total went to the United States. Of
this group, nearly one-third went to the US in the years
1847–54. America, then, got the lion's share of the bitterest
elements, of which nearly half (48 per cent) came from six
counties – Cork, Kerry, Tipperary, Limerick, Galway and
Mayo – where the evils of Ascendancy landlordism were most
prominent. All the same, the impact of the great invasion of
Irish on the American scene was, in part at least, deadened by
the sheer magnitude of the general surge of Europeans across
the Atlantic. Some 25 million of them entered America in this
period. Even in the 1850s, at the most intense stage of Irish
emigration, the Irish constituted only 35.2 per cent of all
immigrants entering America, and were outnumbered by the
Germans. By the 1890s, the Irish constituted only 10.6 per
cent of those coming to America, while the Germans provided

a consistently high proportion.[44]

In Irish terms, the phenomenon was huge and dramatic: in 1860, the US Census Commission noted that for every Irish immigrant in the United States, only five remained in Ireland, whereas the ratio for Germany was 1 to 33, for Norway 1 to 34 and for England 1 to 42. On the other hand, in American terms the arrival of the Irish was only one element in a gigantic problem of absorption. In 1860, the Irish formed 5.1 per cent of the total United States population, the highest it ever attained (thereafter the percentage declined fairly rapidly). The notion that some Irish nationalists entertained in the second half of the nineteenth century, that America would take the place once held by Spain and then France as Ireland's 'natural ally' against oppressive England, and that the Irish (to adapt Canning's famous dictum) would 'call in the New World, to redress the balance of the Old', did not therefore have much substance, quite apart from the fact that America herself had no obvious and fundamental dispute with Britain.

On the other hand, the Irish immigrants in the United States, though comparatively few in absolute numbers, were highly concentrated. If they left Ireland as penniless farm-labourers and smallholders, they entered it as big-city dwellers. Some 75 per cent of them settled in seven states: Massachusetts, Connecticut, New York, New Jersey, Pennsylvania, Ohio and Illinois, and there they were very largely concentrated in seven cities: Boston, New York, Philadelphia, Chicago, Jersey City, Pittsburgh and St Louis. Bearing in mind the fact that a high proportion arrived in America in a state of near-destitution, most of them did well there, thus coining the notable Irish Bull, 'The only place in Ireland where a man can make a fortune is in America'. A famous pair of prints contrasted the rags of the emigrant ('Outward Bound: the Quay of Dublin') with the modest prosperity of the returning Irish-American ('Homeward Bound: the Quay of New York'). In fact comparatively few did return, except on visits. The vision of retribution

> They'll be coming back in ships
> With vengeance on their lips

did not materialize. The primary concern of most Irish-Americans was to make good there. Their first savings were usually remitted home as passage-money to enable other members of their family to join them, though in a large number of cases money sent home was used to purchase family holdings. American-Irish did provide support for Irish nationalism, as we shall see later, and as indeed they still do, but it was never more than marginal.

What the Great Famine and the mass-emigration did accomplish, however, was the final destruction of the native Irish language, at any rate as the speech of the common people. But the decline of Gaelic was the result of a number of factors. During the eighteenth century it had sustained itself remarkably well, retreating slowly in the east and north, but remaining the majority tongue in most of the centre, as well as all the west and nearly all the south. Even at the time of Catholic Emancipation, in 1829, Irishmen west of a line drawn from Cork to Londonderry spoke nothing but Gaelic; and east of the line it was still spoken by a large minority.[45]

The turning point was the creation of the National Education Scheme in 1831. The success of the new schools had a fatal effect on the Irish tongue. Among the nationalists there was an understandable resolve not to be driven into an ever-dwindling Gaelic-speaking ghetto. O'Connell, though he spoke a little Gaelic himself, was emphatic that English had to be the language of Irish nationalism. He always spoke in English at his great open-air meetings. Equally important was the attitude of the Catholic Church. One of the many great consistencies of Irish history has been the hostility of Rome to Gaelic custom and vernacular. Rome was opposed to the Irish-type monasticism of Iona and defeated it at the Synod of Whitby in 663. Its hostility went a stage further with the Bull *Laudabiliter*; and in the mid-nineteenth century it set its face sternly against Gaelic.

Indeed, the defence of Gaelic, let alone efforts to revive it as a language for middle-class Irish intellectuals, was left initially almost entirely to Protestants. The Church of Ireland evangelicals of the early nineteenth century believed that many Catholics in the west could be converted by a combination of school-building and Gaelic-speaking pastors. It was a Protestant, Robert Daly, who edited the first proper Irish–English dictionary; and it was another Protestant, Henry Monck Mason, who endowed the first chair of Irish, at Trinity College. In 1818 Protestant clergy and laity founded a society to develop use of the Irish language with a special view to conversions. Its members challenged Catholic priests to debates in Gaelic on contentious doctrinal points. It was the Protestant interest in Gaelic that stiffened the resolve of the Catholic Church to support teaching in the English language in all elementary schools, and once the priests backed English, no power on earth could have saved Gaelic as the primary tongue of the people. Thus Gaelic declined *pari passu* with the spread of education, and the famine and mass emigration accelerated the process by striking at the very heart of the western *Gaeltacht* itself. The Irish, unlike the Jews, did not take their language with them into the diaspora, and by the time Gaelic again became part of the official armoury of Irish nationalism, it was too late. Yet the loss of Gaelic in no way diminished the thrust of Ireland's drive to independence: quite the contrary. And in place of the predominant Gaelic, Ireland produced a distinguished if fragile and exotic amalgam of its own: the Anglo-Irish culture.

CHAPTER 6

Ascendancy Culture

It is possible that if Edmund Spenser had not been disheartened by the terrible Munster wars, he might have founded a literary school in Ireland, and claimed a place in history as the founder of Anglo-Irish culture. As it is, the role perhaps belongs to the first Duke of Ormonde, not indeed a creator himself but a munificent patron, to whom certainly the great city of Dublin owes its essential character. When Ormonde returned as Lord Lieutenant after the Restoration, in 1662, Dublin was essentially a medieval city and by all accounts a puny one, scarcely one-ninth of a square mile in area. Ormonde laid the foundations of what was to become one of the finest eighteenth-century cities in Europe, rivalled perhaps only by Bath and Nancy. Already, at Ormonde's death, it had 60,000 inhabitants, and by the time of the rebellion in 1798 it was the second city in the British Empire and the seventh largest in the world.[1]

Ormonde had grasped that valuable Restoration notion, shared by his fellow minister Hyde, that a city, to be grand, must have 'lungs to breathe'. His most enduring legacy is Phoenix Park, once over 2,000 acres, even today some 1,752, which makes it larger than Hyde Park, Kensington Gardens, St James's Park and Green Park, Regent's Park, Greenwich and Battersea Parks all put together: no comparable city in the world has such a generous endowment of tamed and civilized nature.[2] Between 1663 and 1669 over £31,000 was spent on it, but the investment repaid itself many times, because the park, with its elegant lodges, set a standard of magnificence and spaciousness which the architects who worked in Dublin throughout the eighteenth century felt compelled to uphold.

The city was soon dotted with the town palaces of the Anglo-Irish nobility, such as the magnificent Leinster House (now the Dail), begun by Richard Cassels in 1745.[3] Yet it must be said that the eighteenth-century Anglo-Irish culture was a gentry and middle-class product rather than an aristocratic one. A man of talent, only provided he was a Protestant, might rise swiftly. Trinity College, like the universities of Edinburgh and Glasgow, was a much more lively and industrious place than Oxford or Cambridge.[4] Anglo-Irish genius flourished among the professions. Oliver Goldsmith and Thomas Sheridan and his brood came from clerical families; Swift and Burke were the sons of lawyers; the great Berkeley's father was a revenue official.

Ireland's weakness, like that of the Scottish lowlands, was the lure of London. The absentee Irish landlord, as we have seen, was a phenomenon going back to the fourteenth century. It remained a problem. Thomas Prior, a typical Irish meritocrat, who founded the Dublin Society in 1731 to promote agriculture and manufactures, went so far as to publish a *List of the Absentees of Ireland*, and calculate their annual cost to the country. For writers it was not easy to make a living of any kind in cities like Cork or Dublin. No one could have been more anti-English than Swift. When a visitor paid tribute to the qualitites of the Irish air, he interjected: 'Hold your peace, Sir, lest the English should tax it.' But he would gladly have thrown up his Dublin Deanery for a comparable English benefice. No one could have had a more Irish foundation than Robert Boyle, the chemist and son of the great Earl of Cork. Aubrey says he was 'nursed by an Irish Nurse, after the Irish manner, where they put the child into a pendulous satchel (instead of a cradle) with a slit for the child's head to peep out'.[5] But all his work was done in England. George Berkeley, an outstanding Trinity College student, went to England, as he said, 'to make acquaintance with men of merit'. Indeed, even Scotland held more attraction for an ambitious young man than Ireland: for it was to Edinburgh that Goldsmith set out in 1752 with the hope of qualifying as a doctor.[6] For men like Burke, Sheridan or Thomas Moore, there was no alternative but to cross the Irish Sea.

The Anglo-Irish writers of the eighteenth century form a group of exceptional distinction. All were highly original. Swift turned satire into great art, and gave it an edge so keen and deadly that, alone of his age, he still cuts to the bone as ruthlessly as in the 1720s. Berkeley, when he had scarcely ceased to be a student, produced his devastating *Treatise Concerning the Principles of Human Understanding*, which was read all over civilized Europe, and makes him, now no less than then, the quintessential 'philosopher's philosopher'. Burke brought originality to everything to which he set his pen. With his *Vindication of Natural Society* he invented sceptical conservatism; with his essay *On the Sublime and Beautiful* he adumbrated the aesthetic theory of the Romantic movement. He is the only eighteenth-century political philosopher whose reputation continues to grow, as modern anti-Utopians find and develop fresh Burkean flashes. It is indicative that Dr Johnson, a harsh judge of North or West Britons who came to London seeking their fortune, paid a number of noble tributes to Burke: 'Burke is the only man whose common conversation corresponds with the general fame he has in the world. Take up whatever topic you please, he is ready to meet you.' Or again: 'Burke *is* an extraordinary man. His stream of mind is perpetual.... That fellow calls forth all my powers.'[7] You could not, said Johnson, be in a shed with him, sheltering from the rain, for ten minutes without becoming aware he was a great man.

Goldsmith was another original, creator of a new kind of novel, and of a new kind of comic play. Johnson said of *She Stoops to Conquer* that he knew of no play which 'Has so much exhilarated an audience, that has answered so much the great end of comedy – making an audience merry' (as indeed it still does). And he wrote for Goldsmith a superb epitaph: *Qui nullum fere scribendi genus non tetigit, nullum quod tetigit non ornavit*.[8] Goldsmith was the first to develop the enormous histrionic talent of the Anglo-Irish genius, which was to flower so generously in the art of Richard Brinsley Sheridan. Indeed, if we subtract from British theatrical history the works of Goldsmith, Sheridan, Oscar Wilde and George Bernard Shaw, we are left with precious little that is durable from the Restoration to the Edwardians.

Men like Goldsmith and Burke made their homes in England and died there; they in no way ceased to be Irish. Goldsmith, with his penny whistle and plaintive songs, his spontaneity and hot pride, strikes us as a very Irish figure. Burke was not a nationalist, because he conceived that Ireland would find her true destiny as part of a great cosmopolitan empire. But he lost his treasured Bristol seat because he would not compromise on the need to give Irish trade free access to the English market. His life-style, too, in his country house at Beaconsfield, had an unmistakable Irish flavour. When Mrs Thrale visited him there in 1774, she found it a scene of (to her) shocking paradox. The defender of Christian chivalry 'was the first man I had ever seen drunk'. The house was filled with splendid statues and paintings, yet there were dirt and cobwebs everywhere and a liveried servant, though polite, 'served tea with a cut finger wrapped in rags'.[9] Sheridan, too, both as writer and politician, had all the marks of an Irishman – one is tempted to say a stage-Irishman. His handsome and gifted progeny enriched the Irish as well as the English aristocracy, for his beautiful granddaughter Helen was the mother of that most versatile of Anglo-Irish Victorian statesmen, the first Marquess of Dufferin; and she herself, a gifted writer of songs, built the most distinguished of Irish follies, Helen's Tower near Clandeboye, where no less than three great poets, Tennyson, Browning and Kipling, wrote lyrics which adorn its walls.[10]

It is no accident that Dublin's hour of architectural glory coincided with the brilliant false dawn of Grattan's parliament. The best thing that John Beresford, Pitt's factotum, ever did for Ireland was to coax there James Gandon, a brilliant young English architect, who had worked under Chambers. Gandon arrived in 1781, and within the next two decades he had created two masterpieces: the Customs House, finished in 1791, and the Four Courts, still building when the Union ended the era, and which together gave Dublin its serene and classical river-skyline.[11] For those twenty years, there was less need to go to London. When Sir Jonah Barrington, a superbly representative Anglo-Irishman (he was related to the Fitzgeralds and the O'Briens), entered the Dublin parliament in 1790, he wrote: 'I felt myself an entirely independent representative of an equally independent nation.' Long after the Union destroyed his world, he wrote a bitter book about it, *The Rise and Fall of the Irish Nation* (1833) and, more good-humouredly, one of the best books of Anglo-Irish memoirs.[12]

The culture embraced Barrington on the one hand and, on the other, a man like Thomas Moore. Moore's origins were lowly – his father was a Dublin grocer – and he was not even a Protestant, travelling to England, as a young man, with a Papist scapular round his neck. But in the Whig drawing-rooms of Regency London, where he was soon very much at home, he was the very essence of the Anglo-Irish spirit. He had a fine, if lachrymose, singing-voice and would brilliantly accompany his own airs. His lament for poor Robert Emmet, executed by the English in 1803 ('O, breathe not his name!'), is the archetypal Irish tearjerker, and for many years he poured forth a gushing stream of romantic lyrics: *Oft in the Stilly Night*, *The Harp that Once in Tara's Halls*, *The Meeting of the Waters*, *The Minstrel Boy to the War is Gone*, *The Last Rose of Summer* and *Believe me, if All those Endearing Young Charms*, to mention only the more celebrated lyrics admired by a spectrum ranging from Byron and Shelley to Max Beerbohm and John Betjeman.

It is tempting, indeed, to argue that the Romantic Age was

the meridian of the Anglo-Irish culture. It certainly coincided with the most munificent era of Irish building. 'Ireland had been absolutely new-built within these twenty years,' wrote Arthur Young of the 1770s. One authority calculates that some 270 medium- and large-sized country houses were erected in the eighteenth century.[13] Many of these were much too ambitious for the purse of the owner, and it was a fact, as Thackeray duly noted, that Ireland was dotted with country houses that had proved too expensive for the families which had created them, and were therefore let. Anglo-Irish literature is, to a great extent, a country-house literature, and its most characteristic symbol is the grandiose rural mansion, usually called a castle, which is barely maintained by its impoverished, though lineage-conscious, owners. *Castle Rackrent* (1800), *The Absentee* (1812), *Ormond* (1817) – the titles of Maria Edgeworth's novels tell their own tale. They are, in fact, very lively, and the Edgeworths of Edgeworthstown in County Longford were undoubtedly a talented and versatile family, not least Maria's father, a prolific inventor, who contrived to speak for the Union and vote against it, and whose life was full of elopements and drama.[14]

Both Maria Edgeworth and her successor as the leading Irish novelist, Lady Morgan, were of course Protestants (the first good Irish Catholic novelist, Charles Kickham, author of *Knocknagow* [1879], did not come till much later), but neither peddled in anti-Papist notions; indeed, Lady Morgan's novels, of which *Wild Irish Girl* (1806), *O'Donnel* (1814), *Florence McCarthy* (1816) and *The O'Briens and the O'Flahertys* (1827) have Irish settings, go to some lengths to try to correct popular Protestant, and still more English, prejudices against Irish Catholicism. She was born Sydney Owenson, and her father, who came from the poorest of all the western counties, Mayo, had Anglicized his name from MacOwen when he went on the stage (he boasted he was related to Goldsmith). She married Charles Morgan, an English doctor practising in Dublin. According to the famous Anglo-Irish critic, William

Maginn, who embodied one of the failings of his race, lack of charity, Morgan was 'an apothecary, who suffered the penalty of knighthood from some facetious Lord Lieutenant – which accounts for her ladyship'. She herself was described as 'hardly more than four feet high, with a slightly curved spine, uneven shoulders and eyes, gliding about in a close-cropped wig, bound by a fillet or solid band of gold, her face all animation and with a witty word for everybody'.[15] Both as a writer and the holder of a literary salon, she fought fiercely for fame. Critics who savaged her books, like John Wilson Croker, the mordant *Quarterly Review*-er from Cork, were liable to end up in her novels, as Croker did in *Florence McCarthy*, much the worse for wear. She is, I imagine, the original of Trollope's sharp portrait of Lady Carbery in his great novel *The Way We Live Now*.[16]

The most prolific, and perhaps the best, of the Irish novelists was Charles Lever, whose *Charles O'Malley* (1841) gives a picture of his own student days at Trinity College. Lever's parentage, be it noted, was entirely English, which in a sense makes him typically Anglo-Irish, ambivalent as to nationality. All the same he was an important figure in Dublin literary life when Thackeray was there in 1842; and another guest at Lever's mansion of Templeogue, four miles from Dublin, has left an account of their meeting:

Thackeray's manner was at first reserved, earnest and quiet, carefully observing and desirous of not being drawn out, at least prematurely . . . he praised some *fricandeau de veau*, of which he had partaken, a thing rarely seen on Irish tables, and the chef d'oeuvre of Lever's German servant, who was cook and butler rolled up into one; which led to mention being made of the artistical arrangements of the kitchen at the Reform Club. This was just what was wanted; we then knew of course what Thackeray's politics were. . . . As dinner proceeded, and after the ladies had retired, the two protagonists began to skirmish, endeavouring to draw each other out. Lever, quickly perceiving his antagonist's game, met his feints with very quiet but perfectly efficacious parries. Thackeray paid Lever the very handsome compliment of saying that he would rather have written Lorrequer's English version of the Student song, 'The Pope he leads a happy life', than anything he had himself hitherto done in literature.[17]

Some of Lever's best works, *Jack Hinton*, as well as *Lorrequer* and *Charles O'Malley*, appeared as serials in the *Dublin University Magazine*, a journal started in 1833, with a policy of literary nationalism, and which for a time he edited. So, in due course, did Isaac Butt, the Nationalist politician. It paid particular attention to Gaelic studies and translation, a new literary fashion first introduced by the Anglo-Irish authoress Charlotte Brooke, who had published *Reliques of Irish Poetry* in 1789.

Anglo-Irish society was eccentric, broadminded, tolerant, inclusive rather than exclusive, above all hospitable. Travel was often by canal-boat, a cheap but tedious method, well described in Trollope's early Irish novel, *The Kellys and the O'Kellys* (1848). The railways were late coming to Ireland, and throughout the south and west, at any rate in the days when Trollope and Thackeray were there, the wonder of communications were 'Bianconis', fast coaches, or 'cars', organized by an enterprising Milanese who had settled at Clonmel. But many places were hard to get to, and Anglo-Irish squires were often glad of a guest. Trollope tells an excellent story of a gentleman in County Cavan who complained bitterly of some Post Office arrangement. Sent out to investigate, Trollope was warmly greeted by a genial host, given a splendid dinner, pressed to stay the night – no question of discussing business before the morning – and entertained to an ample breakfast, the host finally admitting: 'Here I sit all day, with nothing to do – and I like writing letters.'[18]

Such country establishments were notable for their ample
array of servants. Thackeray, in his *Irish Sketch Book*, found
this everywhere:

> There may be many comparisons drawn between English
> and Irish gentlemen's houses; but perhaps the most striking
> point of difference between the two is the immense
> following of the Irish house, such as would make an English
> housekeeper crazy almost. Three comfortable, well-
> clothed, good-humoured fellows walked down with me
> from the car, persisting in carrying one a bag, another a
> sketching-stool and so on. Walking about the premises in
> the morning, sundry others were visible in the courtyard
> and near the kitchen door. In the grounds a gentleman . . .
> began discoursing to me regarding the place, the planting,
> the fish, the grouse and the Master; being himself,
> doubtless, one of the irregulars of the house. As for maids,
> there were half a score of them scurrying about the house;
> and I am not ashamed to confess that some of them were
> exceedingly good-looking.[19]

The servants, of course, were Catholics; only in Ulster
was it thought wise or proper to insist on Protestant domestics.
Apart from periods of particular economic or political stress,
the religious divide never interfered with the amenities of life;
indeed it was astonishing how tolerant the Irish usually were,
when not being, as it were, professionally intolerant. Trollope
had a curious experience while on a tour of inspection. He
arrived after dark at a village, put up at its primitive inn, and
was shown to a room with two beds. Awakened in the night,
he found an elderly person getting ready for bed, and calmly
brushing his coat with Trollope's clothes-brush. Trollope was
a choleric man. He leapt out of bed, seized the man, opened
the door and pushed him out. Unluckily, the door led onto a
steep flight of stairs, down which the man fell, 'and lay as
though dead on the floor'. Roused by the noise, the people of
the inn shrieked out that the Englishman had killed Father

Giles, the parish priest, and an angry mob collected. To Trollope's dismay, a British revenue officer appeared, arrested him and marched him off to the local gaol for the night. In the morning it was explained to him that he might otherwise have been killed by Father Giles's infuriated parishioners. The bedroom was in fact the priest's own, and he had kindly allowed Trollope to use the spare bed. Happily, Trollope and the priest then became good friends, and the incident was recounted in a short story, *Father Giles of Ballymoy*.[20]

In organic alliance with the Anglo-Irish gentry and the urban middle class were the Church of Ireland clergy. It could be argued that if any group, apart from the landowners, lost Ireland for Britain, it was the established clergy. The Irish peasants never had the Reformation, for the simple reason that it was never brought to them. Of course in the sixteenth and seventeenth centuries it was difficult to get good Anglican clergy to serve in Ireland; those who did so tended to hole themselves up in the towns. They did not even attempt to evangelize the country districts, where of course the priests from the Continent, burning with zeal, were very active. The Church of Ireland was never anything but middle or upper class, with the clergy hovering uneasily between. The notion that Protestantism was only for the socially acceptable, so fatal to its survival, is neatly summed up in the eighteenth-century ditty which sought to identify doctrinal gentility with the island's patron:

> St Patrick was a gentleman
> He came of decent people.
> He built a church in Dublin town
> And on it put a steeple.[21]

It must be said, however, that there was an enormous improvement in the Church of Ireland clergy from the early nineteenth century onwards. Low church by English stand-ards, they at last – when it was too late – began to try to evangelize the Irish poor, especially in the west and south-west. That was their principal motive in their rediscovery and revival of Gaelic as a literary tongue. In this process the *Dublin University Magazine* played a leading role until its demise in 1877, the clergy, both as contributors and readers, providing staple support.

Yet the most important figure in the revival was an Anglo-Irish layman, Sir Samuel Ferguson. He hoped that he could somehow underpin and strengthen the existing order. As he put it, 'The Protestant wealth and intelligence of the country must cultivate an acquaintance with its ancient literature and traditions.'[22] He produced his own works, such as *The Hibernian Nights' Entertainment* and *The Lays of Western Gael*, and his narrative poems were greatly admired by William Butler Yeats. 'The author of these poems,' Yeats wrote, 'is the greatest poet Ireland has produced, because the most central and most Celtic.' Yet Yeats was well aware that Ferguson, though a Nationalist in literature, was a Unionist in politics.

At the heart of Anglo-Irish culture there was always this dilemma, and the need to be Janus-faced. Though a Nationalist and a patriot, Yeats was not only intensely aware of his Anglo-Irish and Protestant roots, but proud of them. The Protestant Irish, as he put it, were 'no petty people'. Strongly as he supported the Gaelic revival, he had no wish to rewrite the cultural past – what poet could, given all the riches of Shakespeare's tongue? – and agreed with Shaw that 'English is the native language of Irishmen'. It is characteristic of Yeats, who revelled in the reconciliation of opposites, that the murder of Kevin O'Higgins in 1927, which moved him greatly, led him to write a poem, 'Blood on the Moon', confessing his Irishness as part of the great eighteenth-century tradition:

I declare this tower is my symbol; I declare
This winding, gyring, spiring treadmill of a stair is my
    ancestral stair;

That Goldsmith and the Dean, Berkeley and Burke have
   travelled there.

This, to Yeats, was the true Irish cultural genealogy. The
false one, he seems to have thought, was the kind of
sentimental nationalism, on which most ordinary Irish
Catholics had been brought up, provided by the songs of
Thomas Moore and epitomized by an anthology, compiled by
Sir Charles Gavan Duffy when he had been a leader of the
Young Ireland movement, and republished many times,
called *The Spirit of the Nation*.[23] It was generally supposed that
such verse was the direct descendant (though in English) of
old Gaelic poetry. Through Ferguson, Yeats was aware that
this was not so. Irish literature was too important to be left in
the hands of jejune lyricists and oratorical patriots; much
better that it should relate itself to the sinewy prose of Swift or
the true Celtic of magic – that is, either Protestant or Pagan.
And when the new Irish literature did in fact appear, in the
1890s, those who produced and sponsored it – Yeats himself,
Lady Gregory, Standish, James O'Grady, J. M. Synge,
Douglas Hyde and George Russell (AE) and others – were
overwhelmingly Church of Ireland.[24]

The Irish literary renaissance, of which Yeats, the most
formidable poet of modern times, was the moving force, was
so powerful and coherent, albeit multifaceted, that it has
understandably been compared to the Elizabethan drama.[25]
As it matured, the Independent Irish nation was taking shape
and asserting its rights. There is a close connection between
modern Irish literature and the growth of the nation. Yeats
put it dogmatically: 'No fine nationality without literature . . .
no fine literature without nationality'; or, more nobly:
'To the great poets everything they see has its relation to
the national life and through that to the universal and
divine life.'

But in the long and humbling perspective of history, was
the movement of which Yeats led the beginning a new

national literature or the end of one that began with Swift? It is arguable that the voice and vision Yeats and his contemporaries created prolong themselves in the European drama of Samuel Beckett. It is equally arguable that Yeats has had no Irish successor and that the great literary surge died with him, with James Joyce and with Sean O'Casey. But there is a third possibility: that Yeats's renaissance was both dawn and sunset – the dawn of a new national tradition, the sunset of the Anglo-Irish one.

Yeats was well aware of his own discordant loyalties. He knew he had alternative masks to wear. He could play the high literary card by damning poor Tom Moore's ditties; but he could also play, when he chose, the political card. He would silence a fractious literary gathering by suddenly pronouncing, with total irrelevance and supreme dramatic force, the three words: 'Charles . . . Stewart . . . Parnell.' He made a literary virtue of his bi-focal vision. That was why his key image was of intersecting spirals – gyres, as he called them, spinning cones which interpenetrate, whirling around inside one another. They stood, he said, for objectivity and subjectivity and all complementary opposites, 'beauty and truth, value and fact, particularly and universal, quality and quantity. . . . Man and *Diamon*, the living and the dead, and all other images of our first parents.'[26] They also stood, secretly, for the two elements within the Irish population, one Catholic and subjective, the other Protestant and (so he believed) objective. Yeats used the gyre image in his great poem 'The Second Coming', a lament on the Irish pursuit and illusion of freedom, the horrors of liberation, the agonies of division – 'the centre cannot hold'. The centre was the much-battered Anglo-Irish community, Protestant yet patriotic, shortly to be submerged in the consummation of national freedom.

The last great representative of this spirit was Edith Somerville, born in 1858, who died aged ninety-one in the same year Ireland finally declared itself a republic. Together

with her friend Violet Martin (who wrote under the name
Martin Ross), she produced perhaps the most durable
monument to the old Protestant gentry, the series of short
stories grouped together in the volumes *Some Experiences of an
Irish RM* (1899), *Further Experiences of an Irish RM* (1908) and
In Mr Knox's Country (1915). Written with enviable brilliance
and organized with masterly cunning, these tales present
shamelessly an Ascendancy viewpoint, with the Resident
Magistrate himself as the narrator, the Protestant gentry as
the 'real' people, and the Catholic underlings as an endless
series of comic turns. In their own manner these stories are a
species of 'imperialist' literature no less brazen than some of
Kipling's.

As such they reflect the external image of Edith
Somerville herself, the daughter of the 'big house' at
Skibbereen, the Master of the West Carbery Foxhounds,
a martial and upright figure riding side-saddle, hunting-
horn in hand, as she still appears in her portrait which
hangs in her ancestral home, Drishane House.[27] Yet a
closer reading reveals that it is the RM himself, the very
symbol of imperial authority, who is the bewildered victim of
events, all of which are set in motion and controlled – in so far
as they are controlled at all, since the climax of every tale is
anarchy – by the ordinary people of Ireland. The tales can be
seen as a surrealist forcast of how British rule would dissolve.

This interpretation is strengthened if we look at the more
serious fiction produced under the authorship of Somerville
and Ross: *The Real Charlotte* (1894), *Mount Music* (1919) and
The Big House at Inver (1925), in the last of which the hero is
Catholic, though illegitimate. These provide a closer view of
the sadness, the ambiguities and uncertainties of Anglo-Irish
life. It was always, from first to last, a vulnerable presence.
Certainly once the Great Famine had taken place, it never
looked really secure, except to those who wished to delude
themselves. The stories of the Irish RM were, I suspect, not
documentary but the subconscious recreation of a golden age,

of friendly skirmishes between the races and the religions within a larger harmony of happiness and high spirits – a golden age which had never existed, but which the people of the two communities liked to think had been enjoyed by both, before the Famine years.

CHAPTER 7

Home Rule and the Land

Ireland after the famine was in some ways a Janus-faced, deceptive country, liable to mislead its own spokesmen as well as the British. John Mitchel, a young Irish activist, writing in the *United Irishman*, saw Ireland in 1847 as inert, defeated, dying almost:

> A calm, still horror was over the land. Go where you would, in the heart of the town or in the suburb, on the mountain side or in the level plain, there was the stillness and heavy, pall-like feel of the chamber of death. You stood in the presence of a dread, silent, vast dissolution. An unseen ruin was creeping round you. You saw no war of classes, no open Janissary war of foreigners, no human agency of destruction. You could weep, but the rising curse died unspoken within your heart, like a profanity. Human passion there was none, but inhuman and unearthly quiet.[1]

In 1848, the 'Year of Revolutions' in Europe, stricken Ireland gave little sign of protest. A 'Young Ireland' attempt to raise a revolt in Munster met with virtually no response. Smith O'Brien and other leaders were sentenced to transportation; Mitchel himself was already in Van Dieman's Land, where he wrote his remarkable *Jail Journal*. Was it that Ireland was too exhausted to think of liberty? Apparently not. The next year, the famine still unresolved, Queen Victoria paid a state visit. She wrote to her uncle, the King of the Belgians:

> The entrance at seven o'clock into Kingston harbour was splendid: we came in with ten steamers, and the whole harbour, wharf and every surrounding place was *covered*

with *thousands* and thousands of people, who received us
with the greatest enthusiasm. . . . The most perfect order
was maintained in spite of the immense mass of people
assembled, and a more good-humoured crowd I never saw,
but noisy and excitable beyond belief, talking, jumping
and shrieking instead of cheering. . . . You see more ragged
and wretched people here than I ever saw anywhere else.
En revanche, the women are really very handsome – quite in
the lowest class – as well in Cork as [Dublin]; such beautiful
black eyes and hair and such fine colours and teeth.[2]

Yet there had been a change, and a fundamental one.
Relations between Protestant landlord and Catholic tenant
were never the same again. O'Connell, a landlord himself,
had campaigned very largely on religious and political issues
alone. That was no longer possible. When O'Connell died in
1847, O'Connellism – the divorce of Irish politics from
economic issues – died with him; and so did the notion of
peaceful, constitutional agitation. John Mitchel pronounced
his epitaph:

Poor old Dan! Wonderful, mighty, jovial and mean old
man! With silver tongue and smile of witchery and heart of
melting ruth! Lying tongue, smile of treachery, heart of
unfathomable fraud! What a royal yet vulgar soul! With
the keen eye and potent sweep of a generous eagle of Cairn
Tual – with the base servility of a hound and the cold
cruelty of a spider! Think of his speech for John Magee, the
most powerful forensic achievement since Demosthenes –
and then think of the gorgeous and gossamer theory of
moral and peaceful agitation, the most astounding *organon*
of public swindling since first man bethought him of
obtaining money under false pretences![3]

Until the famine, the grievances of the peasants centred
round tithes. After it, the landlord was the target. In one
sense, it is true, the famine (and emigration) was a Malthusian

catastrophe-corrective, which left the agricultural economy much more healthy by reducing the non-viable sector. During the 1850s, farming incomes, savings and rural living standards all rose, and there was a rapid recovery in agricultural investment, with both landlords and farmers putting more into the land. A good deal of land changed hands during and after the famine. The new landlords tended to be more 'enlightened' (economically), more efficient, and much harsher, especially to smallholders.[4]

The older style landlords, too, wished to get rid of the remaining smallholders. They were hag-ridden by the thought that the famine would return as a result of the multiplication of holdings. Thus the 3rd Earl of Leitrim, rated a good, conscientious landlord who spent his whole life dealing with his estates (he had 90,000 acres in four counties of the North-West), saw his Leitrim tenancies rise from 736 to 776 and his Donegal tenancies rise from 1,572 to 1,664, during the fifteen years 1855–69. His efforts to reverse what he regarded as a disastrous trend led to his murder in 1878.[5] Nor was crime the only weapon. The year 1850 saw two important developments. Despite its obvious disadvantages, the union did at least lock Ireland into the English reform process. The 1850 Irish Franchise Act raised the electorate to 160,000, and it was accompanied by the formation of the Irish Tenant Rights League, which returned no less than fifty MPs at the 1852 election. Traditionally, and in law, Irish tenants had had no specific rights. What the League wanted was that 'legal right under definite law should now become the substitute for equitable right under uncertain custom'.[6] From this point onwards, despite setbacks and delays, the pressure for a transformation of the whole basis on which land in Ireland was owned and occupied was never relaxed. Behind the more spectacular political activity, a silent revolution – which culminated in the years just before the First World War – was taking place.[7]

Against this background of agitation, both legal and illegal, on the land, the Irish Republican Brotherhood was formed in Dublin in 1858 by a group of revolutionaries led by James Stephens.[8] They were called Fenians, a name derived from the *Fianna* or army of the legendary Finn MacCool. But though they looked back to Ireland's remote past, in practical terms they took advantage of the latest development, the growth of a large American-Irish community. As we have seen, during the 1850s and 1860s, the Irish immigrants formed a substantial part of the population in some of the big American cities and for a time the 'American Dimension' became a major factor in Irish politics.[9] In the years 1858–66, the Fenians collected more than $500,000 in America and Canada.[10] Indeed, strictly speaking the American Fenians predated their Dublin colleagues by two years, and for some time they were both more numerous and more active on the far side of the Atlantic – there were 50,000 Fenians in the US at the beginning of the Civil War. In 1861, the body of Terence Bellew MacManus, who had gone to the US after the disastrous 1848 rising, and had died in California, was brought back to Dublin for burial. The Fenians were condemned by the Catholic Church, since they based their organization on the methods of the Italian *Carbonari* and other Continental-type secret societies, to which the Vatican was fiercely opposed. The Archbishop of Dublin, Dr Paul Cullen, refused to allow a Christian burial. Nevertheless, the funeral was a powerful demonstration of the strength the Fenians could command, despite the opposition of the Catholic hierarchy, and the importance of the links with America.

For a time, during the Civil War, the Irish agitation in America, combined with the real anger of the American government towards Britain over the *Alabama* affair, made some kind of direct American intervention in the Irish problem seem possible. In 1863 a National Convention of the Fenian Brotherhood was held in Chicago, and two years later an Irish 'shadow administration', of President, Senate and House of Delegates based on the American model, was set up in Philadelphia. John Mitchel, who had escaped from Australia, was appointed the Fenian agent in Paris, receiving cash from the US and transferring it to Dublin. Many American-Irish veterans of the Civil War volunteered their services for a campaign in Ireland.[11]

The British government was sufficiently concerned to set up a naval patrol off the Irish coast, and an intelligence system in New York and Washington, run from the British consulate and embassy. Meanwhile Lord Odo Russell, at the Vatican, was ordered to bring pressure on Pope Pius IX to restrain what Lord Clarendon, the Foreign Secretary, called 'that truculent body, the Irish priesthood'.[12] Between September 1865 and September 1866, at least eighty-eight American citizens were arrested in Ireland and charged with Fenian conspiracy.

Nevertheless, the danger from America was never very serious. Most of the Irish immigrants, while willing to give the Fenians a few dollars, had no intention of returning to Ireland, let alone fighting there. The British and American governments made up their differences. Attempts by the American Fenians to carry out attacks on Canada from US territory not only ended in military farce but angered and antagonized the American government.[13] A ship called *Erin's Hope*, filled with Civil War veterans, set sail for Ireland, but all aboard were arrested on landing. An attempt by 1,200 Fenians to infiltrate and capture Chester Castle (long an object of hatred to the Irish, as it was the ancient port of embarkation for English armies sent to Ireland) was a ludicrous failure.

All the same, the British authorities received some alarming reports of Fenian strength in Ireland, even in the British forces stationed at the Curragh, the main army camp. The Fenians were organized in 'circles', an early version of the Communist cell structure. Each commander (A) had nine captains; each captain (B), nine sergeants; each sergeant (C) nine privates. A full circle thus had 800 members, but in

practice many of the Irish circles had 2,000, and the
government believed there might well be 150,000 Fenians
altogether. Yet James Stephens and his comrades were
romantics rather than highly-organized and ruthless professional revolutionaries. The manifesto they prepared against a
proposed visit by the Prince of Wales read:

IRISHMEN:

693 years of bloody extermination and rapacious plunder
by British Butchers (countrymen of the Queen of England's son) demand of you silence and contempt, and not
even by your outward appearance to show the slightest
participation in the HOLLOW REJOICINGS THAT
WILL BE PARADED BEFORE YOU BY THE BAS-
TARD descendants of Strongbow and Cromwell . . . Irishmen, testify your loyalty and devotion to Ireland by
meeting in the bonds of brotherhood to HAVE IRELAND
FOR THE IRISH. GOD SAVE THE PEOPLE

By Order of the Vigilance Committee.[14]

The Irish rising itself, planned for 5–6 March 1867, was
betrayed the day before by a letter sent to Superintendent
Ryan of the Dublin Metropolitan Police:

Sir, The Dublin Fenians will assemble on Tallough Hill in
large numbers tomorrow. They will be going out in small
batches all day. They will carry no arms with them. The
arms will be sent out in cabs and vans and carts the best
way they can in the course of the day. I hope you will act on
this information in order to save bloodshed. If you do we
will be troubled in Dublin no more by the Fenians.

I am, Sir,
One Who Would Wish to Save the Lives of the People.[15]

As a result, the police carried out 207 preventative arrests in
Dublin, and small outbreaks in Cork, Tipperary and
Limerick were easily dealt with. Special Commissions tried

169 men charged with high treason or treason-felony. Even those sentenced to death were reprieved as a result of representations by the Catholic Church and pressure from the American government. One of the prisoners, Colonel Kelly, an Irish-American Civil War veteran, was daringly rescued from a police van in Manchester, in the course of which a policeman was killed; and the government refused to commute the sentences on three Irishmen subsequently convicted for the murder. They were hanged in Manchester, became instantly known as 'the Manchester Martyrs', and were added to the ever-lengthening nationalist martyrology. A subsequent explosion at Clerkenwell Gaol, to release another Irishman, killed 12 people and injured over 100.[16]

Some of the elements of the modern Irish problem thus began to emerge: the American connection, the use of terrorism, the need to hang the murderers of policemen to maintain police morale, the consequent martyrdom of those so hanged, the extension of the struggle to England and the murder of innocents – and, not least, the growing feeling among English and Anglo-Irish administrators that it was beyond the wit of man to reach an equitable solution to Ireland's ills; that, in short, Ireland was a problem without a solution. After the Fenian scare was over, at any rate temporarily, the Lord Lieutenant, the Earl of Mayo, wrote to Disraeli:

> Ireland is an infernal country to manage. . . . Impartiality is impossible, statesmanship wholly out of place. The only way to govern is the old plan (which I will not attempt) of taking up violently one faction or the other, putting them like fighting-cocks, and then backing one. I wish you would send me to India. Ireland is the grave of every reputation.[17]

There was a further element, too: the realization among many Irishmen that English governments would yield to force what they had not been prepared to yield to peaceful argument and constitutional protest. Fenianism persuaded

W. E. Gladstone, who became Prime Minister for the first time in 1868, that concessions would have to be made, and he decided to abandon the least defensible aspect of the Ascendancy, the Church of Ireland. He had never been to Ireland, but he had hitherto hotly defended the Establishment there and had even resigned from Peel's ministry over an Irish religious issue. Gladstone's turnabout was so remarkable that he felt it necessary to publish a personal defence;[18] and at the end of his life he rated disestablishment of the Irish Church, carried through parliament in 1869, as one of his four greatest achievements.[19] It helped to make possible a further reorganization of the Irish education system, for some £372,000 of the former revenues of the Church of Ireland were syphoned off to Maynooth College. This was followed in 1878 by the creation of secondary schools, and in the following year of the Royal University of Ireland (Trinity College had opened fellowships and higher degrees to Catholics in 1873), so that within ten years Ireland was provided with a complete educational system to which the Catholic majority had access.[20]

Yet disestablishment in no way satisfied the Irish nationalists. On the contrary, it increased their appetite. It was the first big English surrender, the initial breach in the Act of Union. Moreover, once disestablished, the Protestant clergy no longer had an institutional motive to fight for the union.[21] Even more important, however, was the personal effect of the battle over the Irish Church on Gladstone himself, and on his political priorities. During the 1870s and 1880s he became increasingly committed to nationalism in general, and Irish aspirations in particular; and where he moved, he carried English liberalism – or most of it – in his train.

Gladstone's first idea was to send the Prince of Wales as a permanent viceroy to Dublin, a scheme which had occurred to Henry II. Queen Victoria turned it down flat. In 1870 he produced an Irish Land Bill, which banned certain forms of ejection and extended Ulster tenant right to the rest of

Ireland. The thought behind the measure was that the apparent loyalty of Ulster tenant-farmers to the system must be due to the system of tenure. The suggestion had been made in J. S. Mill's *Principles of Political Economy* (1848), and endorsed by Walter Bagehot in a powerful review. 'The economical condition of Ireland,' he wrote, 'is probably far worse than that of any other country possessing equal natural advantages. . . . The land tenure appears to be about the worst possible.' The landlords had a monopoly of land, the tenants no rights; so the harder they worked, the more the landlords were tempted to raise the rents, with eviction as the alternative. The conventional wisdom saw this as progress, since smallholders were thought to be enemies of efficient agriculture, and the remedy was seen to be the universal conversion to large tillage farms, on the English model, with the lower classes as mere day-labourers. But, said Bagehot, the political cost of this policy was unacceptable. In any case, where tenant right existed, as in Ulster, it worked well: the solution was to extend it to the rest of Ireland.[22] It was on this reasoning that Gladstone acted.[23]

Like all previous concessions to Ireland it came too late. Tenant right in Ulster, though less important than the ties of religion and culture, had helped to solidify Presbyterian opinion behind the union. Had Ulster tenant right been conceded to the southern peasants before the Famine, or even when Mill first proposed it, some of them at least might have been reconciled to British justice. By 1870, however, they had been alienated, and Gladstone's Act was accepted merely as a platform from which to ask for more. More significant, for its impact on Irish politics, was Gladstone's Ballot Act of 1872, which made it possible for Irish tenants to vote in secret, and so against their landlord's wishes. It laid down the legal and parliamentary basis for a strong, homogeneous and tightly disciplined Irish Party at Westminster, whose members would be dependent on the party ticket for their election, and whose votes in the lobbies would therefore be at the disposal of the party whips.

So a new political instrument was handed to the nationalists, and they brandished it with a new slogan: Home Rule. In the autumn of 1873 a nationalist conference laid down that 'it is essentially necessary to the peace and prosperity of Ireland that the right of domestic legislation on all Irish affairs should be restored to our country'.[24] A Protestant lawyer, Isaac Butt, was the leader of the new Home Rule group, and after the election of 1874 he took fifty-nine followers with him to Westminster.

What gave the Home Rule movement an angry edge was a progressive and ominous change in the economy. The mid-1870s were years of depression for the new world economy, and for Britain in particular the end of the long period of sustained growth introduced by the repeal of the Corn Laws in 1846. They also brought agricultural disaster to Britain and Ireland. Up to the harvest of 1876, Irish agriculture had been prosperous. Three bad seasons followed, and they coincided with the first massive deliveries of cheap trans-atlantic grain – free trade coming home to roost. So, for the first time, low yields were accompanied by low prices. The summer and autumn of 1879 were particularly bad: heavy rain in two days out of three. No one actually starved in Ireland but in some areas 60 per cent of the people were on relief in 1880.[25] The combination of misfortunes did for Disraeli's government; it also did for Isaac Butt and the moderate Irish leadership.[26] Introducing his first Home Rule resolution in 1874 (it was voted down 458 to 51), Butt had taken a position not essentially different from O'Connell's:

He believed the Irish people were essentially conservative. It was only misgovernment that had driven them into revolt. Give them fair play, and there was no people on earth who would be more attached to true conservative principles than the Irish nation. The geographical position of Ireland made it her interest to be united with England.

They were allied to England by ties of kindred and ties of self-interest which bound them to maintain inviolate the connection with this country, and the way to maintain that connection was to give them justice in the management of their own internal affairs.[27]

Though Butt's view could not yet command the assent even of advanced English Liberals, it was in a sense – not least in the form it was presented – out of date. The new Irish tone was set by Charles Stewart Parnell, a young Protestant landlord who entered parliament in 1875. A few months later he interrupted the Irish Secretary, who referred to 'the Manchester murderers', with the chilly statement that in Ireland they were universally regarded as martyrs. The next year he and other Irish members systematized a new parliamentary weapon, obstructionism, holding up a Bill for twenty-six hours by making continuous speeches. Parnell seemed to possess the same kind of Anglo-Irish fury which possessed Dean Swift, and he focused it on a hatred of England which recalled Wolfe Tone. In manner he was ice-cold, in purpose unbending, in willpower absolute and fearsome – a combination Ireland would see again in De Valera. He was quite ruthless in exploiting the then easy-going procedure of the Commons and in pursuing Irish nationalist aims to the total disregard of any other consideration. He took over the party from Butt in 1878, and for the next twelve years exercised despotic authority within the nationalist movement.

Parnell came from the Anglo-Irish Ascendancy – indeed, his grandfather, Sir John Parnell, had opposed union to the bitter end – but the man who complemented his leadership, Michael Davitt, though born in the same year (1846), came from the dispossessed peasant poor. His family had been evicted and he himself had served a long term of imprisonment for the abortive assault on Chester Castle. Davitt, who founded the Land League in 1879, linked the agrarian agitation which the Depression made inevitable to give a social and economic underpinning to Parnell's political campaign at Westminster. The fall in agricultural incomes had made Gladstone's 1870 Act irrelevant. What use was tenant right if rents could not be paid? Between 1874 and 1881 there were over 10,000 evictions and, in consequence, a huge increase in agricultural crime and outrage – 2,590 incidents in 1880 alone. What Davitt did was to canalize agricultural unrest into two systematic forms of protest – boycott and rent-strike. The Land League advised tenants to offer the landlord what they felt was a fair rent and, if that was turned down, to pay nothing. Evictions were to be resisted, and anyone taking over an evicted farm was to be boycotted. Evictions were publicized by the League in advance, and became set-pieces in a war of propaganda, attended by press and (increasingly) photographers, and aimed as much at the growing urban electorate of Britain as at the Irish nationalists of the towns.[28]

The 1880 election sent sixty-five Irish nationalists to Westminster, thirty of them pledged to Parnell; it also returned Gladstone to power, a man now hotly determined to do justice to Ireland. At this stage Gladstone believed that, provided the land question could be settled, the union could be maintained. He therefore determined on a double policy: land reform on the one hand, a Coercion Act on the other to maintain order. But he had to contend with many obstacles; a House of Lords which was beginning to reject an increasing number of Liberal Bills; old-fashioned Whig government colleagues, like the Marquess of Lansdowne (who had huge Irish estates) and the Duke of Argyll, who were opposed to reform; an Irish Secretary, W. E. Forster – known as 'Buckshot', because he advocated its use to dispense mobs – who had no sympathy with Gladstone's approach to Ireland; and, not least, Parnell, who was determined not to let Britain solve the land problem without conceding Home Rule too.

Gladstone's first land bill, a temporary measure to force

landlords to compensate evicted tenants, lost him Lansdowne and was, in any case, killed by the Lords. The Coercion Act, which allowed the Irish government to arrest without trial for a wide variety of offences, was forced through despite frantic obstructionism by Parnell, culminating in a sitting of forty-one hours.[29] Much against his will Gladstone was obliged to carry a Closure Act (or guillotine), to limit discussion on any Bill and make obstruction more difficult – typical of the way in which, as he saw it, failure to solve the Irish problem was damaging British institutions.[30]

His 1881 Land Act was a crucial measure. It was said to be so complicated that only Gladstone himself, and his parliamentary draftsman, Sir Henry Thring, could understand all of it. But in essence it conceded to Irish tenants everything the Irish Tenant Rights League had asked for, thirty-one years before: above all, the 'Three Fs' – fair rent, fixity of tenure, and freedom for tenants to sell their holdings. Judicial tribunals were set up to determine fair rents and so long as a tenant paid such rents he could not be evicted. The Act cost Gladstone another Whig resignation, that of his old friend the Duke of Argyll, and it undermined the whole concept of freehold land in Ireland, by giving tenants equal right in the land with landlords. It was the second big surrender, and the Irish landed class took it as a sign that the Williamite land-settlement was to be opened up again, and that they could no longer rely on a British government to protect the interests of property in Ireland. From this time they began to look for a solution which would enable them to sell up at a reasonable price.[31]

Yet the 1881 Act did not satisfy Parnell, partly because about 100,000 tenants in arrears and threatened with eviction were excluded; partly because the sights of the Land League were now raised to accomplish ownership of the land; but most of all because if the Act was successful it threatened (as Gladstone hoped) to blunt the thrust of the agitation for political change.[32] So Parnell and the nationalists tried to wreck the Act by persuading tenants not to use the tribunals, arguing that any rent paid to an alien landlord was contrary to natural justice. This was too much for Gladstone. In a public speech he accused Parnell of preaching 'public plunder'. Nothing, he said, was going to prevent the Irish people from getting the benefits of the Act: if, he said, 'there is still to be fought a final conflict in Ireland between law on the one side, and sheer lawlessness on the other . . . then I say Gentlemen, without hesitation, the resources of civilisation against its enemies are not yet exhausted'.[33] Parnell replied that Gladstone had 'thrown off the mask', and he told the Irish Gladstone was 'prepared to carry fire and sword into your homesteads unless you humbly abase yourselves before him and the landlords of your country'. The next day he was arrested and thrown into Kilmainham Gaol. The Land League began an immediate and total rent-strike.

Yet clearly it made no more sense to throw Parnell into gaol than it had in the case of O'Connell. Moreover, if the Whig element in the Liberal Party disliked land reform, the left-wing element disliked coercion; and this second element was growing, while the Whigs were leaving.[34] John Morley, editor of the *Pall Mall Gazette*, pointed to the weakness in Gladstone's strategy: 'The Irish are more provoked by the application of force than they are gratified by the extension of justice. The English are then in turn disgusted by what they consider to be ingratitude.' So the spiral of hatred continued. Morley argued that coercion increased Irish disorder in the long run because it destroyed Irish respect for the notion of law itself, and drove discontent underground into more violent channels. He maintained that the Land League was a positive force. It was the only friend of the Irish tenants and served them like a trade union; it developed among them a 'habit of self-reliance and self-help' and thus corrected the faults of the Irish character', the consequence of the 'abominable treatment' of Ireland by the English. The League's agitation was abundantly justified and had done 'downright good work in raising up the tenants against their truly detestable tyrants'. Without it, the 1881 Act (which Gladstone was now identifying with civilization) would not have been enacted. In the circumstances, agitation was a natural way of expressing political opinion. The 'all-important thing' was that

> arbitrary powers are not to be used to repress that play of antagonistic social forces which is legitimate in England, which ought to remain legitimate in Ireland, and without which we cannot know how to settle the land system on a secure basis.[35]

Of course the logic of Morley's arguments, which represented the coming trend of Liberal opinion, was that Britain had to choose between continued agitation and devising a more democratic system of government for Ireland. Gladstone had not yet moved to that point. But he was anxious to get Parnell out of gaol; and Parnell was anxious to leave, since he found it increasingly difficult to control his campaign from behind bars. So in 1882 the 'Treaty of Kilmainham' was negotiated, using the Radical Joseph Chamberlain for the government side and Parnell's mistress, Mrs Kitty O'Shea, and her husband on the other. Parnell agreed to support the Land Act as a condition of release, and Gladstone agreed to extend the Act to tenants already in arrears.[36]

The storm of English indignation which greeted Parnell's release was led by Forster, who resigned. Gladstone replied to his letter of resignation in the exalted tone which now began to characterize his approach to Ireland: 'I have received your letter with much grief, but on this it would be selfish to expatiate. I have no choice; followed or not followed, I must go on.'[37] Gladstone replaced Forster with his own nephew, Lord Frederick Cavendish, and the poor young man was murdered almost as soon as he set foot in Dublin. So was his companion, the under-secretary T. H. Burke, the real object of the attack (the killers did not even know who Cavendish was). In the uproar which followed Gladstone had to introduce another Coercion Bill. But he stuck to his Kilmainham bargain and carried through an Arrears Act. By 1884 he was able to announce that agrarian crimes had dropped from 4,438 in 1881 to 870 in 1883.[38]

But what was to be the next step? For Gladstone's 1884 Reform Act, which enormously extended the suffrage, was bound to have a big impact on Ireland, and a next step would therefore be necessary. Joe Chamberlain, who believed passionately in local government, wanted a comprehensive new system for Ireland, with a 'Central Board', or devolved assembly.[39] The Irish Secretary, Sir Henry Campbell-Bannerman, thought such a scheme 'would put the so-called Irish government in a position not only intolerable to itself, but impossible'. Instead, he favoured the next step in Gladstone's land policy, a Bill which would help tenants to buy out their landlords: '. . . we must have a Purchase Bill,' he wrote to the Lord Lieutenant. 'I began with a strong prejudice against it (unless in the most limited form) but I [now] think it is quite necessary in the interests of the landlords, and in order to shut the door and end the question.'[40] Gladstone agreed with him; but the fall of the government in 1885 ended the argument.

By now Ireland had an electorate of 700,000, and the 1885 election gave Parnell 86 out of 103 Irish seats, pretty well the maximum he could ever hope to attain. But that was not the full extent of his electoral power. During the approach to the 1885 election, Parnell negotiated with both Conservatives and Liberals to see which party was prepared to offer more to Ireland. When Gladstone announced that it was vital for the electorate to return 'a party totally independent of the Irish vote', Parnell immediately advised all Irishmen in England, Scotland and Wales to vote Conservative. This manoeuvre, it is calculated, brought about the loss of between 25 and 40 Liberal seats and left the Conservatives with 249 seats, the Liberals with 335 and the Irish Nationalists holding the balance, exactly the result Gladstone had wished to avoid.[41]

Gladstone now decided that to give the Irish Home Rule was a matter of historic necessity. But he wanted the Conservatives to do it, as earlier they had carried Catholic Emancipation and ended the Corn Laws, thus allowing a national consensus to develop on Irish democracy.[42] But when Lord Carnarvon, the Lord Lieutenant, echoing Gladstone, pleaded for Conservative Home Rule and put the proposition to Lord Salisbury's cabinet, it was totally rejected; so was a further proposal by Gladstone for a joint party Bill. At this stage, Gladstone decided he had no alternative but to turn the Conservatives out and proceed with a Home Rule Bill of his own.

Home Rule was opposed within the Liberal Party not only by the Whigs, led by Lord Hartington, but by the Radicals, led by Joe Chamberlain, who thought it had no chance of acceptance by parliament or the English nation, and would waste time better spent on social reform. What is more, all sections of the party had been irritated by Gladstone's exasperating approach to the problem. When Gladstone announced his intention to Sir William Harcourt, the latter said: 'What! Are you prepared to go forward without either Hartington or Chamberlain?' Gladstone replied: 'Yes. I am prepared to go forward without anybody.'[43]

This exchange reflects the almost spiritual exaltation with which Gladstone now regarded the problem of Ireland. Having turned the Tories out, he found he had lost not only nearly all the remaining Whigs, and Chamberlain, but John Bright (whose Liberalism antedated even his own) and G. J. Goschen as well. In other words, the old landed interest and the new business money had both deserted Liberalism. The Grand Old Man was not dismayed. As he told his Midlothian electors in May 1886, he found arrayed against him 'in profuse abundance, station, title, wealth, social influence, the professions, or the large majority of them – in a word, the spirit and power of Class, and the dependants of Class'. But, he added, 'the Classes' had always backed the wrong side, and they now had to fight 'a power very difficult to marshal, but resistless when marshalled – the upright sense of the nation'. He trusted the new electorate he had conjured up out of the cities: 'The heart, the root, the beginning and ending of my trust, is in the wise and generous justice of the nation.'[44]

Not for the only time, Gladstone misjudged the view English electors took of the Irish problem. Not only was his Home Rule Bill lost in the Commons on Second Reading by a vote of 343 to 313 (93 Liberals voting against), but at the subsequent election – which Gladstone turned almost into a plebiscite on Home Rule – he was decisively turned down by the electorate. Some 316 Conservatives and 78 Liberal Unionists had a huge majority of 191 Gladstonians and 85 Parnellites. Lord Randolph Churchill's jibe that the country was asked to rush through Home Rule 'to gratify the ambition of an old man in a hurry' was highly effective.[45]

Unfortunately, it was not so much Gladstone who was in the hurry, as Ireland. Past experience had shown that when legitimate demands were conceded too late – as in the case of Emancipation, disestablishment and tenant right – they were received not with gratitude but with a determination to ask for more. We cannot know whether Ireland, if given Home Rule in 1886, would have been content to remain within a United Kingdom framework. Parnell himself had warned in 1885, in words all Irish schoolchildren were to learn:

We cannot ask for less than restriction of Grattan's parliament (*loud cheers*), with its important privileges and its wide and far-reaching constitution. We cannot under the British constitution ask for more than the restitution of Grattan's parliament (*renewed cheers*), but no man has the right to fix the boundary to the march of a nation (*great cheers*). No man has a right to say to his country, 'Thus far shalt thou go and no further', and we have never attempted to fix the *ne plus ultra* of Ireland's nationhood and we never shall (*cheers*).[46]

The likelihood, then, is that Parnell would have used Home Rule merely as a plinth upon which an independent nation could be constructed. But he was not given the opportunity. For Parnell, the years 1887–90 were ones of intense personal drama. In 1887 *The Times* published a series of articles, entitled 'Parnellism and Crime' which accused him of encouraging the murder of landlords. Worse, it published a facsimile letter which Parnell was alleged to have written (15 May 1882), expressing qualified approval of the murder of Cavendish and Burke, and challenged Parnell to bring an action. After much political manoeuvring on all sides, a Special Commission of three judges was appointed to investigate not only the allegations of *The Times* but to inquire into the whole question of the involvement of Irish MPs with crimes of violence in Ireland. Under fierce cross-examination, the man who had supplied the fatal letter, and others, to *The Times*, Richard Pigott, collapsed in confusion, fled abroad and then shot himself. The letters were forgeries, and Parnell was vindicated.[47] The government lost a number of by-elections. Many believed it would be turned out, and that the electorate would return a Liberal majority strong enough to carry Home Rule.

Then, in November 1890, came the scandalous O'Shea divorce case, Parnell being cited as co-respondent and offering no defence. *The Times*, which had paid out £200,000 over the Parnell–Pigott affair, could be pardoned for exulting:

Domestic treachery, systematic and long-continued deception, the whole squalid apparatus of letters written with the intent of misleading, houses taken under false names, disguises and aliases, secret visits and sudden flights, make up a story of dull and ignoble infidelity untouched, so far as can be seen, by a single ray of sentiment, a single flash of passion, and comparable only to the dreary monotony of

French middle-class vice, over which the scalpel of
Monsieur Zola so lovingly lingers.[48]

Parnell's power was such that, for a moment, it looked as
though his grip on the Nationalist Party would remain. But
Gladstone used an old Scots expression: 'It'll na dee!' and
made public a letter in which he stated that, unless Parnell
resigned as leader of the Nationalists, he himself would cease
to lead the Liberal Party.[49] The Irish Catholic bishops also
disowned Parnell, and after a long and fierce debate among
the Irish MPs, in Committee Room 15 of the House of
Commons, Parnell was deposed.[50] This decision was confirmed by the defeat of the Parnellite candidate in the
Kilkenny by-election.[51] The links with the Liberals were
strained, and as a result the second Liberal Home Rule Bill
was not previously cleared with the Irish Nationalists. The
Nationalists, as a party, never again had the same discipline
or *élan*.

In the circumstances, the Conservatives, who with one brief
intermission (1893–5), ruled Britain for twenty years, could
and did proceed with the alternative to Home Rule. In effect,
this was a return to the position of Gladstone in 1880. It was,
thought Salisbury, the Irish belief that Liberal governments
could be pushed into ever-broader concessions that had led
the Nationalists continually to raise their demands. What
Ireland needed was 'twenty years of resolute government', to
restore confidence in the determination of authority to
uphold the law, while legislation was progressively introduced to solve the land problem.

The Nationalists retaliated with the 'Plan of Campaign',
under which the landlords were to be forced to accept
reductions in rents determined by the Nationalist leaders.
The idea was to direct the campaign against particularly
harsh landlords in notoriously poor areas. The first target was
the Portumna Estate, in Galway, of Lord Clanricarde, a

hard-faced millionaire and permanent absentee, who gouged out his rent down to the last penny and was impervious to criticism or threats. He wrote: 'If you think you can intimidate me by shooting my agent, you are mistaken.' He demanded from the government all the legal protection to which he and his property were entitled, and as he never overstepped the law himself, the authorities had no alternative but to back him. When rent-day came in November 1886, Portumna witnessed a scene carefully rehearsed by William O'Brien MP, described as 'an artist in political melodrama'. The 4,000 Clanricarde tenants, led by a brass band, marched past the estate office, closely guarded by police, and to the hotel, where a committee of Nationalist MPs decided by what percentage their rents should be reduced. They then marched to the estate office, proffered the reduced rent to the agent, who of course refused it, and marched back to the hotel again, to hand in the money to the MPs. It was then used for legal defence, boycotting and other forms of agitation and menace.[52]

A. J. Balfour, Salisbury's nephew, was appointed Irish Secretary to counter this form of protest, which by the beginning of 1887 had already caused two big landlords to accept the reduced rents offered by the Plan of Campaign. Balfour brought in a new Crimes Act (the last Irish Crimes Act ever put on the British statute book) which, unlike its predecessors, gave the executive special powers of arrest without any time limit. Once a district was 'proclaimed', summary powers against specified crimes could be used; this allowed the executive to circumscribe the use of coercion to narrowly limited areas, and was highly effective. Balfour denied any special privileges to those arrested under the Act, and made it clear that he would give unswerving backing to police and magistrates who upheld the law. When a divisional magistrate in Cork, in answer to a police query from Youghal, deliberately sent an uncoded telegram: 'Deal very summarily with any organized resistance to lawful authority. If necessary, do not hesitate to shoot them,'[53] Balfour told the Commons that such action had his unqualified approval. He always backed the police, and he had offenders prosecuted mercilessly, using as his principal counsel a young Dublin Protestant, Edward Carson. As Balfour put it later: 'I made Carson and Carson made me.... Everybody right up to the top was trembling. Some of the RMs [Resident Magistrates] were splendid, but on the whole it was an impossible state of affairs. Carson had nerve, however. I sent him all over the place, prosecuting, getting convictions. We worked together.'[54]

The resistance to the Plan of Campaign earned him the name 'Bloody Balfour'. He made it quite clear that Nationalist MPs would go to prison if they broke the law and could not expect to be pardoned. He told the poet Wilfred Scawen Blunt, an anti-imperialist and sympathizer with the Irish, during a private conversation at a house-party, 'I am sorry for Dillon if he gets into prison, as it is likely to kill him. He will have hard labour, and it will be quite different from Forster's ridiculous imprisonments at Kilmainham.... He is afraid of prison and he is right, as it will probably kill him.'[55] When Blunt went over to Ireland to agitate, Balfour did not hesitate to have him prosecuted (he was given a two-month gaol sentence). Salisbury congratulated his nephew: 'Delighted to see you had Wilfred Blunt run in.'

Balfour wanted powers (which his colleagues would not give him) to coerce bad landlords like Clanricarde. On the other hand, where evictions were legal, he was determined to back them, ordering the police to be equipped with what he called 'proper appliances', which he defined as 'a suitable battering-ram ... and possibly a fire-engine'.[56] He also tried to encourage the landlords to act in concert. But at the same time he put through parliament a mass of constructive legislation – for drainage, railway-construction, relief of congested districts, and above all land legislation. His 1887 Act brought 150,000 tenants within the scope of the 1881 Act, and his 1891 Land Purchase Act, for the first time, deliberately put the backing of the British government behind the move, already under way, to sell the land of Ireland to its people. It pledged £33 million of Exchequer credit to back the loans to finance purchases, and although some of the Irish opposed it, the Act greatly accelerated the progressive transfer of land from landlords to tenants. It was unquestionably popular in Ireland, even among landlords, who saw in it a commitment by the British taxpayer to bail them out.

Balfour's combination of coercion and reform worked better than Gladstone's, chiefly because he convinced the Irish that he meant business. It depressed the Nationalists, who saw the years slip by with Home Rule as far away as ever. For the Liberals, Home Rule was increasingly seen as a source of weakness. It ran against the popular mood of imperialism, so marked a feature of the 1880s and 1890s. In 1886, Lord Randolph Churchill had gone to Ulster, and rallied the Protestants and Presbyterians there to the Tory and Unionist cause under the slogan 'Ulster Will Fight, and Ulster Will be Right'.[57] Home Rule cost the Liberals a great many working-class votes, notably in Birmingham, Liverpool and Glasgow. Many of the Liberal leaders were utterly cynical about the Irish, and even Gladstone was cynical about the Ulstermen. He would not admit the existence of an 'Ulster Problem' within the Irish problem, and never at any stage was prepared to make concessions to them: 'I cannot allow it to be said that a Protestant minority in Ulster is to rule the question at large for Ireland,' he declared. He said that Ulstermen were loyal simply because they had nothing to complain about; and it is not clear whether he was even prepared to admit that the Protestants formed a majority in Ulster itself.[58] The 1886 diary of Sir William Harcourt's son, Lewis, records a conversation at dinner between Gladstone and Harcourt, in which the weaknesses of both men in their approach to Ireland manifested themselves:

> *WVH (Harcourt)* mentioned the 'loyal' Irish. The word seemed to stir Gladstone's wrath extremely, and he said sarcastically: 'Was there ever such a noble race as that! What a beautiful word – loyalist. How much they have done for their country! You say that the Nationalists care for nothing but money, but have not the loyalists the same tastes?' *WVH*: 'Certainly. The only difference is that where you can buy a Nationalist for £5, you must pay £6 for a Loyalist!' (*Turning to Lady Airlie*): 'I once asked your father [Lord Stanley of Alderley] what was the smallest sum he had ever paid for a vote in the House of Commons, and he replied that he had once bought an Irish member for £5 on the morning of the Derby.' *Gladstone*: 'You think Ireland is a little Hell on earth.' *WVH*: 'Yes. I think the only mistake Cromwell ever made was when he offered them the alternative of Connaught.'[59]

Though the Liberals remained officially committed to Home Rule, few were keen on it. When they were returned with a small majority in 1892, Morley, now Irish Secretary, confessed to Lord Acton: 'There never was a government as insincere: they none of them cared for Home Rule but he, Asquith and Mr Gladstone.'[60] They succeeded in getting a Second Home Rule Bill through the Commons, but it was rejected in the Lords by an enormous majority, 419 to 41. Most of Gladstone's colleagues were relieved; the attitude of the country was boredom – it was said 'not a dog barked from Land's End to John O'Groats'.[61] Gladstone wanted to appeal to the country immediately on a 'Peers versus the People' platform; his colleagues refused absolutely – this, too, Gladstone recorded in his *Autobiographica* as one of the four salient episodes of his career when Providence had accorded him special insight.[62] Home Rule became a virtually dead issue for fifteen years.

Meanwhile the Conservatives proceeded to carry their land policy through to a triumphant conclusion. In 1902–3, the last act was entrusted to George Wyndham, a gay, hard-drinking aristocrat whom Balfour (now Prime Minister) made his Irish Secretary. In between hunting with the Kildares, Wyndham got a Land Conference of the interested parties to agree on steps to hasten and enlarge the land transfers. As Lord Mayo was drafting the final report of the Conference, he asked: 'How do you spell grievance?' Wyndham replied: 'You're a nice Irishman, not to know how to spell grievance.'[63] In 1903 Wyndham carried the resulting Act through parliament. It offered bonuses to landlords who sold to tenants, enabling whole estates to be sold together – an important point – with tenants given sixty-eight years in which to pay back. An Irish Land Commission Court dealt with the transfers, and annual interest payments became a charge on the Exchequer.[64]

The Act climaxed a prolonged legislative effort which in time effectively reversed the entire sixteenth- and seventeenth-century land-settlements, and transferred the land of Ireland back into Irish hands. In 1870, only 3 per cent of Irish farmers had owned their own land (20,000 holdings out of 680,000). By 1895, the figure had risen to 12 per cent. In the three years after Wyndham's Act it nearly doubled, to 29 per cent; and by 1918 it had reached 64 per cent.[65]

Yet soon afterwards, Wyndham was driven into resignation, as a result of an indiscretion of one of his officials, which led the Dublin Castle diehards and, still more, the Ulster Protestants to suspect that some plan for Home Rule was afoot.[66] The episode was a reminder that, whether or not the land issue was resolved, the Irish political issue remained. It was also a reminder that while the Irish Protestants of the south were happy enough to sell their land at a good price –

especially with a British government guarantee – the Unionists of Ulster were an altogether different breed, with political, social and economic interests which were peculiarly their own.

CHAPTER 8

Ulster Resists, Dublin Rises

By the beginning of the twentieth century, Ireland, by comparison with her past, was becoming a relatively prosperous country, thanks to the 'killing Home Rule with kindness' policy. The election of a reforming Liberal majority in 1906, and the beginning of the Welfare State with Old Age Pensions, meant that for the first time Ireland became a net financial beneficiary of the union. From 1898, democratic county councils had replaced the old-style Grand Juries in local government, the country was becoming a nation of peasant proprietors, like rural France, and the Irish Agricultural Organizations Society, created by Sir Horace Plunkett, was a token both of the spread of modern farming methods and the changed attitude of many Ascendancy landlords. In 1908 came the formation of the National University. All of the ancient non-political grievances of Ireland had been remedied.

There was, however, a general understanding between the Nationalists and the Liberals that, when the opportunity arose, a Home Rule Bill would be carried. But implicit in this arrangement was the prior reform of the House of Lords, still overwhelmingly Unionist. Hence when the new Liberal government was formed, John Redmond, the Nationalist leader, was content to wait: in any case, the 1906 landslide had given the Liberals a majority of eighty-eight over all other parties, and the government had no need of Nationalist votes. But the Nationalists continued to vote with the government, and John Redmond's relations with Ministers were cordial. He had been Parnell's closest follower and had inherited his mantle; but, as the historian Sir Robert Ensor has put it, 'where Elijah had been Anglophobe, Elisha was Anglophile'.[1]

Yet there were dangers in the relaxed attitude of the Nationalist MPs. Whatever the 'real' Irish nation thought, the 'political nation' could not be killed with kindness. Once again, the constitutional and the revolutionary traditions of Irish nationalism bifurcated. In 1899 Arthur Griffith, a journalist, founded a newspaper, the *United Irishman*, later called *Sinn Fein* (the words mean 'we ourselves'), which preached the doctrine of national self-sufficiency, reviving the Swiftian scheme of a boycott of British goods, and advocating passive resistance to British rule. Griffith did not positively preach the use of force but he saw himself as part of the forceful tradition. As he put it in 1900, hailing the new century: 'Grattan is dead and O'Connell is dead and Parnell is dead, but Emmet and Davis, Mitchel and the Fenian Men are living in the twentieth century.'[2] Then too there was the Irish Republican Brotherhood, founded as long ago as 1858 in the United States, which kept alive the ideas of Wolfe Tone, and was eventually to breed the IRA; and, more important at this stage, Irish offshoots of the great working-class movements of Europe – the trade unions led by James Larkin, and the small Socialist Party run by James Connolly. They echoed Gladstone's note that the struggle for independence was in a sense a class struggle, not to be seen in terms of Catholic versus Protestant. They saw the placid existence of the Nationalist MPs at Westminster as part of a de-nationalizing process and the acceptance of the existing order of society.[3]

Equally determined to preserve a strong Irish national identity were the middle-class supporters of the Irish literary revival, expressed both in English and in a reinvigorated Gaelic tongue. Douglas Hyde who founded the Gaelic League in 1893, 'to keep the Irish language spoken in Ireland', preached an Irish nationalism which transcended any such tidy constitutional arrangement as Home Rule. As he told the Irish National Literary Society in 1892:

Let us suppose for a moment – which is impossible – that there were to arise a series of Cromwells in England for the space of one hundred years, able administrators of the Empire, careful rulers of Ireland, developing to the utmost our national resources, whilst they unremittingly stamped out every spark of national feeling, making Ireland a land of wealth and factories, whilst they extinguished every thought and idea that was Irish, and left us, at last, after a hundred years of good government, fat, wealthy, and populous, but with all our characteristics gone, with every external that at present differentiates us from the English lost or dropped; all our Irish names of places and people turning into English names; the Irish language completely extinct; the O's and the Macs dropped; our Irish intonation changed as far as possible by English school-masters into something English; our history no longer remembered or taught; the names of our rebels and martyrs blotted out; our battlefields and traditions forgotten; the fact that we are not of Saxon origin dropped out of sight and memory. Let me now put the question: how many Irishmen are there who would purchase material prosperity at such a price? It is exactly such a question as this and the answer to it that shows the difference between the English and the Irish race. Nine Englishmen out of ten would jump to make the exchange, and I as firmly believe that nine Irishmen out of ten would indignantly refuse it.[4]

The literary aspect of Irish nationalism was important, not merely because the Irish are a highly imaginative people but because the literary presentation of Irish aspirations tended to favour the revolutionary as opposed to the constitutional tradition. Thus Yeats, though a Protestant and by no means an activist, was a member of the IRB and was elected President of the British branch of the 1898 Wolfe Tone Centenary Celebration.[5] George Bernard Shaw, in his play

John Bull's Other Island, has one of his characters say, cynically, that in order to stir up the Irish 'you've got to call the unfortunate island Cathleen ni Houlihan and pretend she's a little old woman'. This is more or less what Yeats did in his play, *Cathleen ni Houlihan*, first staged at St Teresa's Hall, Dublin, in 1902. The closing exchange of the play was 'Did you see an old woman going down the path?' 'I did not, but I saw a young girl and she had the walk of a Queen.'

Cathleen was played by Maud Gonne, Yeats's Egeria and in a sense the Egeria of the whole romantic-nationalist movement. Half-English, half-Irish, she was an example of the extraordinary appeal the Irish cause exercised for those with no obvious reason of birth to serve it: Wilfred Blunt, Roger Casement, Mary Spring-Rice, Alice Stopford Green, Cathal Brugha, Erskine Childers were others. Maud Gonne was six feet tall, a beautiful giantess. Particularly striking was her hair. It was said 'men could thrash out on a dark night a full barn of corn by the light of one tress of her hair'.[6] Her beauty, wrote Yeats, was of a kind

> That is not natural in an age like this,
> Being high and solitary and most
>   stern[7]

and he noted that, when she made a speech, 'her beauty, backed by her great stature, could instantly affect an assembly'. She had begun her political life as a supporter of the French proto-fascist leader General Boulanger, and towards the end of it she became an admirer of Hitler (she was always anti-semitic). But most of her active life was devoted to Irish affairs, and spent fighting evictions in Donegal, raising funds in the US and France, and as a catalyst and intermediary to a number of nationalist groups. She was much admired by the English liberal journalists, such as H. W. Nevinson, who were gradually swinging English opinion in favour of Irish freedom, and Yeats was passionately in love with her. But, part-*tricoteuse*, part-Valkyrie, she wanted a man

of action, and married Major John MacBride, who com-
mended an Irish Brigade which fought against the British in
the Boer War.[8] Maud Gonne helped to supply the glamour
which the Irish revolutionary tradition needed to balance the
dull puritanism made inevitable by its cohesive Catholicism.

In 1909 the Lords rejected the notorious Lloyd George
budget, and the twin elections of 1910 made a crisis over
Ireland inevitable. The Liberal majority had fallen, so that it
was now dependent on Irish votes; and the Prime Minister,
Asquith, having secured a mandate for a reform of the Lords,
and having passed the Parliament Act which transformed the
Lords' veto into a mere two-year delaying power, had no
alternative but to push Home Rule through at all costs.

It was at this point that the 'Irish Problem' became, in all
essentials, the 'Ulster Problem'. In the light of the South
African settlement, and the development of the British
Commonwealth of Nations, Home Rule as such no longer
seemed so unthinkable to the great mass of the Conservative
Party. In a demographic sense, the significance of Ireland had
declined. In the second half of the nineteenth century, her
population had dropped to little over 4 million, while Great
Britain's had increased from 20.8 million to 37 million, and
was still increasing. Home Rule in 1850 would have meant
putting nearly one-quarter of the people of the United
Kingdom under a Dublin parliament; by 1900 the proportion
would be less than one-ninth, and falling.[9]

But while the threat posed by Home Rule itself had, in
Tory eyes, diminished, the importance of Ulster in the Irish
equation had grown steadily. In the year 1800, Belfast had a
population of only 20,000, less than one-third of Cork
(70,000) and one-seventh of Dublin (172,000). By 1881 it was
186,000 and by the turn of the century 400,000. The 1911
census, the last taken in a united Ireland, produced a return of
4,390,219 in all, with the Catholics making up 75 per cent, the
remaining 25 per cent being divided between 576,611 Church
of Ireland, 440,525 Presbyterians and 60,000 Methodists and

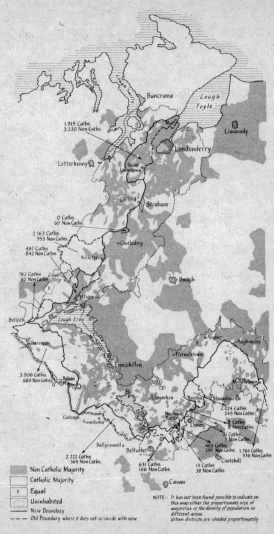

1,919 Caths.
3,230 Non Caths.

0 Caths.
60 Non Caths.

2,163 Caths.
553 Non Caths.

497 Caths.
842 Non Caths.

782 Caths.
80 Non Caths.

3,906 Caths.
680 Non Caths.

2,024 Caths.
245 Non Caths.

8 Caths.
8 Non Caths.

21 Caths.
7 Non Caths.

1,764 Caths.
336 Non Caths.

463 Caths.
235 Non Caths.

2,222 Caths.
369 Non Caths.

631 Caths.
166 Non Caths.

13 Caths.
38 Non Caths.

Buncrana

Lough Foyle

Muff

Limavady

Letterkenny

Londonderry

Saint Johnstown

Lifford

Strabane

Castlederg

Killeter

Lough Derg

Omagh

Pettigoe

Belleek

Lough Erne

Garrison

Augher

Aughnacloy

Fivemiletown

Enniskillen

Middletown

Belcoo

Lisnaskea

Rosslea

Monaghan

Cuilcagh

Newtown Butler

Clones

Swanlinbar

Cootehill

Ballyconnell

Belturbet

Cavan

Non Catholic Majority

Catholic Majority

E　Equal

Uninhabited

New Boundary

Old Boundary where it does not co-incide with new.

NOTE:- It has not been found possible to indicate on
this map either the proportionate size of
majorities or the density of population in
different areas.
Urban districts are shaded proportionately

3.　**North-east Ireland, showing the**

. Dublin castle.

Blarney castle.

3. Richard II's enemy in Ireland, Art MacMurrough, using an Irish-type saddle on his horse. One of sixteen miniatures executed by Jean Creton, who was with the King in Ireland, for his *Histoire du Roi Richard*. (BL Harley 1319, f. 9)

4a. Sir Walter Raleigh, attributed to 'H' and painted in 1588.

4b. Edmund Spenser.

5a. James, 1st Duke of Ormonde, by P. Lely.

5b. Thomas Wentworth, 1st Earl of Strafford (after Van Dyck, 1636).

6. Oliver Cromwell as Lord Lieutenant of Ireland.

7a. Wolfe Tone, the Irish revolutionary leader and French general—after a portrait by Catherine Tone published in Tone's 'Life' in 1826.

7b. The arrest of Lord Edward Fitzgerald. Ryan, mortally wounded, clings to his feet. From an illustration by George Cruikshank for Maxwell's *Irish Rebellion* (1845).

8. Irish loyalists seen through rebel eyes—'Captn. Swayne Pitch Capping the People of Prosperous'. Engraving from Watty Cox's *Irish Magazine* (1810).

9a. Starving peasants at the gate of a workhouse in 1846.

9b. Interior of a peasant's hut during the Irish potato famine of 1847.

10a. Engraving showing the scene the day after an ejectment in 1848.

HERE   AND   THERE;
Or, EMIGRATION A REMEDY.

10b. The revolutionary proceedings in Ireland in 1848 had the effect of rousing the disaffected in England and large bodies of Chartists, many of them earnest and honest men, met to discuss their grievances. *Punch* recommended emigration rather than sedition—a peaceful home rather than rioting and a prison. Cartoon by Leech.

11. Leinster House, Dublin, now the Dail.

12. Charles Stewart Parnell.

13a. Cartoon from *Punch*, 17 December 1881, showing Gladstone and the ghost of Daniel O'Connell. In spite of the suppression of the Land League and the opening of the Land Commission for fixing fair rents, the year 1881 was ending as it had begun, in 'hostility and disaffection'.

13b. *Punch* cartoon of 10 April 1886. Gladstone introduced his Home Rule Bill, and thereby deliberately, as he declared, risked the fortunes of himself and his Party upon the policy of a 'statutory Parliament for Ireland'.

14a. In the country, the peasants were being ejected in the 1880s by means of battering rams.

14b. In the towns, the Irish were travelling by means of the famous Bianconi cars. This photograph, taken in the early 1880s, shows the Galway-Clifden mail car, which ran from 1837-1895, ready to leave.

14c. Horse trams outside the Bank of Ireland in Dublin about 1890. In the foreground is Foley's statue of Henry Grattan; in the background, the ill-fated statue of William III by Grinling Gibbons, which after many mutilations was finally blown up in 1929.

15. The great Ulster Unionist Rally at Blenheim Palace on 27 July 1912.

16a. Gun-running at Howth in 1914: Mrs Erskine Childers (with rifle in hand and wearing the red jumper which was the prearranged signal that all had gone well) and Mary Spring-Rice on board the *Asgard*.

16b. Maud Gonne MacBride, Annie McSwiney (right) and Barry Delaney on hunger strike at Mountjoy Prison in 1922.

17a. In the great gathering which followed the hearse of Thomas Ashe, the Irish Volunteer who died on hunger strike in 1917, were Countess Markievicz, the famous rebel who had been reprieved after being sentenced to death for her part in the Easter Rising, and Cathal O'Shannon, a prominent young Labour and trade union leader, who was later to be 'on the run'. They are seen talking at Glasnevin cemetery after the funeral—the Countess in uniform but without the plumed hat she wore in Easter Week.

17b. Eamon de Valera. A striking study of the newly elected President of Ireland while fund-raising in the USA.

18a. Lloyd George receives men of the RIC and reviews a parade of Auxiliaries in Downing Street in November 1920. With him are Sir Harmar Greenwood and Andrew Bonar Law.

18b. On 6 December 1921 a treaty was signed between the British government and the Irish Delegation here shown. The treaty set up the Irish Free State and, except for a few reservations, gave Southern Ireland the status of a Dominion. Taken at the headquarters of the Delegation in London, the photograph shows (left to right) seated: Arthur Griffith (Chairman of the Delegation), E. J. Duggan, Michael Collins and Robert Barton, standing: Gavan Duffy (with beard).

9. The dilemma of the security forces in Ulster—in the middle trying to contain
wo rival fractions who hate each other.

20a. Aerial view of HM Prison Maze after rioting and burning on 15 October 1974.

20b. Bogside graffiti.

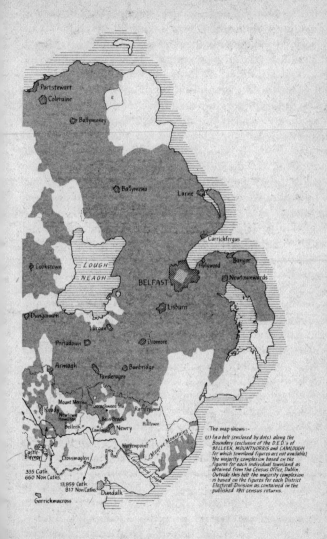

Portstewart
Coleraine
Ballymoney
E
Ballymena
Larne
Carrickfergus
Bangor
Cookstown
LOUGH
NEAGH
Holywood
Newtownards
BELFAST
Lisburn
Dungannon
Dromore
Lurgan
Portadown
Armagh
Banbridge
Tanderagee
Mount Norris
Goraghwood Sta.
Rathfryland
Keady
Newtown
Hamilton
Belleek
Boss Brook
Camlough
Newry
Hilltown
Castle
Blayney
Warrenpoint
Mourne Mountains
Crossmaglen
335 Cath
660 Non Caths
13,959 Cath
817 Non Caths
Dundalk
Garrickmacross

The map shows:—

(1) In a belt (enclosed by dots) along the
Boundary (exclusive of the D.E.D.'s of
BELLEEK, MOUNTNORRIS and CAMLOUGH
for which townland figures are not available)
the majority complexion based on the
figures for each individual townland as
obtained from the Census Office, Dublin,
Outside this belt the majority complexion
is based on the figures for each District
Electoral Division as contained in the
published 1911 census returns.

complexion by religions from the 1911 census.

others. Not only did most of the Protestants live in Ulster; in four counties, Armagh, Down, Londonderry and Antrim, they formed a majority of the population, and in Fermanagh and Tyrone a very large minority. Moreover, Ulster was the only part of Ireland where Protestantism included all classes, not least tenant-farmers and industrial workers. Unfortunately, though Protestants formed a large majority in the east of Ulster, and a majority (chiefly of small farmers) in a border strip enclosing Fermanagh and Tyrone, the Catholics were in the majority in the centre, and there were large Catholic minorities in Belfast and Londonderry.[10] It is important to realize that the Catholics and Protestants in the North could not be separated without large and distressing transfers of population.

Protestantism in the North was multi-class, but throughout the nineteenth century it was becoming increasingly uni-political. Some poor Protestants had 'come out' in 1798, but since then Ulster radicalism had been replaced by Orange-ism.[11] Indeed, it could be argued that the Orange Order, founded in 1795, had been largely confined to the artisans and the labouring element in the Protestant movement until Home Rule became a major threat in the mid-1880s. The modern composition of Orangeism, like the Unionism of which it was part, dates essentially from 1886. Lord Randolph Churchill, with his characteristically sharp eye for a populist phenomenon, realized on his celebrated visit in 1886, that Ulster had a political personality of its own, and would fight to retain it. He thereupon pledged physical support from Britain, and this pledge was inherent in Unionism for the next thirty years. It united Ulster Unionists, Liberal Unionists and Conservative Unionists.

Moreover, the 1884 Act, which gave such strength to Parnell, also created the Ulster unionist group of MPs, who joined together to become a more effective political force, worked with the Tories and helped to polarize the twin forces of Catholic Nationalism and Protestant Unionism.[12] In areas where the Protestants were in a majority, the last decades of the nineteenth century thus saw a paradoxical development; a mass party led by landed aristocrats and successful businessmen.[13] In an age when in the rest of Britain the Labour Party was beginning to oust the Liberals as the 'natural' party of the industrial proletariat, Belfast was a city where Labour candidates might be howled down by shipyard workers who identified radicalism with Popery.[14]

It was one of Parnell's greatest weaknesses that he ignored the strength of unionism among the Ulster working class. Found among Gladstone's papers was a memorandum from Parnell, dated 6 January 1886, which discusses 'the concession of a full measure of autonomy to Ireland'; Parnell stated that 'the Protestants, other than the owners of land, are not really opposed to such concessions'.[15] Gladstone accepted this assertion, coming from an Irish Protestant. But of course Parnell knew nothing of industrial Ulster. Long after his death, the party he led still did not comprehend the strength of Ulster feeling; and the nationalist MPs in turn misled the Liberal leaders.

Ulster resistance, in fact, was growing, partly as a result of the reactionary Pontificate of Pius X (1903–14), who condemned 'Modernism' in all forms and laid down new rules for 'mixed' marriages which Protestants found insulting and unacceptable. In February 1910, immediately it became clear that the Liberal government would henceforth be dependent on Irish parliamentary votes – thus opening the road to Home Rule at any cost – the Ulstermen elected Edward Carson, the grim ascendancy lawyer from Dublin, as their leader. He was a man in the Parnell mould in more ways than one, but above all in his determination to put Irish interests – as he conceived them – before any other consideration in public affairs.[16] In the 1880s, the Irish nationalists had shown themselves ready to disrupt, even destroy, British public life to gain their ends; now it was the turn of the Unionists.

The passing of the 1911 Parliament Act had already raised the political temperature to white heat, since it was thought that Asquith had tricked the new and inexperienced King, George V, into agreeing to create peers to get the Bill through the Lords.[17] Both sides accused each other of treason, and there were scenes of near-violence in the Commons. The passing of the Act meant that the Liberals could now put a Home Rule Bill into law by the middle of 1914. Even before it was tabled, Carson went to Ulster to organize resistance. On 23 September 1911, in Craigavon, the home of James Craig, leader of the Ulster-born Unionists, Carson told a parade of 50,000 men:

> We must be prepared, in the possible event of a Home Rule Bill passing, with such measures as will carry on for ourselves the government of those districts of which we have control. We must be prepared . . . the morning Home Rule passes, ourselves to become responsible for the Government of the Protestant Province of Ulster (*cheers*).

Two days later the Ulster Unionist Council appointed a five-man commission 'to frame and submit a Constitution for a Provisional Government of Ulster'.[18] From this point onwards there was never any doubt that Home Rule would be followed by the formation of an Ulster Government.

The position of the Ulster wing of the Unionists was further strengthened by the resignation of Balfour as party leader and his replacement, at the end of 1911, by Andrew Bonar Law, a man in emotional sympathy with the Ulstermen (he was Canadian-born but with a Scots Presbyterian background). Bonar Law quickly made it clear that he approved of their planned resistance. Under Irish law, any two magistrates were empowered to authorize the raising and drilling of men, 'provided such authority is sought and will be used by them only to make them more efficient citizens for the purpose of maintaining the constitution of the United Kingdom as now established and protecting their rights and liberties thereunder'.[19] In January 1912 Belfast magistrates gave this authority, and the Ulster Volunteer Force, which soon numbered 80,000 men, came into existence. On 27 March Carson wrote to Lady Londonderry:

> I dine tonight with Craig to meet Lord Roberts and I hope something may come of it. This is very private. I have made up my mind to recommend very drastic action in Ulster during this year. . . . There is a growing feeling that we do not mean business. I certainly think this is the critical year and am prepared for any risks.[20]

On 9 April 1912, two days before the Home Rule Bill was due to be tabled, Bonar Law and Carson took the salute at a review of the new force. There were seventy MPs, the Primate of all Ireland and the Moderator of the Presbyterian Church on the platform to hear the Conservative leader pledge support and promise that 'the help will come'.[21]

Asquith might have met this show of force in two ways. First, he might have sought to ban all para-military organizations in Ireland. But this would have been difficult. Ireland had always had its private armies. It was a country where the ruling class had traditionally expected to have to defend its property by force, and where the legal structure and social custom allowed it – indeed encouraged it – to do so. Secondly, Asquith might have excluded Ulster from the provisions of his Bill. In June 1912, while the Bill was in committee, a Liberal back-bencher moved an amendment to exclude Antrim, Down, Armagh and Londonderry. If the government had accepted this as a basis for negotiation, they might have split the Unionist camp, for the Southern Unionists were against Home Rule as such, while even Carson at this stage saw Ulster resistance as a means to destroy the Home Rule idea; on the other hand, the Ulstermen might have been open to an offer.

But Asquith, who had a patrician contempt for Bonar Law and the Ulstermen, had the amendment voted down, and allowed events to take their course. As the Bill inched its way through the parliamentary process, the Unionists raised the temperature. On 29 July at a huge rally at Blenheim Palace (attended by 120 MPs and 40 peers, including the head of the English Catholic laity, the Duke of Norfolk), F. E. Smith, who spoke for the Liverpool Unionists, told the gathering: 'Should it happen that Ulster is threatened with a violent attempt to incorporate her in an Irish parliament with no appeal to the English electors, I say to Sir Edward Carson "Appeal to the young men of England".' [22] Bonar Law capped this by saying that the Ulstermen 'would be justified in resisting by all means in their power, including force' any attempt to 'deprive them of their birthright'. 'I can imagine,' he added, 'no length of resistance to which Ulster will go in which I shall not be ready to support them, and in which they will not be supported by the overwhelming majority of the British people.' [23]

One young Tory MP, Lord Winterton, testified later that he was 'among many young Conservative MPs who were ready to support Ulster in a physical sense and took effective means to that end. . . . I formed what would now be described as a Commando which was ready to give physical assistance to Northen Ireland and the Ulster Volunteers if the need arose.' [24] Tory MPs, in the expectation of fisticuffs in the Commons, drafted their youngest and burliest members to positions near the gangway, as a secret set of instructions found in the Astor Papers makes clear. [25] It was one of those rare occasions in British politics when party venom spilled over into social life; as Asquith's daughter, Violet, told me many years later: 'The drawing rooms of high society were closed to us, and as F. E. Smith gleefully asserted, we were "condemned to the society of knights' ladies".'

The next step was to embody Ulster's resolve in one of the traditional Irish oath-taking ceremonies. While drafting a form of words in the Constitution Club in London, James Craig was reminded by a fellow-member of the old Scottish

Covenant of 1581. The ancient oath was updated:

> Being convinced in our consciences that Home Rule would
> be disastrous to the material well-being of Ulster as well as
> the whole of Ireland, subversive of our civil and religious
> freedom, destructive of our citizenship, and perilous to the
> unity of the Empire, we, whose names are underwritten,
> men of Ulster, loyal subjects of His Gracious Majesty, King
> George V, humbly relying on the God whom our fathers in
> days of stress and trial confidently trusted, do hereby
> pledge ourselves in solemn Covenant throughout this our
> time of threatened calamity, to stand by one another in
> defending for ourselves and our children our cherished
> position of equal citizenship in the United Kingdom, and
> in using all means which may be found necessary to defeat
> the present conspiracy to set up a Home Rule parliament
> in Ireland.[26]

The Ulstermen were no less gifted at presenting political
drama than the Nationalists. On 28 September 1912, a
solemn signing of the Covenant was held in the Belfast City
Hall. The document itself was on a table spread with the
Union Jack and, for the occasion, the Orange Standard
which had been carried before William III at the Battle of the
Boyne was unfurled. It was a sign of the times that the woman
who owned it, Mrs Burgess Watson, wanted her name kept
secret because, as Admiral Lord Charles Beresford, who had
discovered the standard's existence, said in a letter to Craig:
'She has two sons in the navy. You know how unscrupulous
the present government are, and now that that mulatto Fisher
is back supreme at the Admiralty, vengeance would surely be
wreaked on the boys.'[27] Carson signed the pledge first, and
altogether 471,414 names of Covenanters were recorded.
when Carson, in triumph, crossed back to Liverpool in the
Patriotic, he was met at 7.30 in the morning by 150,000
Liverpool Protestants, led by F. E. Smith, who told him
publicly: 'We will undertake to give you three ships that will

take over 10,000 young men of Liverpool.' Alderman Salvidge, the celebrated Unionist boss of Liverpool, recorded in his diary that an excited admirer told Carson on the steps of the Conservative Club: 'It's been marvellous, Sir. Nothing like it has been seen at the Liverpool landing-stage since Crippen was brought back from America.'[28]

Nevertheless, the legislative process moved on inexorably, and it became certain that the Bill would become law. In September 1913, Lord Loreburn, a former Liberal Chancellor, wrote to *The Times* suggesting a compromise over Ulster to avert civil war. The suggestion was taken up by Winston Churchill, First Lord of the Admiralty. The Ulster claim 'for special consideration', Churchill said, 'if put forward with sincerity, cannot be ignored by a government depending on the existing House'. The idea was angrily rejected by John Redmond, looking anxiously over his shoulder at the IRB: 'Irish Nationalists can never be assenting parties to the mutilation of the Irish nation. Ireland is a unit. . . . The two-nation theory is to us an abomination and a blasphemy.' When Asquith and Bonar Law met for secret talks on the exclusion idea, in October, no agreement was reached.

On his side, Carson was becoming convinced that Asquith could not now 'go on to the bitter end', as he put it, and coerce Ulster into accepting Home Rule. He took the precaution of obtaining a secret 'waiver' from the southern Unionists, in a series of questions. 'Is it your decision that I am to go on fighting for Ulster?' 'Yes.' 'Will my fight in Ulster interfere in any way with your fighting in the South?' 'No.' 'If I win in Ulster, am I to refuse the fruits of victory because you have lost?' 'No.' So Carson, the Dubliner, moved sadly towards the notion of partition. He was losing faith in the willingness of southern Unionists to fight. 'They are so different from the North,' he told Lady Londonderry, 'and do so little to help themselves.'[29] But when the fertile Lloyd George put forward a plan for separate options for each Ulster County, to remain outside the Home Rule Bill for six years – a plan reluctantly accepted by Redmond – Carson flatly replied on 9 March 1914: 'Ulster wants this question settled now and for ever. We do not want sentence of death with a stay of execution for six years.'

No doubt Carson thought he was acting from a position of strength; and it may be that Asquith had privately assured him that the exclusion of Ulster would be permanent. Certainly, Asquith was saying different things to the different sides (as Lloyd George was to do later), as the Redmond Papers make plain.[30] Ulster resistance was now organized: 'This place is an armed camp, with the General and officers here,' Carson wrote to Bonar Law from Craigavon, on 20 March 1914.[31] He was aware that Bonar Law had a secret plan for the Lords to amend the Army Act. In the event, it was not needed. In a clumsy attempt to prepare the way for the use of the army in Ulster, Colonel Seely, the Secretary for War, authorized Sir Arthur Paget, Commander-in-Chief in Ireland, to give his subordinates the choice: officers who did not wish to 'coerce' Ulster could resign their commissions, and those whose homes were in Ireland could go on leave. These 'orders' were an absurd mockery of military discipline, and the same day that Carson was in his 'armed camp' in Ulster, the real camp at the Curragh was the scene of unseemly wrangling and argument between officers junior and senior – more reminiscent of a French army than a British one – which ended with General Hubert Gough and fifty-seven officers of the 3rd Cavalry Brigade opting to leave the service. Gough said later that if he had simply been told to go to Ulster he would have obeyed; given the choice, however, he naturally followed his sentiments. As it was, he was given a signed assurance that the cavalry would not be ordered to coerce Ulster. Seely, who had been responsible for the assurance, resigned, as soon as the 'Mutiny at the Curragh' became known, and Asquith took over political direction of the army himself. But by this point it was patently obvious that army coercion was out of the question.[32] Meanwhile,

Churchill had switched the Third Battle Squadron from Spain to Lamlash on the Scottish coast, seventy miles from Belfast, allegedly for gun practice. The move was authorized by the Cabinet, though Asquith at the time concealed his responsibility.[33] Undeterred, Carson continued with his plans. On the night of 24–25 April, the Ulster Volunteers, who were short of guns, succeeded in landing a shipment of 35,000 rifles and 3 million rounds of ammunition; at the same time plans were afoot for printing an Ulster currency.[34]

Why did not Asquith have Carson arrested? Asquith himself claimed that the reason was 'it was as certain as any of the sequences of nature that no Irish jury would convict'.[35] The Irish Attorney-General did in fact prepare a charge against Carson and others under the Treason-Felony Act, but it was never used. Asquith told the King it would be like throwing a lighted match into a powder-barrel. The truth is that Asquith believed, probably correctly, that Carson's boldness in fact kept the wilder Protestant Ulstermen in check and prevented a Belfast pogrom.

A further reason was that action against Carson would have had to be accompanied by action against the Nationalist extremists, who were arming too, though less publicly. Indeed, perhaps the most serious and lasting consequence of Ulster Protestant bellicosity was that it undermined the authority of Redmond and his constitutional followers and increased the importance of those Irish Nationalists who not only looked further than Home Rule but sought a decision by force.

The new Nationalists were of two kinds. On the one hand there were the militant trade union leaders and socialists. The years immediately preceding World War I were characterized by large-scale strikes and industrial violence all over the British Isles. In Ireland the great transport-workers' strike of 1913–14, led by James Larkin, brought 20,000 workers out; and in Ireland any strike tended to have political overtones. During a police baton charge to break up a strikers' meeting in Dublin in August 1913, two of the strikers were killed, and a woman was shot dead by 'free labour' hired by the transport employers. This led directly to the creation of the radical Irish Citizen Army.[36] From October 1913, the Irish Republican Brotherhood also assumed a military form, though it preferred to operate through the official and respectable Nationalist response to the Ulster Volunteers, which took the name of the Irish Volunteers.

This body was born in November 1913, at a mass-meeting in the Dublin Rotunda, where 4,000 signed an enrolment form drafted to sound innocuous: 'I, the undersigned, desire to be enrolled in the Irish Volunteers, founded to secure and maintain the rights and liberties common to all the people of Ireland without distinction of creed, class or politics.' The force's motto was 'Defence, not Defiance', and its manifesto emphasized that the duties of the Volunteers 'will be defensive and protective, and they will not contemplate either aggression or domination'.[37]

In reality, it was planned that, while Establishment people fronted the Volunteers, the IRB would in fact hold key positions within it. Colonel Maurice Moore, brother of the novelist George Moore, became the Inspector-General of the IVs, and the treasurer was the former British consular official, Sir Roger Casement. But a leading organizer was also of mixed descent, Patrick Pearse, whose father came from Devon, but who had held extremist views on Ireland from youth (his mother was Irish). He told his brother William: 'I swear before God and before you that I will free Ireland or die fighting the English.' In the spring of 1914 he told an audience in Brooklyn: 'Today Ireland is once more arming, once more learning the noble trade of arms. There is again in Ireland the murmur of a marching, a talk of guns and tactics.' Pearse was of the puritan-nationalist type: a bachelor, teetotaller, non-smoker, whose dearest possession was a lock of Napoleon's hair. Another signatory at the Rotunda was likewise of the puritanical cast, also half-Irish: Eamon de Valera, a mathematics professor, son of a Spaniard, tall, lean, sombre, looking, as Oliver St John Gogarty put it, 'like something uncoiled from the Book of Kells'.[38]

Inevitably, the Volunteers became the object of a struggle between the constitutionalists, led by Redmond and his fellow MPs, and the militants. By May 1914 Redmond had decided that, in the light of the Ulster gun-running and the Curragh business, the Irish were not going to get Home Rule without a fight, and he was determined to control the Volunteers. He successfully insisted that twenty-five of his nominees should be drafted to the twenty-five 'provisional committee'. Casement – outwardly 'respectable', at heart a fanatic – wrote to Alice Stopford Green:

> The cause of Ireland seems so hopeless in the hands of such men. How can any freedom arise in the land with such narrow-minded, intolerant bigots as John Dillon, tool and agent of English Liberalism – and Joe Devlin, ignorant, forceful, greedy, ambitious.... I really think I'll join the Orangemen. They are better *men* – even better Irishmen than this gang of tricky schemers and place-hunters.[39]

Not surprisingly, it was not the Redmonites who engaged in gun-running on behalf of the Nationalists. That was the work of Erskine Childers, a former House of Commons clerk, Alice Spring-Rice, cousin of the British ambassador in Washington, Cathal Brugha, De Valera and other hard-liners, who managed to get 1,500 rifles ashore at Howth on 26 July.

The next day, however, Austria declared war on Serbia, and within nine days Britain was at war too. The rapid and unexpected development of the long-feared World Crisis caught the Irish problem at a complete *impasse*. On 23 June the government had introduced in the Lords an Amending Bill to give each of the Ulster counties a separate option for six years – a proposal Carson had already rejected. This, in turn, led to a three-day conference at Buckingham Palace (21–3 July), attended by Asquith, Lloyd George, Bonar Law,

Lansdowne (Tory leader in the Lords), Redmond and Dillon, Carson and Craig. The bargaining ranged around Separate County Option (supported by Redmond, because this would give the Nationalists Fermanagh and Tyrone), the *en bloc* exclusion of the Six Counties (the Unionist position), and a compromise put forward by Asquith which would leave the Ulstermen with the six counties, excluding parts of Fermanagh, Tyrone and Armagh. But no agreement could be reached.[40] Thereafter, the European war engulfed everything in its maw, and the Ulster and Nationalist leaders in the Commons realized that they could avoid fighting each other by fighting the Germans instead.[41]

With the declaration of war, Asquith put the Home Rule crisis into cold storage by withdrawing the Amending Bill and passing a Suspension Act, which made the Home Rule Act, which would otherwise have become law automatically, inoperative until after the war. Carson promptly offered to form an active service division out of the Ulster Volunteers, with the Red Hand of Ulster for its emblem. Kitchener, the new War Minister, accepted. But he turned down a similar offer by Redmond, on the grounds that there was no place in the new army he intended to form for soldiers who did not conform to the standard British pattern. He turned down a similar offer from Wales, until Lloyd George forced him to change his mind. Even when Redmond persisted, and a division of Irish Volunteers was formed, Kitchener refused to allow the Irish Harp to be blazoned on its colours unless the crown was carried too.[42]

To be fair to Kitchener, one of Redmond's motives in offering men was to get the Irish Volunteers armed at British expense. And many of those in influential positions in the Volunteers did not support Britain at all. On the contrary, they believed in John Mitchel's watchword: 'England's difficulty is Ireland's opportunity'. On 5 September 1914 a meeting of the Supreme Council of the IRB, attended by other nationalist hawks, took a secret decision to make a protest in arms during the war, either if the Germans invaded England, or if the English tried to force conscription on Ireland. When the IRB elements within the Volunteers broke with Redmond, who was busy recruiting for the war effort, 12,000 of them (out of a total of 180,000) deserted the Redmond camp.[43] Some of the extremists actively favoured the Germans. Casement's tone varied from the maudlin to the Messianic. 'My heart bleeds for those poor people, beset by a world of hatred,' he wrote to Alice Stopford Green, 'their crime is their efficiency.' He claimed that Britain and Russia had formed a new Holy Alliance to plunder the Old World:

> England's crime in this war is the most flagrant of all – she made it inevitable – she leagued herself with the Powers of Darkness against Teutonic commerce and industry. May the Sword of the Just destroy and annihilate the League of Enmity – the conspiracy of assassins formed against them. I pray for the Salvation of Germany night and day – and God save Ireland now is another form of God Save Germany![44]

Casement's views took him to Germany, whence he plotted vengeance on Britain. In Dublin, Connolly, who had taken over the leadership of the transport workers in October 1914, trained his Citizen Army in street-fighting. Though the militant section of the Volunteers was a small minority, they contrived to keep the title – it was Redmond's army which had to change, to the National Volunteers, and his band ceased to be significant as its members left for the Flanders trenches, where southern Irish volunteers formed two whole divisions.

The authorities in Ireland now had the provisions of the Defence of the Realm Act to deal with Irish subversion, and between November 1914 and April 1916 there were nearly 500 prosecutions under DORA for possession of arms, seditious speeches and other offences. But curiously enough, Dublin Castle made no attempt to prevent the IRB from holding marches and parades, even when they drilled with rifles and fixed bayonets. On St Patrick's Day 1916 about 2,000 of them drilled on College Green, without any interference by the police. Among the Citizen Army contingents were a number of women, led by Countess Constance Markievicz, who had run the soup-kitchens during the great strike. Like Maud Gonne, she was a beauty, the daughter of a Sligo baronet, married to an expatriate Polish count. She had designed her own uniform: dark-green breeches and blouse, black stockings, and a black velour hat with plume – all in the best traditions of Wolfe Tone. The Dubliners called her 'a Rosalind in green tights'.[45]

The constant drilling was dictated by the lessons, or perhaps mythology, of 1798, the determination not to be caught by a government pre-emptive strike. The decision of the authorities to allow drilling was in the belief that it was all bluff. Certainly there was no large body of opinion in Ireland in favour of an armed rising. The highly respectable head of the Volunteers, Eoin MacNeill, knew nothing of any plans. In fact the rising, which had been concocted by Pearse and a few IRB intimates, was timed for Easter Monday 1916. A German cargo of arms was to be landed, 10,000 Volunteers and the Citizen Army called out over the weekend, and a Provisional Government set up, with Pearse as President. But ill-fortune dogged them, as it had dogged Tone. The ship carrying the German arms was pounced on by the Royal Navy, and its German captain blew it up, cargo and all. A German U-boat, carrying Casement and two companions, landed them safely at Banna beach in Kerry. But Casement was taken by a suspicious constable of the Royal Irish Constabulary, quickly recognized and spirited away to London.

When news of these events reached Dublin, MacNeill, who had become suspicious and demanded the truth from Pearse, decided to cancel all plans to raise the Volunteers. He sent out messages on Holy Saturday, and published an announcement in the *Sunday Independent*, which stated: 'Owing to the very critical position all orders given for tomorrow, Easter Sunday, are hereby rescinded, and no parades, marches or other movements of Irish Volunteers will take place'. Despite this, the IRB and the Citizen Army decided to go on with the rising.[46] Final confirmatory orders went out in Dublin on Easter Monday morning.

The consequences confirmed the old military maxim: 'Order – Counter-order – Disorder'. Only about 1,000 of the Dublin Volunteers were mobilized. But Connolly managed to get nearly all his Citizen Army out – 192 men and 27 women. And Dublin Castle was taken completely by surprise: this was one Irish revolt which was not betrayed, doubtless because it had such a narrow popular base. Indeed, the Castle itself could have been taken without the slightest difficulty. When twenty of the insurgents approached its gates at 11 a.m. on Monday morning, there were precisely six men of a corporal's guard within the fortress, armed only with blanks, and with a mere unarmed constable at the entrance. Taking the castle would not have been decisive, but it would have disrupted British communications even more effectively than the 1798 stopping of the mails. The insurgents shot the constable, but took alarm when the guard tumbled out, and fled. If the Castle knew nothing of the rising, the IRB seems to have known nothing about the Castle either.

In the event it made little difference, for Dublin refused to 'rise'. The rebel leadership, ignoring Connolly's advice that the Bank of Ireland (the old, if much altered, Parliament House on College Green) would make the best stronghold, from both a military and a symbolic viewpoint, chose to hole themselves up in the General Post Office in O'Connell Street, and wait for the nation to join them. Other buildings were occupied: thus De Valera, adjutant of the Dublin brigade, commanded a battalion which held Boland's Mills, on the south-east of the city. From the portico of the GPO, Pearse read out a proclamation announcing that a provisional government had been formed, and the flag of the Republic was run up the mast. About 400 people heard the proclamation and it was later posted at various parts of the city. But only a dozen or so of the Redmondites appeared to have joined the rising, which was effectively confined to the revolutionary groups.

The failure of the rising was obvious to all. An Englishman in the Metropole Hotel, opposite the GPO, recorded:

> I was able to secure a unique snapshot of the hoisting of the new flag of the Republic, and took another of the cheering of the crowd – though this was very insignificant and in no way represented any considerable body of citizens. . . . I realized at once that the movement was at that time a dismal failure as far as the vast majority of Nationalist Ireland was concerned. There was practically no response from the people. [47]

If the rising did not bring out the Nationalists, it led to an orgy of looting. The same observer noted:

> Little guttersnipes wearing high silk hats and new bowlers and straws, who had never worn headgear before; barefoot little devils with legs buried in Wellington top-boots, unable to bend their knees, and drunken women brandishing satin shoes and Russian boots till it seemed the whole revolution would collapse in ridicule or pandemonium. . . . I saw a tussle between two drunken harlots for the possession of a headless dummy taken from a tailor's shop. . . .

The looting seems to have continued in places even after the British forces, which rapidly gathered in and around the city, began serious fighting. Another witness, Mrs Hamilton Norway, said she saw

> a woman was hanging out of a window dropping loot to a friend when she was shot through the head by a

sniper. . . . The body dropped in the street and the mob cleared. In a few minutes, a handcart appeared and gathered up the body, and instantly all the mob swarmed back to continue the dreadful proceedings.[48]

The insurgents' training had been based on the assumption that they would have to face nothing more than small-arms fire; they thought it impossible that the British would use artillery in the centre of an historic city. But from Britain's point of view it was essential to crush the rising quickly before the familiar reflexes of Irish nationalism – up to now dormant, apparently – began to operate. They not only used field guns from the Wednesday onwards, but brought a gunboat up the River Liffey. The first surrender took place that day. On Friday the GPO had to be evacuated, and the following day Pearse agreed to an unconditional surrender. Countess Markievicz kissed her revolver before handing it over. By Monday 1 May all the insurgents were under arrest.

The first reactions to the Dublin Rising were almost universally hostile. A great many people had been killed in a futile undertaking: the British Army listed 103 dead, 357 wounded, 9 missing; the Royal Irish Constabulary 14 killed, 23 wounded; the Dublin police 3 killed, 3 wounded; and there were 450 Volunteers and civilians killed, 2,614 wounded. The destruction was enormous and irreparable; St John Ervine penned a description of the fire in O'Connell Street – 'the finest street in Europe was consumed in a night'. In the House of Commons John Redmond expressed his 'feeling of detestation and horror' which he said was shared by 'the overwhelming mass of the people of Ireland'.

Then the executions began, and the syndrome of Irish nationalism began at last to make its appearance. Even before the surrender there had been a gruesome judicial murder. Francis Sheehy-Skeffington, a well-known Dublin eccentric and advocate of minority causes, a comic Shavian figure in beard, knickerbocker suit and cloak, had been arrested and shot (together with two Irish journalists) at the orders of a demented captain in the Royal Irish Rifles. The officer, J. C. Bowen-Colthurst, had not a shred of authority for his action, and was afterwards proved to be criminally insane. The British did their best to retrieve the business, court-martialling the man, who was sent to Broadmoor, and having a Royal Commission sit on the incident. But soon rumours spread that it was all a British trick and that Bowen-Colthurst had been secretly released and was now commanding troops in Ulster.

The other shootings, fourteen in Dublin and one in Cork, were deliberate. Martial law had been declared, and General Sir John Maxwell, the British Commander-in-Chief, proceeded methodically to try the rebel leaders by court martial, and then execute them between 3 and 12 May. De Valera, who was technically stateless, was saved by his status, and went to prison. The Countess ended up in a women's gaol in Aylesbury. Pearse and most of the other leaders were put in front of firing-squads, two or three at a time. The hearings were in secret, and only the announcements of the shootings told the public what was going on. Maxwell was later criticized for dragging out the business. But martial law has its forms, too, and he would certainly have been in worse trouble if he had not observed them. The worst case was Connolly's, who had been wounded. Unlike Fitzgerald and Tone, he was not allowed to die in his bed. The priest who was with him at the execution later gave this description:

> They carried him from his bed in a stretcher to an ambulance and drove him to Kilmainham Gaol. They carried the stretcher from the ambulance to the gaol yard. They put him in a chair. . . . I asked him: 'Will you pray for the men who are about to shoot you?' And he answered: 'I will say a prayer for all brave men who do their duty.' . . . And then they shot him.[49]

Of course Maxwell, and the court-martial officers, saw the

whole Dublin business as a squalid act of treason, betraying
the army in France, where thousands were being killed and
mutilated every week. Less justifiable was the execution of
Casement, who was tried at the Old Bailey and hanged early
in August. President Wilson might have saved him, but
Wilson sympathized with the Ulstermen and declined to
intervene. Other sympathizers in high places were discouraged by the discreet use the government made of
Casement's captured diaries, which told a sordid tale of his
homosexual activities.[50] But this and the other executions
seemed, at the time, only incidents in a summer of
unmitigated horror. A month before Casement was hanged,
on 1 July, the British army on the opening day of the Battle of
the Somme suffered 60,000 casualties in less than twelve
hours. Among them were many Protestants and Catholics of
the Ulster Division, which fought with conspicuous heroism
and appalling slaughter, losing half its men in that single,
terrible day.[51]

Nevertheless, in the south of Ireland, it was the Dublin
executions that were remembered. It is sometimes argued
that the revulsion against Britain began with the firing
squads. This does not seem to be correct. Yeats, himself a one-
time member of the IRB, but in many ways an accurate
barometer of middle-class nationalist opinion, not only had
no sympathy with the rising but at first felt no pang at the
executions either. One of those who died was John MacBride,
the 'drunken vainglorious lout' who had stolen Maud Gonne
from him. When it was reported that MacBride had refused to
be blindfolded in front of the firing-squad, saying 'I've been
staring down rifle-barrels all my life', Yeats remarked that he
should more truthfully have said he had been staring down
pint-pots all his life – and then went off to propose to the
widow, on condition she gave up politics.[52]

What seems to have begun the change of mood was the
decision to intern 1,862 of the rebels without trial, and ship
them off to Wales. When they were marched to the quays for

embarkation, the Dubliners' change of mood was apparent. Yeats, too, began to wonder at his own part in the affair, which began to seem less like a blunder, more like an exploit:

> Did that play of mine send out
> Certain men the English shot?

Moreover, as the war proceeded and changed its object, and became (in Allied propaganda) a crusade for the self-determination of peoples, Alsacians, Lorrainers, Poles, Czechs, Finns, Yugoslavs – even Arabs – the notion that the Irish could conceivably be denied their liberty in a post-war world began to seem increasingly absurd, and the rising, therefore, as part of the spirit of the times, noble even. Yeats had already anticipated this change of assessment. 'The late Dublin rebellion,' he wrote in July 1916, 'whatever one can say of its wisdom, will long be remembered for its heroism.' On 25 September he went further, and wrote one of his best-remembered poems, an elegy:

> I write it out in verse –
> MacDonagh and MacBride
> And Connolly and Pearse
> Now and in time to be,
> Wherever green is worn,
> Are changed, changed utterly:
> A terrible beauty is born.

CHAPTER 9

Freedom and Partition

During the last two years of the Great War, the modern configuration of Irish politics began to take shape. Of the 3,000 Irish arrested without charge after the Easter Rising, the largest contingent was sent to an internment camp at a disused distillery at Frongoch, near Lake Bala in North Wales. Many were released in bunches during the summer and autumn of 1916, for there was no evidence against them; and the remaining 600 were sent home by Lloyd George in December 1916, as soon as he became Prime Minister. But by that time Frongoch had served not only as a seminary for the new Irish nationalism, in which Sinn Fein was absolutely dominant, but as a training-centre for the military resistance to which Sinn Fein was pledged. In particular it saw the emergence of the man who was to command the Irish Republican Army, a twenty-six-year-old former post office worker, Michael Collins, soon to be known as 'the big fellow', to distinguish him from De Valera, 'the tall fellow'.[1]

By the time the Easter rebels returned, a great transformation had taken place in Irish Catholic opinion, and support for the constitutionalists of the parliamentary party was evaporating fast. In 1917 the first quantitative assessment of the new mood was provided by a by-election in North Roscommon, where the Nationalist candidate polled only 1,708 against 3,022 for Sinn Fein. The winning candidate, Count Plunkett, was himself a portent. Though his three sons were Sinn Feiners, he was a venerable establishment figure and, even more important, stood high in the esteem of the Catholic hierarchy and the Vatican. He was a witness to a new and vital development: the consolidation behind Sinn Fein of the support of the Catholic Church.[2] This helps to explain Sinn Fein's electoral success, confirmed at a further by-election in South Longford. The Church and Sinn Fein joined hands in a campaign to resist any attempts by Britain, which adopted conscription in 1916, to impose it in Ireland, a campaign which was both popular and successful.

Neither of the two Sinn Fein MPs agreed to take his seat at Westminster (one, in fact, was in gaol). Sinn Fein also flatly refused to take any part in an Irish constitutional convention which Lloyd George proposed in May, accompanying it with the release of all Irish convicted prisoners, including De Valera. The latter was soon elected at a third Sinn Fein by-election victory, by a huge majority. Though the police reported that Sinn Fein militants used a great deal of intimidation to secure this result, it was clear that a convention without Sinn Fein was meaningless. It met, nonetheless, between July 1917 and April 1918, and was notable for the formalization of the split between Northern and Southern Unionists, and for the last appearance of the Anglo-Irish political personality on the stage of history. The aim of this group was to avert partition and secure the closest possible links to the United Kingdom; they were defeated when the Ulster Unionists joined hands with the Home Rule extremists, led by three Catholic bishops. The shift in the pattern of power was confirmed when the death of John Redmond, in March 1918, was treated as a non-event in Ireland. One Catholic bishop even refused to allow a requiem mass in his cathedral, a striking indication of the shift in the hierarchy's sympathies, skilfully accelerated by the diplomacy of De Valera.[3]

At its own convention in October 1917, Sinn Fein had declared for a Republic and elected De Valera president. Everything Lloyd George did in the closing months of the war tended to play into the hands of the extremists. There was a considerable degree of coercion and use of special powers. Though most Irish advice was against applying conscription, Lloyd George, hag-ridden by the German successes in France in the spring of 1918 and under fierce pressure from his new Chief of the General Staff, Sir Henry Wilson – a zealous Ulster Unionist – pushed forward an Irish Conscription Bill. With the turn of the tide in France, conscription was in practice never applied in Ireland; but Britain incurred the maximum odium nonetheless. At the General Election which followed after the Armistice, the polarization of Irish opinion was completed. Before the dissolution, the score had been Nationalists 68, Unionists 18, Sinn Fein 7, plus a few independents. The December 1918 election returned 73 Sinn Fein (26 unopposed), 26 Unionists, and only 6 Nationalists. To complete the triumph of Sinn Fein, De Valera defeated the Nationalist leader, John Dillon, in his own heartland of East Mayo.

It may be asked, why did not Lloyd George, then negotiating a European peace treaty based upon the principles of self-determination, concede independence to Ireland also, since the Irish had apparently voted for it? The answer is that it was not clear what the Irish had voted for. In contested constituencies in Ireland only 69 per cent of the electors had voted; and of these only 47 per cent had voted Sinn Fein. Independence, then, was the wish only of a minority of Irishmen. Moreover, it was a central plank of Sinn Fein policy that independence must be accorded to a united Ireland. And Ulster, whether considered as a historical eight-county unit or as the six-county unit now in contention, had voted by a substantial majority to remain in the union. Sinn Fein might argue that Ulster had no intrinsic right to take a separate decision. But in that case the British government could argue that Ireland had no such right either, and they could point out that the British government, whose policy was Home Rule with safeguards for Ulster, had also, in the same election, won an overwhelming majority. In England, Scotland and Wales, Lloyd George had had an astounding triumph. As Bonar Law put it, 'He can now be Prime Minister for life if he wishes'. The Asquithian Liberals, traditionally the British partner of the Irish Nationalists, had been massacred. The truth is, that while Griffith and De Valera had won in southern Ireland, the Unionists had won everywhere else in the British Isles, which was still a legal and constitutional unity.

It is also necessary to place the Irish problem in its European context. The Versailles conference was systematically redrawing the map of Europe to accommodate the principle of self-determination now enshrined in the League of Nations Covenant. But nowhere was the principle in fact conceded without the use or threat of force. The people of Alsace and Lorraine had rejoined France under the custody of a triumphant French army. Elsewhere, the issue was being settled, throughout most of 1919 and 1920, in accordance with Thomas Hobbes's grim dictum: 'Covenants without swords are but words'. In Finland and the Baltic States, in the Ukraine, White Russia, the Caucasus, Poland, East Prussia, Bohemia, Hungary, Slovenia, Austrian Italy, Dalmatia, European Turkey, Western Anatolia and elsewhere, frontiers were being settled as much by guns as by plebiscites, and by guns largely wielded by 'free corps' formed from the returning armies of Armageddon.

This helps to explain the speed with which the Sinn Fein acted. The election results were announced on 28 December 1918. Less than three weeks later, on 15 January, a Sinn Fein congress met, decided its seventy-six MPs would boycott the Westminster Parliament, and set up an assembly (or 'Dail Eireann') of its own. Other Irish MPs were invited to attend – Carson, to his disgust, received an invitation in Gaelic – and on their failure to do so, the Sinn Fein MPs, on 21 January, adopted a Declaration of Independence.[4] A government, with Cathal Brugha at its head, was appointed, and its first act was decisively successful – to release De Valera, President of Sinn Fein, from Lincoln Gaol, and bring him back to Ireland.

There was, at this stage, still a possibility that the Irish problem might be resolved by negotiation. The Earl of Ypres, the Lord Lieutenant, was under orders from Lloyd George to avoid violence if possible. On the Sinn Fein side, too, there had been a policy of restraint. In the two years and eight months since the Easter Rising, no soldier or policeman had been killed in Ireland. But the Declaration of Independence was in effect a declaration of war, since it denied the legal rights of the existing authorities, and placed responsibility in the hands of individual IRA commanders, most of whom were very young. The same day, two policemen were killed in an IRA ambush; and ten days later, on 31 January, Brugha, acting head of the executive as well as Chief of Staff of the provisional army, issued an order in *An-t-Oglach*, the official organ of the Irish Volunteers: 'Every Volunteer is entitled, legally and morally, when in the execution of his military duties, to use all legitimate methods of warfare against the soldiers and policemen of the English usurper, and to slay them if it is necessary to do so to overcome their resistance.'[5]

When De Valera returned to Ireland to take charge of Sinn Fein, he flung wide the gates of violence. He chose to make a frontal attack on the Royal Irish Constabulary, which had been created in the nineteenth century precisely to enforce the law impartially between the two communities, from both of which it was drawn, and had hitherto remained above serious reproach. The RIC, said De Valera, 'are given full licence by their superiors to work their will on an unarmed populace. The more brutal the commands given them by their superiors, the more they seem to revel in carrying them out, against their own flesh and blood be it remembered. Their history is a continuity of brutal treason against their own people.'[6] He accordingly moved a resolution of the Dail on 10 April 1919 that the police 'be ostracized socially and publicly by the people of Ireland'. The Clerk of the Dail recorded what was meant:

. . . that the police forces must receive no social recognition from the people; that no intercourse, except such as is absolutely necessary on business, is permitted with them; that they should not be saluted or spoken to in the streets or elsewhere nor their salutes returned; that they should not be invited to nor received in private houses as friends or guests; that they be debarred from participation in games, sports, dances and all social functions conducted by the people; that intermarriage with them be discouraged; that, in a word, the police should be treated as persons, who having been adjudged guilty of treason to their country, are regarded as unworthy to enjoy any of the privileges or comforts which arise from cordial relations with the public.[7]

It is important to note that this fatal resolution was passed a whole year before the first of the 'Black and Tans' set foot in Ireland. It led directly to many acts of violence against the RIC, a progressive decline in their moral authority, and a consequential collapse in their morale – leading, inevitably, to a weakening in their restraint in the face of provocative acts. The RIC grew to fit the ugly mask De Valera had carved for it. That, in turn, played into the hands of Sir Henry Wilson, the Chief of the Imperial General Staff, who all along urged in Lloyd George a government policy of 'thorough'.[8] In August Sinn Fein was proscribed and in September the Dail declared illegal. Acts of violence against government servants continued, eighteen (mostly police and soldiers) being killed in 1919. Both Irish communities demanded diametrically opposed lines of action from the government. As Winston Churchill, now War Secretary, put it: 'We saw the flames of orange and green flash out from the Irish furnace.'[9]

To accommodate the post-war developments, the Cabinet decided to produce a new Home Rule Bill. Introduced on 25 February 1920, this proposed a Northern Ireland Parliament of 52 MPs, a Southern Irish Parliament of 128 MPs, representation at Westminster by 42 all-Ireland MPs, and a Council of Ireland consisting of 20 members of each Irish

Parliament. Westminster was to retain control over peace and war, foreign affairs, customs and excise, army and navy, land and agricultural policy and law and order.[10] On 4 March 1920, the Ulster Unionist Council, with considerable reluctance, accepted the scheme. The Dail, or rather Sinn Fein, rejected it totally. This was the fatal moment of Ireland's bifurcation; for after the Sinn Fein rejection, there was no alternative but to pass the Bill and create a Northern Ireland Parliament.

In the South, meanwhile, the scale and frequency of violent incidents steadily increased. On 4 April, Sinn Fein formally opened a guerrilla war, with raids on tax offices and other government record centres all over Ireland. Civil authority was now in the hands of Sir Harmar Greenwood, with the army under the former Adjutant-General, Sir Nevil Macready, both regarded as hard-liners.[11] On 11 May the Cabinet adopted a proposal by Churchill that 'a special force of 8,000 old soldiers be raised at once to reinforce the RIC'.[12] This was made necessary by the effect of ostracism and murder on RIC recruitment. Up to the end of August 1922, 12,000 auxiliaries were enrolled, serving in two categories: the RIC Auxiliary Division and the Auxiliary Cadets. The ADs, dressed in khaki, owing to the shortage of RIC uniforms, with the black belts and dark green caps of the RIC, were called the Black and Tans, after the famous pack of hounds at Scarteen, County Limerick. To Wilson they were '8,000 scalliwags' or 'mobs'. The Cadets were an elite group of ex-officers, who had to have exemplary war records. The training of both groups was essentially military, and this reflects a confusion of ideas in the mind of the Cabinet, bitterly attested to by both Wilson and Macready: though these auxiliaries were intended to reinforce the police, they were in fact the politicians' alternative to strengthening the army garrison.[13]

Thanks to the verbatim diary kept by the Assistant-Secretary to the Cabinet, Tom Jones, we have a revealing insight into the way in which British policy was determined, especially at a meeting between the Cabinet and the Irish Executive on 31 May 1920, which opened on a sombre note with Lloyd George greeting Macready and Greenwood: 'I am glad to see you back alive.'[14] Greenwood reported:

> The vital point is to deal with the thugs, a number of whom are going about shooting in Dublin, Limerick and Cork. We are certain that they are handsomely paid, that the money comes from the USA, that it is passed through Bishop Fogarty [Bishop of Killalie, 1904–55, prominent Sinn Fein supporter] and Arthur Griffith by means of cheques issued to Michael Collins, the Adjutant-General of the Irish Republican Army. The money is paid out to the murderers in public houses. . . . The community is hostile, indifferent or terrorised.

The Lord Lieutenant disagreed: 'In my view the mischief originates with the Irish Volunteers, and unless you knock them on the head you make no progress.' There was no clear agreement on remedies, either – notably on the imposition of martial law.

> *Walter Long*: The complaints from soldiers and sailors are that owing to the non-existence of martial law they are liable to be tried for murder and found guilty. They have no protection if they shoot first.
> *Prime Minister*: The Cork jury has found the Lord Lieutenant and myself guilty of murder! . . . Another way would be to act indirectly on the opinion of the peasants – to make the rates liable for compensation for damage to barracks, etc.
> *Greenwood*: That is the law now.
> *Denis Henry* (Irish Attorney-General): They are refusing to strike a rate.
> *Greenwood*: The County Council system is breaking down.
> *Prime Minister*: Deduct it out of the Grants-in-Aid.

Greenwood: We have a draft Bill for that now in hand.

A. J. Balfour: It should be forced through.

Churchill: You should include in the Bill a special tribunal for trying murderers. It is monstrous that we should have 200 murders and no one hung. . . . After a person is caught he should pay the penalty within a week. Look at the tribunals which the Russian Government have devised. You should get three or four judges whose scope should be universal and they should move quickly over the country and do summary justice.

Henry: When that was put to the judges some months ago they did not want to touch it.

Churchill: Shows all the more need for extraordinary action. Get three generals if you cannot get three judges. . . . (*To the Prime Minister*) You agreed six or seven months ago that there should be hanging.

Prime Minister: I feel certain you should hang. Can you get convictions from Catholics?

Henry: Substantially, no.

The argument circulated round the table. Martial law or not? The Forster Act or the Balfour Act? Lord Curzon wanted progressive fines and (making use of his Indian experience) burning the bodies of convicted murderers. Lloyd George wanted a blockade, Bonar Law penal servitude for anyone caught with arms, Churchill 'to make life intolerable in a particular area'; no real agreement was reached, and it was left to the Irish government to 'frame suggestions'. As a result, the Restoration of Order in Ireland Act (August 1920) gave the military administration the powers of court martial in cases of treason and treason-felony, and replaced coroners' inquests with military courts of inquiry, sitting in secret to protect witnesses. When these proved inadequate, both police and military began to carry out unofficial reprisals.

A good deal of mythology surrounds the murders and counter-murders which took place in the second half of 1920 and the first half of 1921. The most famous incident, the 'sack' of Balbriggan, a small town twenty miles north of Dublin, on 20 September 1920, is a case in point. Two members of the RIC, a popular pair of brothers called Burke, were shot to death in a pub there. Instant retaliation was carried out by RIC men from the nearest depot at Gormantown (not, as is often stated, by the Black and Tans).[15] What exactly happened at Balbriggan? Asquith, attacking the whole policy of repression in Parliament, gave the Sinn Fein version and compared Balbriggan to a Belgian town wrecked in the Great War – and then admitted he had not visited the place.[16] General Macready, who visited Balbriggan a few days after the incident, wrote: 'A person ignorant of what had happened might have motored through the village without being aware that anything unusual had occurred.'[17] Harmar Green-wood's official report stated 'the police ... executed summary vengeance for the death of their comrades by killing two reputed Sinn Fein leaders in Balbriggan and committing extensive destruction of property in that town'. In all they destroyed nineteen houses and a hosiery factory.[18]

Balbriggan was not the first reprisal. It simply seems to have caught the interest of the press, since it was near Dublin. Reprisals at Limerick, Ennistymon, Lahinch, Milltown-Malbay and elsewhere were scarcely covered. Hence Balbriggan became a 'fighting word'. A poster, attributed to the Black and Tans and seen in Drogheda by an English writer, read:

DROGHEDA BEWARE!

If in the vicinity a policeman is shot, five Sinn Feiners will be shot. It is not coercion, it is an eye for an eye. . . . Are we to lie down while our comrades are shot by the cornerboys and raggamuffins of Ireland? We say – 'Never!' and all the inquiries in the world will not stop our desire for revenge. Stop the shooting of the police, or we will lay low every house that smells Sinn Fein – and remember Balbriggan![19]

In September 1920, Sinn Fein threatened to destroy all houses occupied by officials and other persons loyal to the government. Macready then announced that 'for every house destroyed the house of a Republican leader will be similarly dealt with'. He later claimed this was effective; he also claimed that his threat to shut down racing succeeded to the point where an Irish race-course was the one place a British officer could feel absolutely safe.[20] Macready's assertion that soldiers carried out only four reprisals, however, is not quite correct. On one occasion, as reported by Hugh Martin of the *Daily News*, the most reliable and objective of the British correspondents, men of the Northamptonshire regiment dressed up as Black and Tans to carry out a reprisal; and Martin also recorded that the Black and Tans had fought fires in Tipperary, displaying 'considerable gallantry'.[21] He argued: 'The police in Ireland are themselves the victims of a condition of terrorism which is only equalled by the condition of terrorism that they themselves endeavour to impose.' But of course it has to be remembered that many of the police had never been trained in police work. The Auxiliary Cadets, in particular, of whom Macready said 'they can best be described as a pretty tough lot', were fighters – 'super fighters and all but invincible', as one IRA commander called them afterwards.[22]

There were two particularly bad incidents. The first was 'Bloody Sunday' on 21 November 1920. This followed the early morning murder of seven officers, three ex-officers, two RIC and two civilians; most were in bed and killed in front of their wives. One of the victims had lost a leg in the Great War. During the afternoon, Black and Tans opened fire indiscriminately at a football crowd in Croke Park. The second incident was the firing of Cork City by Auxiliaries in December.[23]

It was not clear at the time precisely what government policy was; and the historian also has trouble in making sense of it. Colonel Hankey, the normally phlegmatic Secretary to the Cabinet, had written in his diary on 28 May 1920: 'My view is that terror must be met by greater terror.' [24] Macready was against reprisals, as he thought they would alienate public opinion in Britain, as indeed they did. General Crozier, commanding the Auxiliaries, was also against repression, to the point that he resigned in February 1921 and wrote a critical letter to *The Times*. General Tudor, commander of the RIC, was more ambivalent. Greenwood favoured a tough policy; so, from time to time, did Lloyd George and Churchill. [25] Wilson, whose diary is an important source for the real attitudes of ministers, generals, policemen and officials, favoured official and legal reprisals, rather than unofficial and illegal ones. On 29 September 1920 he records:

> I had 1½ hours this evening with Lloyd George and Bonar Law. I told them what I thought of reprisals by the 'Black and Tans' and how this must lead to chaos and ruin. . . . It was the business of the government to govern. If these men ought to be murdered, then the government ought to murder them. Lloyd George danced at all this, said no government could possibly take this responsibility.

Wilson added on 29 November that Britain should 'declare martial law in Ireland and stamp the vermin out'. [26] The official War Office view, put by General Sir Percy Radcliffe, Director of Military Operations, was that 'the only solution to this problem is to institute the principle of *official* reprisals and to impress on the troops that by taking the law into their own hands they damage the cause instead of furthering it'. [27] On 14 October Lloyd George told Wilson that he agreed with this view but he 'wanted to wait until the American elections are over. . . . The cursed elections take place next month. He told me the Cabinet this morning discussed Ireland, and many of them wanted to give way on Ireland. Lloyd George said he never would.' [28] Official reprisals were duly authorized, and took place with effect from 1 January 1921. They took the form of dynamiting selected buildings after due notice had been given. At no point did official action involve murder.

There is no doubt that some ministers sympathized with unofficial reprisals. H. A. L. Fisher quotes in his diary a remark by Lloyd George: 'You cannot in the existing state of Ireland punish a policeman who shoots a man whom he has every reason to suspect is concerned with police murders. This kind of thing can only be met with reprisals.' The Cabinet was provided with plausible evidence that reprisals in fact led to the volunteering of important intelligence, and that they tended to split the moderate Sinn Fein from the extremists. Austen Chamberlain wrote to his sister Hilda on 31 October 1920: 'it is a fact that the reprisals have secured the safety of police in places where previously they were shot down like vermin . . . [the policy] is getting the murder gang on the run by degrees'.[29] To some extent ministers were even prepared to defend the policy in public. 'If it is war,' Lloyd George told a cheering audience at Guildhall in November, 'they [the IRA] cannot complain if we apply some of the rules of war.' Greenwood told the Commons on 29 October: 'the best and surest way to stop the reprisals is for [the IRA] to stop the murder of policemen, soldiers and loyal citizens'.

It is a matter of opinion whether the policy of coercion and official reprisals would have succeeded if carried on long enough. This is the view taken by the historian of the Black and Tans, who quotes an Irish Volunteer commander: 'The IRA never beat the Tans, it was the British people who did it.'[30] Up to the autumn of 1920, only the Liberal and Labour papers had opposed the policy of repression. But *The Times* joined the critics on 30 November and other papers followed. Lloyd George denounced those who attended a protest meeting at the Albert Hall as 'Bolshevists and Sinn Feiners and faddists and cranks of all sorts'. But during the winter and spring of 1920–1, more and more highly respectable citizens – led by Anglican bishops – joined the opposition. Official reprisals did not end the terror: more people were murdered in March 1921 than in any previous month. Throughout this period the Sinn Fein 'government' had a Director of Propaganda – something the authorities lacked – a former Nationalist MP called Laurence Ginnell, who seems to have been highly effective. One striking indication of the mood in Ireland occurred at Templemore in Tipperary, which had been set on fire by both the Black and Tans and the military. In one of the sacked shops a seminarist saw a holy statue 'bleeding', and pilgrims and sick people from all over Ireland flocked to see the miracle.

Meanwhile the Government of Ireland Bill, which became law on 23 December 1920, set in motion the new constitutional machinery. In April 1921 a new Lord Lieutenant was appointed: Lord Fitzalan was a Catholic, the first since the days of James II. On 24 May the elections were held for both the Irish parliaments. In the North, the Unionists won 40 out of 52 seats, and went ahead to form a government and set up the new constitutional machinery; the famous B-specials had already been created in Ulster to put down Catholic and Protestant rioting, and maintain order. In the South, all 124 Sinn Fein were returned unopposed, with only Trinity College electing 4 Unionists. These four alone took the oath, met once, and then adjourned for ever. The response of Sinn Fein, on the day after the election, was to seize the Dublin Customs House and destroy the public records there.

The Cabinet had held an inconclusive discussion on Ireland on 27 April, at which the idea of a truce was mooted; there was a further discussion on 12 May, indicating that the truce party was growing – Churchill and four others voted for a truce, Lloyd George and eight others against.[31] The King, too, had now revolted against the coercion policy: 'In punishing the guilty,' he protested to Greenwood in May, 'we are inflicting punishment no less severe on the innocent.' Finally, on 15 June, the Cabinet 'Irish Situation Committee' heard an exceedingly gloomy report from Macready. What he called 'half-hearted coercion' was not working. The position of the troops was 'farcical'. 'It must be all out or

another policy,' he said. He made no secret of his own
personal belief that the policy of coercion would not succeed
and would merely 'land this country in the mire'. 'Throughout the discussions,' Jones minuted, 'Macready reiterated his
main point: does the Cabinet realize what is involved? Will
they go through with it? Will they begin to howl when they
hear of our shooting a hundred men in one week?' [32]

   The scale of the killing was, of course, an important point.
Irish sources give the number killed by the authorities from 1
January 1919 to 12 July 1921 as 752 IRA and civilians, with
866 wounded. British sources give 276 IRA and 288 civilians
killed from January 1920 to July 1921, with government losses
as 366 police and 162 soldiers killed, and 600 police and 566
soldiers wounded. [33] For comparative purposes, it must be
remembered that British ministers had just conducted a
successful world war, lasting more than four years, in which
British casualties alone had averaged over 1,500 a day. But
throughout the Great War military advice had been that the
appalling casualty rate was justified; now Macready –
Wilson, of course, opposing – gave his voice decisively in
favour of a new policy.

   The Cabinet took up a suggestion of General Smuts,
himself a notable resistance fighter in his day, that King
George V should use the occasion of the state opening of the
new Belfast parliament, on 22 June, to make a conciliatory
speech. This was done; and the rapidity with which the
gesture was reciprocated indicated that the Sinn Fein, who
had never numbered more than 3,000 active gunmen, were
also feeling the strain and anxious to talk. [34] A truce took effect
from 11 July 1921, and on 13 July De Valera crossed over to
Britain and met Lloyd George. The occasion was notable for a
superb example of gamesmanship by Lloyd George. Know-
ing De Valera's obsessive regard for Gaelic – he had said on
one occasion: 'Were I to get my choice, freedom without the
language or the language without freedom, I would far rather
have the language without freedom' – Lloyd George, on

being handed by De Valera a document in Irish, asked innocently for a literal translation of the title, 'Saorstat Eireann', on the grounds that it did not strike his ear as Irish. De Valera replied: 'Free State.' 'Yes,' replied Lloyd George, 'but what is the Irish word for Republic?' While De Valera conferred hastily with a colleague, Lloyd George conversed loudly with Tom Jones in Welsh, finally – after getting no satisfactory answer – exclaiming: 'Must we not admit that the Celts never were Republicans and have no native word for the idea?'[35]

So began the negotiation of what one historian has called 'peace by ordeal'.[36] The point Lloyd George made was not academic, since acceptance of the crown by the Irish, in some form, as the ultimate guarantee of Irish membership of the Empire, was the crux of the whole negotiation, in some ways an even more emotional issue for the Irish than Ulster itself. The talks began on 11 October, with Griffith, Collins, Robert Barton, Gavan Duffy and E. J. Duggan (with Erskine Childers as secretary) representing Ireland, and Lloyd George, the Lord Chancellor, Lord Birkenhead (formerly F. E. Smith), Harmar Greenwood, Churchill and Chamberlain as the principal British negotiators.

Lloyd George's extraordinary dexterity was in evidence throughout; indeed, without him it is most improbable that a successful treaty could have been negotiated at this stage, for he had to reconcile the Ulstermen to virtual independence in the South, reconcile the South to a separate Ulster and to the crown and empire, and at the same time keep his own coalition, in which his Liberal followers were greatly outnumbered, intact. He told Griffith: 'You have never made a treaty with the people of this country before. Treaties in the past have been made with oligarchies ruling this country.' In fact the negotiations were conducted like any other, though the Prime Minister was always available to supply fresh ideas and drama.

Lloyd George made it clear from the start that if the Irish

wanted Ulster coerced, they would have to do it themselves.
He told the Irish on 14 October:

> Ulster defeated Gladstone, Ulster would have defeated us.
> Mr Churchill and I were for the Bill, Mr Chamberlain and
> the Lord Chancellor were opposed. They with the instinct
> of trained politicians saw that Ulster was the stumbling
> block. They got the whole force of the opposition
> concentrated on Ulster. Ulster was arming and would
> fight. We were powerless. It is no use ignoring facts
> however unpleasant they may be. . . . We could not do it. If
> we tried, the instrument would have broken in our hands.
> Their case was: 'Let us remain with you.' Our case was:
> 'Out we go or we fight you.' We could not have done it. Mr
> Churchill and I warned our colleagues. Mr Gladstone and
> Mr Asquith discovered it. I cannot say I discovered it
> because I was always of that opinion. You have got to
> accept facts. The first axiom is, whatever happens, we
> could not coerce Ulster.[37]

He offered an Ulster Boundary Commission as a palliative,
the alternative being his own resignation, leading to a
Conservative government which might resume coercion. To
Craig, he offered the alternative of civil war. He himself had
now turned completely against further British involvement in
the south, and was serious about resigning. He told Jones (8
November): 'I will not be a party to firing another shot in the
South of Ireland. I have told the King. I have told my wife,
and I have told my secretaries today that there may be
someone else here next week.'[38] As one historian has put it,
'there was hardly a day when he was not making progress in
one of two directions. Either he was extracting more
provisional concessions from Sinn Fein to induce them to
continue with Craig, or he was working out proposals which,
even if he failed with Craig, would give Ireland no excuse for a
break.'[39]

　The decisive argument in the Irish acceptance of a separate

Ulster was Collins's belief, implanted by Lloyd George, that the Boundary Commission would so reduce Ulster as to render it economically unviable. That left the crown as the only issue. The draft treaty was taken back to Dublin by the Irish for a debate in their Cabinet on 3 December. Back in London two days later, Griffith told Jones that 'he and Collins had been completely won over to belief in your desire for peace and recognize that you had gone far in your efforts to secure it. This belief was not shared by their Dublin colleagues.'[40] Nevertheless, in the early hours of the morning of 6 December, the Irish delegation signed the Treaty.

Lloyd George had kept up the drama to the end, telling Griffith that a destroyer was waiting to take the notification of success or failure to the Northern Irish government, and must leave that night. Would they sign, or face the British army? Griffith signed. 'A braver man than Arthur Griffith I have never met,' said Austen Chamberlain. Collins's signature was even more important: Griffith had told Jones that, whatever Collins accepted, '90 per cent of the gunmen will follow'. Lloyd George held up in front of him two letters, both addressed to Craig, one containing the Articles of Agreement, the other the refusal of Sinn Fein to come to terms: which should he send? Collins signed, 'looking,' as Churchill recorded, 'as if he would like to shoot somebody, preferably himself'.[41] Birkenhead, gloomily anticipating how he would be savaged by Carson, said to Collins: 'I may have signed my political death-warrant tonight.' Collins replied: 'I may have signed my actual death warrant.'[42] Home in the early hours, Griffith said to his wife that after the signing Lloyd George looked like 'a benevolent old gentleman, with white hair and a smooth face with no lines on it'. Mrs Griffith: 'He must have an easy conscience.' Griffith: 'He has no conscience.'[43]

The Treaty brought bitterness for many. Carson attacked it inside and outside the House of Lords. He was particularly angry about the failure (in his view) to protect or compensate adequately former servants of the crown left in the South:

'Was there any reason why we should walk off the battlefield and leave our wounded behind?' He denounced the British delegates: 'Austen's a coward. Lloyd George is a mass of corruption.'[44] Most of the Irish on both sides of the Border, and in both communities, accepted it with relief. But at the Irish Cabinet meeting on 8 December, while Griffith, Collins, Barton and William Cosgrave voted to accept it, De Valera, Brugha and Austin Stack would not do so. It is a curious fact that nearly all the most implacable opponents of the Treaty had non-Irish fathers, and derived their sense of nationalism from their mothers; and it is another related fact that all six women members of the Dail voted against the Treaty, finally passed, after a two-week debate, by 64 votes to 57.

Women played a notable part in the debate, which has been described as 'a literary production'. One woman deputy accused Michael Collins, who was a bachelor, of planning to seal the Treaty by an arranged marriage with King George's daughter, Princess Mary. Another, urging continued resistance against Britain, said:

> If she exterminates the men, the women will take their place, and if she exterminates the women, the children are rising fast. And if she exterminates the men, women and children of this generation the blades of grass, dyed with their blood, will rise, like dragon's teeth of old, into armed men, and the fight will begin again in the next generation (*interjection*: She would not leave us even the grasshoppers).

De Valera, arguing for rejection, took his stand on Parnell's principle: acceptance of the Treaty was an attempt to set boundaries to the march of a people (cries of 'No' and 'Yes'). But it was notable that nearly all the military men wanted the Treaty. The Minister of Local Government poured scorn on those who argued that honour came before practical sense: 'Here in the capital of Ireland there are something like 20,000 families living in single-room tenement dwellings, and are they the people who are going to fight for you?' Griffith steered the Treaty through. He refused to answer a question from Childers, whom the British regarded as their bitterest opponent, but whom Griffith privately thought a British agent: 'I will not reply to any damned Englishman.' Otherwise, 'never did he become personal, never lose his coolness or depart from the solid rock of argument'. This quiet, shy man, who walked on the balls of his feet (damaged Achilles tendons necessitated raised shoes), and moved like a Dalek, was the real hero of Irish self-government.[45]

But the Irish ordeal was not over: the 'Troubles' with the British of 1919–21 were a mere prelude to civil war. On 18 March 1922, the IRA split, the Irregulars or 'Army of the Irish Republic' joining De Valera's newly-formed Republican Party. Fighting broke out in various parts of Ireland and along the Ulster Border. On 14 April, Rory O'Connor and a group of Irregulars seized and fortified the famous Four Courts building in Dublin. The plan of O'Connor and De Valera was to involve British troops, who were still in Dublin (the process of evacuating the South was not yet complete), in the fighting, calculating that this could lead to a collapse of support for Collins and his official army. But the British, while supplying arms and ammunition to Collins, wisely kept out of the struggle. Elections on 9 June, which gave the Provisional Government 58 seats to 35 for De Valera's Republicans, strengthened Collins's hand. On 28 June his men attacked the Four Courts. Two days later the rebels surrendered, but the splendid building blew up, taking with it most of what remained of Ireland's public records.

The slaughter and destruction continued, on a scale which made the struggle with Britain the previous year seem minor. As in the final scene of a Shakespearean tragedy, there was a rapid clearance of the cast. In June Sir Henry Wilson, who had been assiduously stirring up the die-hards in Ulster, was murdered by the IRA on the steps of his London house. In July Brugha was shot to death, rushing out of a blazing building, a pistol in each hand. Griffith, sad and weary, had a

stroke and died on 12 August, being succeeded as President by
Cosgrave. Ten days later Collins was killed in an ambush. In
November Childers was executed for possessing firearms; and
the next month Rory O'Connor was executed as a reprisal for
the killing of a Dail member. Altogether 77 rebels were
executed by the new Irish government. Fighting went on
through the winter, with General Mulcahy, Collins's deputy,
and Kevin O'Higgins, the Minister of Justice, gradually
getting the upper hand and restoring the authority of the
government. De Valera effectively surrendered in April, and
in May he ordered his followers to lay down their arms. The
damage was so enormous that there was no possibility of
Ulster coming into a united Ireland. Equally decisive was the
rapid decline of the Anglo-Irish community, many of whose
members took refuge in Britain, never to return. But peace of
a sort descended. In July 1923 the Treaty party won the
election, and in September the new Irish Free State joined the
League of Nations.

What of the Border? The Irish Boundary Commission Bill
was passed in 1924. A South African, a former member of
Milner's 'Kindergarten', Mr Justice Featham, was appointed
the independent chairman. The Irish nominated old Eoin
MacNeill, their Minister of Education, and the British J. R.
Fisher as the Ulster member. But the Chairman took a
narrowly legalistic view of the commission's terms of
reference, and as a result the award made few important
changes. The net effect of transfers to both sides would have
left the Free State with a gain of a mere 134,048 acres and
23,725 people. The draft report was agreed on 5 November
1925, and leaked to the *Morning Post* two days later. Craig,
who had hitherto opposed the commission, agreed to accept
the findings. But O'Neill, who had agreed to the draft report,
now insisted on resigning, and the Irish government made it
clear that it could not accept the changes in full settlement on
its claim. In the light of all this, and by general agreement, the
Report was never officially published, and the six-county

border remained as it was.[46]

In 1926 De Valera formed a quasi-constitutional party, Fianna Fail. His members won forty-four seats in the election, but refused to occupy them. Spasmodic violence continued. On 10 July 1927, a Sunday, Kevin O'Higgins, to whom Yeats had given the accolade 'Sole statesman', was murdered on his way to Mass; nobody was ever convicted of this crime. The next month, De Valera and his men were forced into the Dail by a new Electoral Act, which obliged candidates to take a constitutional oath, or forfeit their seats – thus Ireland remained a land of oaths.

What finally reconciled De Valera to the Free State was the passage of the Statute of Westminster, governing Dominion Status, in 1931. The relevant passage reads: 'The parliament of a dominion shall have power to repeal or amend any existing or future Act of Parliament of the United Kingdom in so far as the same is part of the law of the dominion.' Though De Valera had nothing to do with it, he was able to argue that his object – the securing of an 'external relationship' with the Commonwealth – had been secured. Hence after the defeat of the Cosgrave government in 1932, De Valera was able to take office. Using the new powers conferred by the Statute, he abolished the Oath of Allegiance to the Crown, degraded the office of Governor-General, and created a separate Irish citizenship. At the same time he signified that he did not endorse the recognition by the Cosgrave government in 1925 of the present status of Northern Ireland, by standing for and winning the South Down seat in the Ulster parliament. This repudiation of Cosgrave was formalized by a new constitution, which De Valera had enacted by referendum in 1937. It made Eire (as it was then called) a virtual republic and declared that Ireland, as constituted, meant 'the whole of Ireland'. At the same time he refused to continue to pay the land-transfer annuities to Britain. This led to an Anglo-Irish tariff-war, settled by agreement the following year.

As part of this agreement, Ireland recovered control of

three western ports, retained as British naval bases under the 1921 Treaty.[47] When the war broke out in 1939, De Valera declared Eire neutral. His attitude towards the fascist dictators had been, and remained, ambivalent. The 'thirties had not, unfortunately, brought an end to the private armies of Ireland. The IRA continued in being after De Valera became a constitutionalist. To match it, an Army Comrades Association was formed, and at the 1933 election the AGA and the IRA 'fought it out with knuckleduster and cosh'.[48] General O'Duffy, dismissed in February 1933 as Commissioner of Police, became leader of the Blueshirt Movement in July. To counter the Blueshirts, De Valera's government formed the S Division, known as the 'Broy Harriers', from the anti-Treaty members of the IRA. The years 1933–6 were marked by a number of political murders and reprisals.[49] When the Spanish Civil War broke out, O'Duffy sent a detachment of 700 Blueshirts to fight for Franco. About 200 IRA fought for the Republicans. But the IRA also operated against Britain, causing a number of bomb-explosions in 1939. After the declaration of war, it pledged support for Germany. Its so-called Chief of Staff, Sean Russell, went to Berlin, where he was joined by another IRA gunman, Frank Ryan. They were trained in bomb-making at the Nazi Legel Laboratory, and put aboard a U-boat; but neither reached Ireland, and both were dead by the end of the war. IRA efforts within Ireland to help the Nazis by sabotage and espionage were similarly ineffectual.[50]

De Valera's wartime policy was to exploit hostilities for Irish purposes. On the one hand he dealt severely with the IRA, using military courts and internal camps. On the other, he discouraged, but could not actually prevent, some 50,000 Southern Irish from volunteering for service in the British forces. In general, he observed neutrality strictly in accordance with international law.[51] The German Embassy in Dublin broadcast weather-reports to Germany, and the Luftwaffe must have benefited from this service during the ferocious raids on Belfast (in one raid in April 1941, 700 people, Protestants and Catholics, were killed). But they were entitled to do this under the neutrality protocols. De Valera seems to have turned down various approaches from the Germans, as he turned down a British offer on 26 June 1940 to publish a declaration 'accepting the principle of a United Ireland' in return for Irish support and the use of naval ports.[52]

In the United States De Valera sought to strengthen the isolationist elements, believing that American entry into the war would increase the pressure on Ireland to help the Allies. The US ambassador in Dublin, David Grey, was a personal friend of Roosevelt and a staunch supporter of Britain. He cabled home in January 1941: '[De Valera] has capitalized on hatred of Great Britain for political reasons. . . . He began to talk about his rights. I told him that . . . the only right he and myself enjoyed was to believe in our religion, and be burned for it if need be. Every other right depended on force to maintain it.' America was, in fact, much more hostile than Britain to the Irish maintenance of neutrality. Up to 13 December 1941 Britain had brought 400,000 tons of food supplies to neutral Ireland at the risk of her ships and the lives of her seamen. After the United States entered the war, such services ceased; and in the years 1942–4 it was Roosevelt and Cordell Hull who wished to put more pressure on Dublin, Churchill being more cautious.[53] In June 1943 David Grey proposed to Admiral Leahy that the naval bases in Ireland should be seized; and in 1944, the State Department delivered to De Valera a note which read: 'Despite the declared desire of the Irish government that its neutrality should not operate in favour of either of the belligerents, it has in fact operated and continues to operate in favour of the Axis Powers.' America demanded that De Valera should ask for the recall of the German and Japanese representatives in Dublin, fearful that they might jeopardize the security of the Overlord invasion of Europe. De Valera did not even finish the note before saying: 'Of course our answer shall be no.' He likewise refused an Allied request that he reject any attempt by the Nazi war criminals to seek asylum in Ireland. Indeed, when the Nazis surrendered, Irish students stoned the American consulate-general; and when news of Hitler's suicide reached Dublin, De Valera paid a call on the Nazi Minister, Herr Hempel, to express sympathy over the death of his Chancellor. He claimed he was merely following protocol. An Editorial in the *New York Times* commented: 'Considering the character and record of the man for whose death he was expressing grief, there is obviously something wrong with the protocol, the neutrality, or Mr De Valera.'[54]

Throughout the war, however, Churchill was determined not to be provoked; he, at any rate, had learnt a lesson from Ireland. But he did see fit to remark in his Victory Broadcast of 13 May 1945, referring to the years 1940–2:

> This was indeed a deadly moment in our life, and if it had not been for the loyalty and friendship of Northern Ireland, we should have been forced to come to close quarters with Mr de Valera, or perish forever from the earth. However, with a restraint and poise to which, I say, history will find few parallels, His Majesty's Government never laid a hand on them, though at times it would have been quite easy, and quite natural.[55]

These wartime events provide the background to the post-war development of the constitutional relationship between Ireland and the United Kingdom. In 1948, Fianna Fail lost the elections, being replaced by the Fine Gael coalition. In the next year the new government completed the break with Britain by passing legislation which turned Eire into the Republic of Ireland and took it out of the Commonwealth, besides laying claim to all thirty-two counties. The Labour government in Britain responded by making what is known as the 'Attlee Declaration', given the force of law in the Ireland Act, 1947. This guarantees that 'in no event will Northern

Ireland or any part thereof cease to be part of the United Kingdom without the consent of the parliament of Northern Ireland'. It was this pledge which forms the constitutional setting for the present problem of Northern Ireland.

CHAPTER 10

From Revolt to Stalemate

The constitutional entity called Northern Ireland, which came into existence in 1921, had a substantial built-in Protestant majority. In 1926 Protestants constituted 66.5 per cent of the population, against 33.5 per cent Catholics. By 1961 this ratio had changed somewhat in favour of the Catholics, whose percentage rose to 34.9, the Protestant share falling to 65.1, but not in such a way as to constitute any challenge to Protestant hegemony in the foreseeable future.

However, Northern Ireland was in no constitutional sense a confessional state. The Government of Ireland Act 1920 which, as subsequently amended, became the constitution of Northern Ireland, provides specific religious safeguards. Section 5(1) states:

> In the exercise of their power to make laws under this act neither the Parliament of Southern Ireland nor the Parliament of Northern Ireland shall make a law so as either directly or indirectly to establish or endow any religion, or prohibit or restrict the free exercise thereof, or give a preference, privilege or advantage, or impose any disability or disadvantage, on account of religious belief.[1]

This remains constitutional law in Northern Ireland, and in this respect is quite different from the Republic of Ireland, which dropped Section 5(1), and whose 1937 constitution recognized 'the special position of the Holy Catholic Apostolic and Roman Church as the guardian of the Faith professed by the great majority of the citizens', a constitutional provision which inevitably had a direct bearing on laws governing divorce, the sale of contraceptives, censorship and other quasi-religious issues.

However, Northern Ireland has not been in practice a unitary state. Carson, who did most to bring it into existence, saw Ireland as two races, one superior to the other, religion being merely the external distinguishing characteristic. At the close of his life, he wrote to the historian Sir John Marriott: 'In the end, it is a question of nationhood. The Celts have done nothing in Ireland but create trouble and disorder. Irishmen who have turned out successful have not in any case that I know of been of true Celtic origin.'[2]

The leaders of Ulster, led by its first Prime Minister, Sir James Craig, always maintained that Ulster was essentially Protestant, with the Orange Order the symbol of its ruling force. 'Ours is a Protestant government,' said Craig in 1932, 'and I am an Orangeman.' He repeated this in the parliament at Stormont two years later: 'I have always said that I am an Orangeman first and a politician and a member of this parliament afterwards. . . . All I boast is that we have a Protestant Parliament and a Protestant State.'[3] In practice, Protestantism was identified with Unionism. Thomas Lyons MP, later Deputy Speaker of the Commons from 1955–69, said in 1947: 'A man who was a Protestant and not a Unionist had a "kink" in his make-up. Such a man was not normal.'[4] Equally, Protestantism was identified with the Orange Order. When the question of Catholics belonging to the Unionist Party or the Orange Order came up in 1959, the Grand Master of the Orange Order, Sir George Clark, said that while Catholics might support Unionism through the ballot box, membership either of the Party or of the Orange Order was a different matter:

I would draw your attention to the words 'civil and religious liberty'. This liberty, as we know it, is the liberty of the Protestant religion. In view of this, it is difficult to see how a Roman Catholic, with the vast differences in our religious outlook, could be either acceptable within the Unionist Party as a member or, for that matter, bring himself unconditionally to support its ideals. Further to this, an Orangeman is pledged to resist by all lawful means the ascendancy of the Church of Rome, abstaining from uncharitable words, actions and sentiments towards his Roman Catholic brethren.[5]

In practice, then, Ulster had always tended to be a one-party state, and the tendency was reinforced by a number of constitutional factors. The Government of Ireland Act 1920 had introduced the principle of proportional representation to mitigate the dangers of confessional voting. Southern Ireland retained it, and a survey of its workings there over fifty-seven years has produced the conclusion: 'It is safe to assert that at present it enjoys widespread public acceptance.'[6] In Ulster, however, proportional representation for parliamentary elections was abolished in 1922, and for local elections in 1929. This may not have affected the results of parliamentary elections, but it led to many more uncontested seats – 40 per cent as a rule, sometimes rising to nearly 70 per cent – which emphasized the element of one-party rule and the atrophy of politics. Even after the last Stormont election in 1969, the Unionists had 39 seats against 13 opposition; and they never held less than 33 seats out of 52.[7] Despite their abolition in Britain, plural voting and university representation remained in Ulster until 1968 (the Republic of Ireland still keeps university seats). In local elections, the change from PR undoubtedly helped the Unionists. Indeed, the under-representation of the Catholic minority in local government was their biggest single legitimate grievance: in 1967, for instance, the Nationalists controlled only eight out of sixty-eight local authorities. This was produced by the 'first past the post' system, the alleged rigging of local government boundaries and by the Northern Ireland Elections and Franchise Act of 1947, which continued to make it possible for one elector to have six local government votes.[8] In turn, the local government 'gerrymander' led to widespread allegation of persistent Unionist favouritism in the allocation of public housing, and to political bias in the location of public housing estates.

It was also claimed that Unionist rule was underpinned by the system of maintaining public order. Under the 1920 Act, the northern units of the old RIC became the Royal Ulster Constabulary. Carson and Craig claimed that they did not want an armed force for Ulster. But during the Treaty negotiations the Southern Irish insisted on having their own armed force, which Lloyd George conceded. Once the South had such a force, the North had to have one too. The Ulster Volunteers were transformed into a special constabulary to put down the Belfast riots of summer 1920, in which the Catholics were the victims, and they continued under arms to meet the threat to the Border posed by De Valera and his IRA units after the Treaty came into force. There were three kinds of 'Special' Constables: the B-Specials, the most famous (or notorious), who performed part-time duties in their own localities; the C-Specials, who were available only for emergencies; and the A-Specials, who were on full-time service throughout the province.

The Ulster Special Constabulary at one time numbered 44,000, and was in effect the residuary legatee of Carson's Ulster Volunteers. In 1969 it still had 425 full-time and 8,481 part-time members. It was alleged that the Specials were exclusively Protestant, and this charge was borne out by the report of the Cameron Commission, set up in 1968 to investigate disturbances in Northern Ireland. It reported:

The recruitment of this force, for traditional and historical reasons, is in practice limited to members of the Protestant faith. . . . Until very recent years, for drill and training purposes, the Ulster Special Constabulary made large use of Orange Lodges and this . . . tended to accentuate in the eyes of the Catholic minority the assumed partisan and sectarian character of the force.[9]

4. Ireland in the present day.

The RUC itself was intended, from the start, to be one-third Catholic, and thus retain the objective character of its progenitor, the RIC. But partly as a result of a boycott by Nationalists, and partly because of a decision to allow constables to form Orange Lodges, the proportion of Catholics in the force never rose above 11 per cent. Hence allegations of sectarian bias were levelled against the RUC also. These seem to have been unfounded. A tribunal under Lord Justice Scarman, set up to investigate such complaints in 1969, reported: 'The general case of a partisan force co-operating with Protestant mobs to attack Catholic people is devoid of substance, and we reject it utterly.'[10]

What gave additional force to the charges of bias in administering the law was the existence, from the very foundation of the state, of relics of the old coercion policy. Craig had promised, in his first speech to the Ulster Parliament: 'Every person inside our particular boundary may rest assured that there will be nothing meted out to them but the strictest justice. None need be afraid, the laws must be obeyed. We will be cautious in our legislation. We will be absolutely honest and fair in administering the law.'[11] This intention was frustrated first by the efforts of the De Valera Nationalists in the South to destroy Ulster as a state, and their refusal ever to recognize its legal existence, and secondly by the refusals of the Nationalists within Northern Ireland to accept their citizenship of the United Kingdom, and their proclaimed intention to overthrow the state. While contesting some seats in the elections, the Nationalists often refused to attend Stormont, and only in February 1965 did the Nationalist Party accept the role of official opposition.

Hence in 1922 the Ulster government passed the Civil Authorities (Special Powers) Act, and it remained on the Statute Book. Section 2(4) created a catch-all offence of the type beloved of emergency law draftsmen throughout the civilized world:

If any person does any act of such a nature as to be calculated to be prejudicial to the preservation of the peace or maintenance of order in Northern Ireland and not specifically provided for in the regulations, he shall be deemed to be guilty of an offence against the regulations.[12]

A constitutional lawyer has defined the 1922 Act as 'a desperate measure taken to deal with a desperate situation', as indeed it was. But the need to keep it became, as the Cameron Commission reported, 'a continuing cause of irritation and friction within the body politic' which had 'borne most heavily upon the Roman Catholic part of the population'. What tended to confirm the notion of a one-party state was the combination produced by the existence of the Special Powers Act and its enforcement by B-Specials, especially in raids on private houses.[13]

Despite the existence of Stormont, Ulster was still a part of the United Kingdom of Great Britain and Northern Ireland, to give it its full title, and therefore subject to the ultimate rule of the Westminster Parliament, to which it sent twelve MPs. Yet Westminster did not prove in practice an effective check on Stormont. Section 75 of the 1920 Act emphasized the subordinate nature of the Stormont Parliament, but it must be remembered that this Act was originally drafted to satisfy the demands of the Irish Nationalists, and therefore gave wide powers to the devolved legislatures. Thus Stormont was able to opt out of Westminster legislation which it did not like, by passing its own Bills, and Westminster did not normally legislate, except by agreement, for Northern Ireland in matters where responsibility had been transferred to Stormont. Moreover, in 1923, the Speaker at Westminster had ruled: 'With regard to those subjects which have been delegated to the Government of Northern Ireland, questions must be asked of Ministers in Northern Ireland and not in this House.' This convention, which strictly speaking had no force of law, meant that British or even Ulster MPs who were

critical of the Stormont regime were unable to raise the
subject in the House of Commons.[14] Thus complaints about
discrimination in housing and public appointments, in
breach of the safeguards provided by the 1920 Act, of the
manipulation of electoral boundaries, and of the restrictive
franchise in local government, could not be given an airing at
Westminster. As a 1972 Conservative government paper on
Northern Ireland put it, 'many members of the minority felt
that they could not expect redress of grievances through
parliament or through the constitutional safeguards which
had been written into the Act of 1920'.[15] British ministers who
tried to get Stormont to make changes ran into heavy
opposition, as James Callaghan found when he was Home
Secretary, and recorded in his account of the Ulster
problem.[16]

In view, then, of the many weaknesses of the Ulster political
structure, and the absence of means of redress, why did it
continue to operate with the acquiescence of the minority
until 1968? The reason is largely economic. Although many
had believed the six-county territory was not a viable
economic unit, in practice it performed much better than its
critics foresaw, and certainly better than its southern
neighbour. It also benefited from British Exchequer subsidies,
especially after the introduction of massive welfare provisions
by the post-1945 British Labour government. The Southern
Irish might not be prepared to recognize Ulster legally, but as
individuals many voted for it with their feet. In 1947,
Stormont was obliged to pass a Safeguarding of Employment
Act to limit rising emigration from the South. And it is
significant that when, in 1949, the Stormont Prime Minister,
Sir Basil Brooke, held a general election, in response to
Ireland's Republican constitution, on the issue of Ulster's
separate identity, he received an impressive endorsement, the
Unionists polling over 63 per cent of the electorate.[17]
Throughout the post-war period, the financial advantages
Ulster derived from her constitutional links with Britain

continued to increase. Thus, in the mid-'sixties, one authority calculated that 'if Ulster were independent and had to pay for her own defence and for diplomatic, consular and other "imperial" services, she would either have to cut domestic spending by some £50 million a year or raise that sum by taxation. Either course would be catastrophic.'[18]

Southern Ireland's limping economic performance was due to a number of reasons. One was the damage wreaked by the 1922–3 civil war, and the continuing insecurity thereafter. This in turn led to an exodus of the Anglo-Irish element, a high proportion of which had professional qualifications and technical skills and, not least, capital. In the 1930s, De Valera's policy of national isolation and introspection added to the problems caused by the Great Depression. To give only one example: De Valera was obsessed by the need to promote Gaelic, and the efforts to advance this cause, symptomatic of the state he was trying to create, took priority over all other *desiderata*, including government efficiency, educational progress and investment. Yet the language policy was doomed to failure. By 1966 the population of native Irish speakers had declined to under 70,000, that is less than 20 per cent of what it had been at the foundation of the state.[19] Since then the situation has deteriorated still further, and the population in the authentic Gaeltacht areas may now be as low as 32,000.[20] In so far as the Irish had any choice in the matter, they have tended to reject the narrow concept of nationalism represented by the language policy.[21]

Certainly, the emigration figures may be taken as a negative verdict on De Valera's Ireland. Emigration continued during the 1930s and was resumed after the war: between 1945 and 1961 the Republic of Ireland lost a further 500,000 people – to Ulster, to Britain and to the world. An official report on economic development noted in 1958:

After 35 years of native government people are asking whether we can achieve an acceptable degree of economic progress. The common talk among parents in the towns, as well as in rural Ireland, is of their children having to emigrate as soon as their education is completed in order to secure a reasonable standard of living.[22]

The gap between living standards in the North and in the South, and the continuing emigration from the Republic, was almost certainly the underlying cause of the complete failure of a renewed IRA campaign in the North during the years 1956-62. Though there were some violent incidents (including the murder of an RUC sergeant), it was significant that IRA gunmen were forced to operate from behind the Republic border and could not find refuge within Ulster territory. On 26 February 1962, the IRA Publicity Bureau in Dublin announced that they were ending the campaign. The *New York Times* wrote: 'They have been condemned by the most deadly of all judgments, political indifference... the present generation know that if Partition is ever to be ended it must be by peaceful arrangements.'[23]

The late 1950s were probably the lowest point in the fortunes of the Irish Republic, however. The accession to power of Sean Lemass, who put business and common sense before nationalist ideology, was the watershed.[24] He was helped by a radical change in the attitude of the Finance Department, hitherto hostile to economic expansion, introduced by T. K. Whitaker, which produced the highly successful 'Programme for Economic Expansion 1958'.[25] During the 1960s, emigration was virtually halted. The marriage-rate went up, and the age of marriage (a highly sensitive index in Ireland) went down.[26] The process of economic change was assisted by the emergence, at the head of affairs, of men who had played no part in 'the Troubles' and who were relatively unfettered by the past.[27]

During the 1960s the Unionist government in Ulster, not unmindful of the Republic's progress, made strenuous efforts to maintain the economic differential which it saw as the best guarantee of its political hegemony. During the Premiership of Terence O'Neill (1963–9), the Minister of Commerce, Brian Faulkner, put into effect the recommendations of a report made in December 1964 by Professor Thomas Wilson, which called for the rapid creation of 65,000 new jobs in manufacturing and service history.[28] Over the seven-year period 1963–9, Faulkner managed to establish nearly sixty new factories in the province. Unemployment went down from four times to three times the United Kingdom average.

Yet these efforts in themselves were used to draw attention to the duality of Ulster's political system. Spokesmen for the minority pointed out that, of fifty-eight new factories, only eight were sited in West Ulster, beyond the River Bann – that is, beyond the traditional area of Protestant predominance. The very name of Ulster's New Town, Craigavon, was offensive to the Nationalists, and the fact that it was sited in Protestant Armagh was a further grievance; so, too, was the decision to create Ulster's new university in Protestant Coleraine, rather than in Londonderry.

The more liberal Unionist elements were aware that political changes were both necessary and overdue. Their spokesman, Terence O'Neill, began to edge towards them in 1965, when he exchanged visits with Sean Lemass, an exchange which bore immediate fruit in the acceptance by the Ulster Nationalists of official opposition status at Stormont. But O'Neill was hampered by the fact that the parties reflected not so much economic interests as religious categories and historic attitudes. This phenomenon was by no means confined to the North. In the Republic, the Fine Gael party is economically conservative, but its historic alliance with Labour against the Anti-Treaty Party, Fianna Fail, means that Irish politics cannot develop a normal left-right polarization, and tend therefore to dwell in the past and especially on issues of nationalism.[29] Equally, north of the Border, the Unionist Party was inhibited by its sheer comprehensiveness. Just because it embraced such a wide class spectrum, it has preserved its cohesion by emphasizing the religious issues which unite it, but which divide Ulster as a whole. The moment the Unionist leadership drops this emphasis, the party begins to disintegrate and the elite can no longer deliver their followers.[30]

There were signs of this happening under O'Neill even before the events of 1968. O'Neill's action in inviting Lemass to Ulster was strongly resented by many Unionists. The Unionist Party itself told O'Neill that, in future, such moves should be made only after it had been consulted, and had approved. The year 1966 saw the emergence of the Reverend Ian Paisley as a leader of extremist Protestant-Unionist opinion, with the foundation both of his newspaper, the *Protestant Telegraph*, and the revival, as a new activist group, of the Ulster Volunteer Force, which was promptly proscribed as an illegal organization – under the Special Powers Act. In 1966 and again in 1967 there were revolts against O'Neill's leadership within the Unionist Party; and Brian Faulkner, in his memoirs, says that the 1966 rebels were only one short of forming a majority of the parliamentary party at Stormont.[31]

Extremism on the right almost inevitably stimulated extremism on the left. And O'Neill's more liberal policy may, in itself, have helped to detonate the explosion of discontent which occurred in 1968. To vary the metaphor, O'Neill's invitation to the Nationalists to emerge from their political ghetto was taken, as his Unionist critics predicted it would be, as a licence to assault the entire Stormont structure. Yet fundamentally the Ulster crisis was not provoked by events in Ulster itself. The prime cause was the relatively poor performance of the British economy, in relation to the rest of the developed world, which became increasingly apparent as the 1960s progressed. This was reflected in a general decline in Britain's prestige, and a growing feeling that the British way of doing things was no longer working. Stability in Ulster was founded on a high valuation of the British connection; as this fell, so stability was undermined. Ulster was not alone in feeling these tremors: Scotland and Wales felt them too, and there was a moment, in the late 1970s, when it seemed quite possible that the United Kingdom would disintegrate as a political unit.

But if British decline was the deep-seated cause of the Ulster revolt, the proximate cause lay in the events which took place in Paris in May 1968. Just as the French Revolution inspired the 1798 rising, and the adoption of self-determination as an Allied war aim spurred on Sinn Fein in 1916–18, so the student revolt at Paris university, the progenitor of youthful radicalism all over the western world, led directly to the great marches of summer 1968 in Ulster. The Northern Ireland Civil Rights Association was formed in January 1967, primarily to tackle the inequities of the local government franchise. But it was the excitement aroused by the French effervescence, glamorized by intense publicity, which gave the Civil Rights Movement a mass and predominantly youthful following. Moreover, the 'student revolt', as an international phenomenon, was at first greeted with approval, even delight, in liberal circles everywhere; and this cordiality was extended to the Ulster protest. Not for some considerable time was it realized that a Frankenstein monster had broken loose.

The Civil Rights movement made the first move to raise the political temperature by holding a march of 2,500 demonstrators from Coalisland to Dungannon, on Saturday 24 August 1968, to protest about the allocation of public housing in the area. When the intention to hold this march was announced, Paisley's organization, the Ulster Protestant Volunteers, made public plans for a counter-demonstration in Dungannon. About 1,500 turned up for this rival meeting, and the police had great difficulty in keeping the two mobs apart. A fortnight later the Civil Rights movement announced they would hold a second march at Londonderry on 5 October. The Protestant Group, the 'Apprentice Boys of Derry', countered with plans for a rival march for the same day. The

Minister of Home Affairs, William Craig, then banned both marches. The Civil Rights executive decided to hold their march nevertheless, and 2,000 demonstrators formed the procession, accompanied by three Westminster MPs – Eddie McAteer, leader of the Nationalists at Stormont, and two of his colleagues, Gerry Fitt and Austin Currie. At the beginning of the march, which was now illegal, the RUC reminded its organizers of the existence of the banning order, and when the marchers tried to make their way across the Craigavon Bridge, the police made a baton-charge. Riot equipment was used, stones were thrown, and there were 88 injured – 77 civilians and 11 police.[32]

The incidents at Londonderry were undoubtedly the real beginning of the Ulster crisis, and it is therefore important to determine to what extent the clash was planned. The Report of the Cameron Commission, which inquired into the affair, said the intentions of the organizers were peaceful; but it accused them of 'inefficiency' and wrote of 'the absence of any effective Civil Rights Association control'.[33] It added that the Civil Rights Association itself was 'dedicated to a policy of non-violence' and was 'non-sectarian in origin and purpose'. But there were 'IRA sympathizers and members within the Association' who acted as stewards for marches and demonstrations.

The truth of the matter seems to have been that the IRA had comparatively little to do with the beginnings of the Civil Rights movement, which was genuinely non-sectarian. After the abandonment of active campaigning in 1962, the organization was penetrated by Marxists, led by Roy Johnston, a computer-operator. Tomas Mac Giolla became president of Sinn Fein, the political arm, and Cathal Goulding Chief of Staff of the IRA itself; the decision was taken to concentrate on social issues. Hence, though members of the IRA found the Civil Rights Association a useful front, they originally saw it as a political rather than a military instrument, to stimulate protest on a class, not a communal,

basis. Like most other people, including the politicians at
Stormont and Westminster, they were astounded by the
strength of the primitive communal feeling which the
marches revealed. At this point the IRA split. A new, ultra-
militant and pro-violence wing was formed, to take advantage of the communal unrest; it called itself the 'Provisional
IRA', and was led (we are not surprised to find) by an
Englishman living in the South under the name of Sean Mac
Stiofain. It took up all the traditional IRA attitudes – anti-
Border, anti-British, anti-Protestant, and pro-Catholic –
dropped its social beliefs, turned to the conventional sources
of finance in the American-Irish community and began to
arm itself in the winter of 1968–9.[34]

At this stage, then, everything depended on the willingness
of the government to satisfy legitimate grievances and thus
prevent the men of violence from taking over the protest
movement. O'Neill was certainly willing. On 22 November
1968, after a cabinet meeting, he announced a five-point
reform programme, which included a new system for
allocating housing, the abolition of the business vote in local
elections, and a review of the Special Powers Act. A week
later, his Electoral Law (Amendment) Act was passed,
abolishing the university seats and multiple votes in
parliamentary elections and providing for a new boundary
commission to answer charges of gerrymandering in the
Stormont seats. On 9 December he made a television
broadcast, starting with the words 'Ulster stands at the
crossroads', asking for co-operation by both communities in
getting the new reforms working, and warning Unionists that
both Harold Wilson, the British Prime Minister, and Edward
Heath the Conservative leader, had told him that any
attempt to sabotage the reform programme could lead to
direct intervention by Westminster.

The next stage in the tragedy was the refusal of the Unionist
Party as a whole to heed this warning. It is at least arguable
that the bulk of the Catholic community was willing to accept

reform within a Stormont framework. After his retirement, O'Neill claimed: 'I had won the trust of the Catholics as no previous Prime Minister had ever been able to do. But I was unable to restore to them the rights which small-minded men had removed from them during the first years of Northern Ireland's existence.'[35] The movement to unseat O'Neill was begun by William Craig the next day, when he disputed the right of Britain to intervene under Section 75 of the 1920 Act, and accused O'Neill of submitting to British blackmail. Craig was dismissed. Marches, counter-marches and violence continued, however, as did accusations of bias and brutality against the RUC. When, on 15 January 1969, O'Neill announced the appointment of a Commission under Lord Cameron to inquire into the disturbances, their causes and the composition of the bodies involved in them, he lost another member of his cabinet – indeed, the most important man in it – Brian Faulkner.

O'Neill, like the IRA, underestimated the power of sectarian feeling on either side of the religious dividing line. He believed in sweet reason; indeed, he once described himself to me as 'an eighteenth-century politician trying to govern a seventeenth-century country'. Encouraged, per- haps, by the favourable inter-party response from ordinary people to his broadcast, he called a General Election for 24 February, in the hope of unseating some of the Unionist die- hards. It was a dismaying failure. Some pro-O'Neill Unionists stood in die-hard seats, and there were more contested seats than at any election since 1925. But none of O'Neill's opponents within the party was defeated, and the election brought to Stormont a number of Civil Rights leaders, such as John Hume and Ivan Cooper, which in turn tended to produce a closing of Unionist ranks around ancient shibbo- leths. O'Neill was confirmed as leader by his MPs, but the pressure on him from both extremes rose steadily There was a fearful riot at Londonderry on 19 April, in which 209 policemen and 79 civilians were hurt, petrol bombs were thrown, and the authorities had to use armoured vehicles. The next day the first bomb explosions took place, and on the following Wednesday O'Neill lost his Minister of Agriculture, James Chichester-Clark, who said that the government's franchise reforms, though right in principle, were premature. At this, O'Neill threw in his hand.

Most of the Unionist rank-and-file wanted Faulkner, seen as a hawk, but an efficient and able one, to succeed as Prime Minister. The parliamentary party was less sure, and in their indecision they picked Chichester-Clark, a squire-figure from the same landed background as O'Neill, by a narrow vote of seventeen to sixteen for Faulkner. James Callaghan, the British Home Secretary, described him as 'a very even-tempered man . . . absolutely straight and usually came to the point without much embroidery'.[36] But his mandate was neither coercion nor reform, but the mixture as before; in practice this meant keeping the party together at all costs. The British, meanwhile, moved steadily closer to direct intervention. On 18 May 1969 the Civil Rights Association announced that it would continue and intensify its civil disobedience campaign until the government produced a definite timetable on reforms, which it listed as: one man, one vote in local government elections, votes at eighteen, an independent Boundary Commission for electoral boundaries, a fair housing allocation system, anti-discrimination laws for employment, a review of the Special Powers Act and disbandment of the B-specials. The British Labour Government was in general sympathy with these aims. A month before, Labour MPs, ministers included, had been mesmer-ized by an extraordinary maiden speech made by young Bernadette Devlin, a Nationalist firebrand who had won a by-election in mid-Ulster. In his diary, R. H. S. Crossman described 'Members falling over themselves to congratulate her', though, as he noted, all she was doing was 'building the barricades'.[37]

The real barricades went up on 12 August, in the Catholic

Bogside area of Londonderry, whose inhabitants claimed they were being attacked by the combined forces of the RUC and Protestant mobs. Republican flags appeared and the Bogside was declared 'Free Derry'. Skilfully exploiting the riots, Jack Lynch, the Fianna Fail Prime Minister of the Republic, made a broadcast the following evening, in which he said his government was asking Britain to apply for a United Nations peacekeeping force. Stormont, he claimed, was no longer in control. There were many injured and he had therefore arranged for Army field-hospitals to be located along the border. Thus the Irish sense of drama took over; and thereafter the Ulster problem was no longer under the control of any, or indeed all, of the parties to it.

Chichester-Clark signified his incapacity to master events the very next day by invoking British military support. After a hurried meeting with Harold Wilson in Cornwall (Wilson was holidaying in the Scilly Isles), Callaghan agreed to put in troops. Even at this stage, no one, and certainly not British ministers, had any idea of the horrors ahead. Crossman describes Callaghan as exhilarated at the challenge: 'By God,' he said, 'it is enjoyable being a Minister. It is much more fun being Home Secretary than Chancellor. This is what I like doing, taking decisions, and I had to take the decision to put the troops in while I was in the plane on the way back from Cornwall.'[38]

British troops moved into Londonderry on 14 August, immediately after Callaghan gave the order, and into Belfast the following day. By the next week there were 6,000 British soldiers in Northern Ireland. But Chichester-Clark had to pay the price. The B-Specials were put under the British Commander-in-Chief, and a commission under Lord Hunt was set up to inquire into the future of the force.[39] A Tribunal of Inquiry, under Mr Justice Scarman, was appointed to inquire into the disturbances.[40] Two senior civil servants were sent out to Stormont to keep watch over the administration; and Callaghan attended two Northern Ireland cabinet meetings to speed on the reform programme. The Stormont regime was thus already, to some extent, the prisoner of the Westminster government. The old convention of non-interference had been abandoned. Indeed, the Crossman Diaries reveal that Direct Rule by Westminster was envisaged and prepared for as early as April 1969.[41]

With Stormont firmly under control, British ministers were confident that the combination of reforms and British troops, to provide an impartial system of law and order, would gradually damp down the flames. But as O'Neill pointed out: 'What I think everyone failed to understand is that you cannot have a situation where Catholic houses are burnt down and Catholics shot in the street, and then say "Here are some reforms, let's forget about the past".'[42] The Hunt Committee reported in October, recommending the disbanding of the Ulster Special Constabulary and its replacement by a new, 4,000-strong force, the Ulster Defence Regiment, which would be recruited from all sections of the population and placed under the British Commander-in-Chief. But tension did not die down. Too much blood had already been shed, too much misery caused. In the five years of the O'Neill government, only three people had died by sectarian violence. In the summer of 1969 eight people were killed, over 150 wounded by gunfire, 500 houses destroyed and over 2,000 made homeless.

At first the British troops had been welcomed. But the IRA, now armed, was moving into the Catholic areas of Belfast and Londonderry, and setting up arms caches, bases and 'safe houses' elsewhere in Ulster. Its object was to lure British units further and further into the Catholic ghetto areas, provoke incidents, force the troops into firing, ensure that Catholics were killed or hit, make house-to-house searches unavoidable, and thus progressively turn the Catholic population against the troops, as a prelude to a 'Get British Troops Out' movement and the revival of the Border issue. The strategy began to succeed. On 13 October Callaghan was obliged to tell parliament that, for the first time, rioters in Belfast seemed to be equipped with firearms, and British troops – they now numbered 9,000 – had been obliged to return fire. Once the troops began to use firearms in Catholic ghetto-areas, the IRA – which earlier had been accused of cowardice and inactivity by the Catholics of the Falls Road area – could pose as the defenders of the Catholic streets. With the open appearance of the new Provisional IRA towards the end of 1969, the Catholic population became the natural habitat of the gunmen. As Conor Cruise O'Brien put it:

> The formidable thing about the new IRA, the Pro-
> visionals, was its simple relevance to the situation. Any
> ordinary patriotic Catholic, clinging to the dual pieties of
> his community, could identify with the Provisionals. There
> was no 'taint of Communism' about them, nothing
> puzzling or foreign at all. And there was no nonsense about
> them either. They were not forever telling people that the
> Protestant workers were really on the same side as
> ourselves, when anyone could see – especially in and after
> August 1969 – that these same Protestant workers were out
> to kill us. The Provisionals weren't telling people to turn
> the other cheek if a misguided Protestant brother had a
> bash at them. There had been enough of that. If the
> Protestants wanted trouble now, they could have it. These
> Provisionals weren't like the old crowd – they were getting
> the guns and they were ready to use them.[43]

The victory of the Conservatives in the June 1970 elections was taken by Ulster Catholics as a signal that tougher measures would be used against them. In fact there was bi-party agreement at Westminster, and the Conservatives, though traditionally allies of the Ulster Unionists, were just as insistent that the reforms should be applied with all possible speed. But the emotional mechanics in which an army was poised on the edge of a Belfast ghetto already thickly penetrated by the IRA almost inevitably took over from deliberate policy. Early in July, the Army carried out its first house-to-house search in the Falls area. They unearthed an impressive quantity of weapons: 28 rifles, 2 carbines, 52 hand-guns, 100 bombs, 20 pounds of gelignite and 20,000 rounds of ammunition But four civilians were killed, and it was the end of the love-affair between the Catholic population and British troops. On 6 February 1971 the IRA killed their first British soldier on duty, followed by the murder of three British off-duty soldiers on 11 March. Thereafter it was war.

The first, and perhaps inevitable, political casualty was Chichester-Clark. He had really stood for nothing, except perhaps the 'good old days', now gone beyond recall. He was replaced by Brian Faulkner, who did stand for something: the stick as opposed to the carrot. Faulkner took over on 23 March 1971, and declared that his object was to restore confidence throughout the whole community. For this purpose he appointed a Labour MP, David Bleakley, as Minister of Community Relations, and in July held an 'inter-party meeting' with members of the Social Democratic Labour Party (which had largely replaced the old Nationalist Party). But rioting, bombing, shootings, killings, marches, demonstrations and arson continued to increase, and in Britain influential voices began to be raised urging that the British army, which was now involved in daily incidents with Catholics, should be pulled out.

Faulkner's response came on 9 August 1971, when he invoked Section 12 of the Special Powers Act and introduced internment without trial. The first arrests were carried out by the Army at 4 a.m. that morning in raids throughout the province. The next day riots in Belfast and Londonderry led to the deaths of thirteen people, the burning of hundreds of houses, and the flight of 7,000 refugees to the Republic of Ireland. The authorities claimed that the internment policy had been successful, some 70 per cent of the 'wanted' men being in custody; but there was no notable decline in the number of explosions and other incidents attributable to the

IRA. In August the government issued a White Paper enumerating the list of reforms carried out since 1969; it was impressive, and might have been highly effective if carried through in the mid-1960s.[44] But by the end of 1971 the Catholics were more concerned by the numbers of those held without trial, and British Ministers by the rising total of deaths: 173 in 1971 against a mere 25 the year before. What also worried London was the boycott of Stormont by all the Catholic Members, the withdrawal of Catholics from local government, and the refusal of over 20,000 Catholics to pay rent and rates. And on 30 January 1972 came 'Bloody Sunday' in Londonderry, when British paratroops shot dead thirteen Catholic demonstrators.

On 22 March 1972, the Westminster government acted. Faulkner and his deputy, Senator John Andrews, were summoned to 10 Downing Street, and in effect given an ultimatum: to accept the transfer of responsibility for law and order to Westminster, and the phasing out of internment, or to see the end of Stormont. After two days of argument, well described in Faulkner's memoirs, the demand was rejected, and direct rule imposed.[45] Internment had alienated the Catholic population, and had clearly been a failure. But what was direct rule designed to do? Its first effect was to alienate the bulk of the Protestant population, which had regarded Stormont as 'their' parliament. A natural consequence was the disintegration of the old Unionist Party. Two groups had already formed: the Democratic Unionist Party, under Ian Paisley, and the Vanguard Movement under William Craig. Obviously, having demolished the Unionist edifice at Stormont, the Conservative government had to replace it with something which united, rather than divided, the province. Secondly, they had to show that direct rule was more acceptable to the Catholics than Stormont, and more effective in restoring order.

They failed on both counts. William Whitelaw, Secretary of State for Northern Ireland, began releasing detainees, and even had Sean Mac Stiofain and two other IRA leaders secretly flown to London for a meeting on 7 July 1972. This was immediately followed by a spasm of appalling violence in which twenty-one civilians, eleven soldiers and one police-man were killed, and 7,000 refugees fled to the Republic. On one day alone – 21 July or 'Bloody Friday' – twenty-two IRA bombs killed eleven people. Thereafter the destruction of life and property continued without respite. On the political side, the government summoned an all-party conference at Darlington on 25 September 1972. Only three groups, the Unionists, the SDLP and the centre Alliance Party, sent delegates, but all parties produced proposals, which were printed as appendices to the government's views in a Green Paper for discussion, *The Future of Northern Ireland*.[46] What the discussion and the papers presented revealed was general agreement on a wider-based Assembly, with some sort of committee system for spreading the responsibility for power across the sectarian divide.

In March 1973, having held a poll in Northern Ireland which revealed that a majority (57.4 per cent of the total electorate) still favoured the province remaining part of the United Kingdom, the British government presented its own constitutional proposals. These were for an Assembly of eighty members, elected by proportional representation for four-year periods and an Executive composed of Heads of Departments chosen from the Assembly, each assisted by an inter-party committee, chosen from different parties, under the general guidance of a UK Secretary of State. The Secretary of State would have to be satisfied that the Executive was representative of Northern Ireland opinion as a whole before he authorized the devolution of political power from Westminster to the Assembly.[47]

The proposals also laid down that the maintenance of law and order was to be a 'reserved matter', under Westminster control; that a Charter of Human Rights would provide against discrimination; and that the government favoured, and would facilitate, any institutional arrangements to bring about co-operation between the governments of Northern Ireland and the Republic. Catholic reaction to the proposals was more cordial than Protestant; but the government pressed ahead with the Northern Ireland Act, which became law on 18 July 1973. It abolished the 1920 Act and replaced Stormont with the new Assembly. If no Executive had been formed and was functioning by the end of March 1974, the whole scheme would lapse.

With this pistol held at his head, Brian Faulkner consented on 21 November 1973 to head an executive formed from the Unionist, SDLP and Alliance parties. At a conference at Sunningdale in Berkshire, held in December and attended by the Irish Prime Minister, Liam Cosgrave, two principal points were agreed: the Irish government accepted that no change in the status of Northern Ireland could take place until a majority of the people of Ulster desired it; the Unionists, on the other hand, accepted the idea of a Council of Ireland, resurrected from the old 1920 Act, formed from the Dail and the new Assembly. The Executive took office in January.

This fragile edifice soon came apart. At the Westminster elections in February 1974, it became apparent that Faulkner could not deliver his party: of the twelve Ulster seats, anti-Faulkner 'Loyalists' captured eleven. In May, the Ulster Workers' Council, backed by Protestant trade unionists, called a general strike, demanding the rejection of the Sunningdale Agreement and the repeal of the 1973 Constitution Act.[48] The strike was so successful that Faulkner urged the new Secretary of State, Merlyn Rees, that he had no alternative but to negotiate with the Workers' Council. When Rees refused, the Unionists resigned, and the whole Executive collapsed on 28 May.

Since the failure of the new Assembly and the Sunningdale Agreement, neither Labour nor Conservative ministers have been able to devise any constitutional formula which

commands general acceptance in Northern Ireland. Within
Ulster, there has been a general fragmentation of the political
structure. No political leader and no organized group has
been able to speak for the whole, or even the majority, of the
Catholic community in Ulster. No commanding figure of the
centre has arisen to bridge the daunting gap between the two
communities. No new Carson has emerged to reunite and
lead the Unionists. From 1974 Enoch Powell attempted to be
such a charismatic figure, and failed. In May 1977 Ian Paisley
touched the limits of his influence when he called a general
strike and met with only a puny response. Since the death of
Brian Faulkner in March 1977, the Unionist Party has failed
to produce an acceptable and forceful successor. The
imposition of direct rule has produced a foreseeable result: the
destruction of the representative nature of Ulster politics.

In the meantime, the British government has continued to
discharge its elementary obligation to keep the peace, after a
fashion. The Army, which reached a maximum strength of
21,266 in July 1972 during 'Operation Motorman', to clear
'no-go' areas in Londonderry and Belfast, has since settled
down at a level of around 14,000.[49] It has not succeeded in
destroying the IRA or in imposing an acceptable level of
security. It has had to face many accusations of brutality and
excessive use of force.[50] A number of official bodies have
inquired into various aspects of the security operations, have
pronounced judgments, made criticisms, offered suggestions
and laid down new procedures and recommendations.[51]
These official findings have, in turn, led to minority reports
and vociferous objections by private bodies and individuals.[52]
Both the United Nations and the European Courts have
looked into such allegations. Seldom, perhaps never before, in
history has a military force been subjected to such close
scrutiny of its conduct, over so long a period, and by such a
variety of umpires, and emerged with such credit. Indeed, if
nothing else has been achieved, the British Army has
contrived to prove, by its conduct over the past decade, that

Britain has no other object in Ulster but to secure a lasting peace and a just settlement. And that, perhaps, is a more important object gained than military victory. If there is one lesson the history of Ireland teaches, it is that military victory is not enough.

Epilogue

In his book about his ministerial dealings with Ireland, James Callaghan recounts a significant little exchange with the Reverend Ian Paisley. In the course of a difficult conversation, and thinking to utter a sentiment with which no one – not even an Ulster religious leader – could conceivably disagree, Callaghan remarked: 'You know, Mr Paisley, we are all the children of God.' Quick as a flash came the implacable answer: 'No, we are not, Mr Callaghan. *We are all the children of wrath.*'

Are the Irish, indeed, the children of wrath? Looking back over their history, we are tempted to think so, and to credit Edmund Spenser with a gift of prophecy when he wrote of Ireland that 'Almighty God hath not yet appointed the time of her reformation', but 'reserveth her in this unquiet state still for some secret scourge, which shall by her come into England'. The outstanding fact of the British–Irish connection has been the fearful toll it has exacted of human life, and not merely of the anonymous multitude. How many holders of famous names in that long story have died by violence or on the scaffold! 'Silken Thomas' Kildare and Thomas Wentworth, Archbishop Plunkett and Phelim O'Neill, Lord Edward Fitzgerald and Wolfe Tone, Robert Emmet and Lord Frederick Cavendish, Pearse and Connolly, Casement and MacBride, Collins and Henry Wilson, Childers and Rory O'Connor, Brugha and O'Higgins, Airey Neave and Mountbatten – and how many more to come?

Nor must we forget those men who were crushed by the Irish problem and died disheartened or despairing: Tyrone and Tyrconnell, Grattan and Flood, O'Connell and Mitchel, Isaac Butt and Parnell, Redmond and Griffith, Carson and

Faulkner – all of them believing their life's work had been ruined or wasted. It is sad to think how few of those who have devoted their whole careers to Ireland have died in their beds, full of years and honours and fulfilment, De Valera and Craig being perhaps the only instances.

It is often argued that, except for short periods of crisis, Ireland has never stood in the forefront of British policy or attracted the services of her best statesmen and thinkers. It is true that, for the British, Ireland has proved a well-stocked graveyard of reputations. It effectively destroyed Richard II and the Earl of Essex, it fatally damaged the cause of Charles I and James II, it wrecked the careers of a long procession of Lords Lieutenant and ministers, of whom we remember only a handful – Forster and Wyndham, Seely and Greenwood, for instance. A few used Ireland to add to their contemporary fame: Mountjoy and Cromwell, Castlereagh and Balfour. But today Mountjoy survives only as the name of a prison, and the other three have been condemned by posterity. It must be admitted that few great men have willingly sought out Ireland as a life-work: therein, perhaps, lies one reason for Britain's failure there. On the other hand, the list of those who, at one time or another, have marshalled their wits and energies to settling Ireland is impressive: Henry II and William Marshall, Sir Henry Sidney and Sir Walter Raleigh, Edmund Spenser and Sir John Davies, Thomas Wentworth and William of Orange, Ormonde and Chesterfield, Dean Swift and Edmund Burke, Pitt the Younger and Robert Peel, Morley and Lecky, Gladstone and Asquith, Lloyd George and Churchill – no mean roll-call.

Most of these men failed because Ireland was merely a passing episode in otherwise fruitful lives of public service and creative labour. But most of them accepted the fundamental misconception to which even the more enlightened British statesmen and pundits have clung: that if only Britain gave Ireland justice, prosperity and wise government, the British connection would be accepted by her people. Alas, it is of the essence of wise government to know when to absent itself. Britain has learned by bitter experience in Ireland that there is no substitute for independence.

But it is not the only conclusion we may draw from the past. British–Irish relations are not so much a matter of human choice as of geographical determinism. 'God hath so placed us together unavoidably', to use a phrase of Milton's. If Irishmen who have resisted the British presence have sought aid from Britain's enemies – Spain and Rome, France and Germany, and today from those who finance and profit from international terrorism – so also Britain, in defending herself, has been obliged to bring Ireland into her calculations. There never will be a time when Britain will be able to remain indifferent to events in Ireland. To that extent, Britain will always have an 'Irish problem'; and, *a fortiori*, Ireland will always have an 'English problem'.

Yet we need not end on a note of despondency. Despite all the clashes between the English and the Irish, which necessarily form the substance of such a book as this, we must remember there is also a great unwritten and largely unrecorded story of Anglo-Irish relations: a story of countless friendships and innumerable intermarriages, of shared enthusiasms and dangers, mutual interests and common objectives. We have the same language and literature, the same legal tradition and parliamentary matrix. Whatever happens in the future, we can be sure that Irish and English will always have more to unite than to divide them.

At the moment a stalemate has been reached in Ulster. In that stricken province, whose living standard has now fallen behind the Republic's, courts judging political crimes operate without juries, one of the salient features of English and Irish law. Yet political crime remains unconquered, and spreads from time to time to Britain and the Republic also. No acceptable solution seems to be in sight. But, if history is any guide, the present phase of violence may now be nearing its end, and the Irish problem may be about to subside into one of the prolonged periods of uneasy calm which punctuate its disorders. If so, we must try to make use of another lesson our history teaches: to profit from such a relaxation of tension and to use the calm thus granted to devise 'a new reformation of that realm' – rather than to wait for the next explosion.

Sources

Chapter One: Gaelic Ireland and the English Pale

1. Francis John Byrne, *Irish Kings and High Kings* (London 1973), 7ff.

2. Richard Howlett (ed.), *Chronicles of the Reigns of Stephen, Henry II and John* (Rolls Series, London 1884–5), I, 167.

3. Byrne, *op. cit.*, 270–3.

4. W. L. Warren, *Henry II* (London 1973), 189.

5. D. A. Binchy, 'The linguistic and historical value of the Irish law tracts', *Proceedings of the British Academy*, xxix (1943).

6. A. O. Gwynne, *History of Irish Catholicism*, vol. II: 'The Twelfth-Century Reform' (Dublin 1968); J. A. Watt, *The Church and the Two Nations in Medieval Ireland* (Cambridge 1970).

7. Byrne, *op. cit.*, 270ff.

8. A. Saltman, *Theobald Archbishop of Canterbury* (London 1956), 95.

9. Text of *Laudabiliter* in Edmund Curtis and R. B. McDowell (eds), *Irish Historical Documents, 1172–1922* (London 1943), 17–18.

10. E. H. Scott and P. X. Martin (eds and trns), *Expugnatio Hibernica* (Dublin 1978), 145–7.

11. Cf. J. F. O'Doherty, 'Rome and the Anglo-Norman invasion of Ireland', *Irish Ecclesiastical Record*, 42 (1933), 31–45; and M. P. Sheehy, 'The Bull *Laudabiliter*: A Problem in Medieval diplomatique and history', *Journal of the Galway Archaeological and Historical Society*, 29 (1961), 45–70.

12. C. C. J. Webb (ed.), *Metalogicon* (Oxford 1929), 217–18.

13. Robert de Torigny in *Chronicles of the Reign of Stephen, Henry II and Richard I*, IV, 81–315. See Warren, *op. cit.*, 195.

14. Warren, *op. cit.*, 192.

15. For the Norman invasion see G. H. Orpen, *Ireland under*

the Normans (Oxford 1911–20), I, 141ff.

16. Warren, *op. cit.*, 199.

17. The pipe rolls of 17 Henry II and 18 Henry II give details of the expedition's equipment.

18. *Expugnatio Hibernica*, 98–9.

19. *Ibid.*, 101.

20. Text of Alexander's letters in *Irish Historical Documents*, 19ff.

21. Text of treaty in *Irish Historical Documents*, 22ff.

22. Warren, *op. cit.*, 205.

23. Sidney Painter, *William Marshall* (Baltimore 1933).

24. Edmund Curtis, *History of Medieval Ireland from 1086–1513* (2nd edn, London 1938).

25. J. F. Lydon, *The Lordship of Ireland in the Middle Ages* (Dublin 1972).

26. Harold G. Leask, *Irish Castles and Castellated Houses* (Dundalk 1941).

27. Orpen, *op. cit.*, IV, 274.

28. A. J. Otway-Ruthven, *A History of Medieval Ireland* (London 1968), and in *Irish Historical Studies*, VI, 261–70 and VII, 1–16.

29. A. McKerrall, 'West Highland mercenaries in Scotland', *Scottish Historical Review*, xxx (1951).

30. Text in *Irish Historical Documents*, 38ff.

31. *Annals of Ulster* (Rolls Series), II, 433.

32. Robin Frame, 'Power and Society in the Lordship of Ireland, 1272–1377', *Past and Present*, 76 (August 1977).

33. *Annals of the Four Masters*, III, 761.

34. For examples, between James Butler Earl of Ormonde and the O'Kennedys in 1336 and 1356, see *Irish Historical Documents*, 48ff.

35. Text in *Irish Historical Documents*, 52ff.

36. *Ibid.*, 59f.

37. *A Discovery of the True Causes why Ireland was never Entirely Subdued and brought under Obedience of the Crown of England*, in *Historical Tracts by Sir John Davies* (Dublin 1787).

38. Edmund Curtis, *A History of Ireland* (Dublin 1964), Chapter 9.

39. Leask, *op. cit.*

40. Text in *Irish Historical Documents*, 72ff.; see H. G. Richardson and G. O. Sayles, *The Irish Parliament in the Middle Ages* (Philadelphia 1952).

41. Richardson and Sayles, *op. cit.*, 274; *Documents* 83ff.

42. S. B. Chrimes, *Henry VII* (London 1972), 257ff.

43. Text in *Documents*, 78f.

Chapter Two: Conquest and Plantation

1. Quoted in Nicholas P. Canny, *The Elizabethan Conquest of Ireland* (London 1976).

2. Wotton to Throgmorton, 25 December 1561, British Museum Addit. Mss 35, 380, f.230.

3. Canny, *op. cit.*, 30.

4. Curtis, *History of Ireland*, 185.

5. Quoted in Canny, *op. cit.*

6. Quoted in A. L. Rowse, *The Expansion of Elizabethan England* (London 1955).

7. Smith to Burghley, 6 March 1574.

8. Quoted in Canny, *op. cit.*

9. James Spedding, *Life and Times of Sir Francis Bacon*, VI, 207.

10. Edmund Spenser, *A View of the State of Ireland in 1596*, printed in W. L. Renwick (ed.), *Complete Works of Spenser* (London 1934), IV.

11. E. Edwards, *Life of Sir Walter Ralegh* (London 1868), I, 108.

12. *HMC Salisbury, Mss*, X, 18.

13. Quoted by J. B. Black, *The Reign of Elizabeth* (Oxford 1936), 473–4.

14. Arthur Collins (ed.), *Sidney Papers* (London 1746), I, 23.

15. *Ibid.*, 24–5.

16. Edwards, *op. cit.*

17. Rokeby to Cecil, 15 April 1570, quoted in Canny, *op. cit.*

18. Cyril Falls, *Elizabeth's Irish Wars* (London 1950).

19. William Camden, *Annals* (London 1688).

20. Cyril Falls, *Mountjoy: Elizabethan General* (London 1955).

21. J. Maclean (ed.), *Letters from Sir Robert Cecil to Sir George Carew* (Camden Society, London 1864), 148.

22. Fynes Moryson, *An itinerary containing his ten years' travel* (London 1617), II, 268.

23. *Ibid.*, 191.

24. *Ibid.*, 262.

25. *Ibid.*, 454.

26. *Ibid.*, III, 189–90.

27. G. B. Harrison, *Letters of Queen Elizabeth* (London 1968), 296–301.

28. For the decision ending gavelkind, see *Documents*, 126ff.

29. Davies, *op. cit.*, 199.

30. *Ibid.*, 201, 211.

31. For the 'Conditions to be Observed by the British Undertakers', 1610, see *Documents*, 128ff.

32. Curtis, *History of Ireland*, 226–34.

33. Text in *Documents*, 133ff.

34. For Omonde, see Thomas Carte, *Life of James Duke of Ormonde*, 6 vols (Oxford 1851).

35. Thomas L. Coonan, *The Irish Catholic Confederacy and the Puritan Revolution* (Dublin 1954), 45.

36. Oliver Lawson Dick (ed.), *Aubrey's Brief Lives* (London 1962), 138.

37. For Boyle's diary and correspondence see A. B. Grosart (ed.), *The Lismore Papers*, 10 vols (London 1886–8).

38. R. Bagwell, *Ireland under the Stuarts*, 3 vols (London 1906–16), I, 203–4.

39. H. F. Kearney, *Strafford in Ireland, 1633–41* (New York 1960).

40. A selection is published in Mary Agnes Hickson, *Ireland in the Seventeenth Century, or the Irish Massacres of 1641–42*, 2 vols (London 1884).

41. W. D. Love, 'Civil War in Ireland: Appearance in

three centuries of historical Writing', *Emery University Quarterly* (Summer 1966).

42. Quoted in M. Percival-Maxwell, 'The Ulster Rising of 1641 and the Depositions', *Irish Historical Studies* (September 1978).

43. *Ibid.*, 165, especially for references in fn. 78.

44. Texts in *Documents*, 152ff and 156ff.

45. For the role of Ormonde in the 'War of the Three Kingdoms', see Winifred, Lady Burghclere, *Life of James, First Duke of Ormonde*, 2 vols (London 1912).

Chapter Three: From Cromwell to the Boyne

1. W. C. Abbott, *Writings and Speeches of Oliver Cromwell*, 4 vols (Cambridge, Mass. 1937–47).

2. *Ibid.*, II, 107.

3. For Cromwell's behaviour, see Antonia Fraser, *Cromwell: our Chief of Men* (London 1973), 326ff.

4. S. R. Gardiner, *History of the Commonwealth and Protectorate*, 4 vols (London 1903), I, 118 and fn. 2.

5. According to Grotius, *De Jure Belli ac Pacis* (1625), then the standard authority.

6. Abbott, *op. cit.*

7. Fraser, *op. cit.*, 337 fn.

8. A. Clark (ed.), *Wood's Life and Times*, 2 vols (Oxford 1891), I, 171–2.

9. Abbott, *op. cit.*, II, 127.

10. Fraser, *op. cit.*, 339.

11. Abbott, *op. cit.*, II, 140.

12. For Catholic documents on the civil war in Ireland, see S. J. Kavanagh (ed.), *Commentarius Rinucinianus etc*, 6 vols (Irish Manuscripts Commission, Dublin 1932–49); for the royalist side, see J. T. Gilbert (ed.), *Sir Richard Bellings, History of the Irish Confederation and War in Ireland*, 7 vols (Dublin 1882–91).

13. For the radical side of Cromwell, see Christopher Hill, *God's Englishman: Oliver Cromwell and the English Revolution*

(London 1970).

14. Abbott, *op. cit.*, II, 145.

15. Clarendon's historical writings on Ireland are in *The history of the rebellion and civil wars in Ireland* (Dublin 1720).

16. Texts in C. S. Firth and R. S. Rait (eds), *Acts and Ordinances of the Interregnum*, 3 vols (London 1911); Summarized in Peter Berresford Ellis, *Hell or Connaught: the Cromwellian Colonisation of Ireland, 1652–1660* (London 1975), 50ff.

17. Ellis, *op. cit.*; see also Coonan, *op. cit.*, and J. P. Prendergast, *The Cromwellian Settlement of Ireland* (Dublin 1922 edn.).

18. Dick, *op. cit.*, 302ff.

19. For Petty's writing, see *The history of the survey of Ireland, commonly called the Down survey, 1655–6*, edited by T. A. Larcom (Dublin 1851); and *The Political Anatomy of Ireland* (London 1672).

20. Gerard Boate, *Ireland's Natural History* (London 1652).

21. Ellis, *op. cit.*, 28–9.

22. Curtis, *op. cit.*, 256ff.

23. Text of 1662 Act in *Documents*, 158ff.

24. Karl S. Bottigheimer, 'The Restoration Land Settlements: a structural view', *Irish Historical Studies*, xviii (1972–3).

25. W. D. Macray (ed.), 'Notes which passed at meetings of the Privy Council, between Charles II and the Earl of Clarendon, 1660–7', *Roxburgh Club* (London 1896), 498.

26. For the church, see W. A. Phillips (ed.), *History of the Church of Ireland*, 3 vols (London 1933–4).

27. Antonia Fraser, *Charles II* (London 1979), 409; A. Curtayne, *The Trial of Oliver Plunkett* (London 1953).

28. For James II's Declaratory Act 1689, see *Documents*, 169ff.

29. For William III in Ireland, see Stephen B. Baxter, *William III* (London 1966).

30. Text of civil treaty in *Documents*, 171ff.

31. J. G. Simms, *The Williamite Confiscation in Ireland* (London 1956).

32. James Hewitt, *Eye-witnesses to Ireland in Revolt* (Reading 1974), 33.

Chapter Four: Rebellion and Union

1. Text in *Documents*, 186.

2. For the eighteenth-century church see Phillips, *op. cit.*

3. M. J. MacManus, *Irish Cavalcade, 1550–1850* (London 1939), 126.

4. Text of 1666 Act in *Documents*, 179f.

5. G. N. Clark, *The Later Stuarts, 1660–1714* (2nd edn, Oxford 1955), 320–1.

6. Letter to Alexander Pope, 1 June 1728.

7. Letter to Bolingbroke, 21 March 1729.

8. Thomas Sheridan, *Life of Dean Swift* (London 1785), 227.

9. For Berkeley's ideas see L. C. Tipton, *Berkeley: the Philosophy of Immaterialism* (London 1974).

10. Quoted in Isaac Krammick, *The Rage of Edmund Burke: Portraits of an Ambivalent Conservative* (New York 1977), 61.

11. Curtis, *op. cit.*, 300.

12. Arthur Young, *A Tour in Ireland* (London 1780).

13. James Boswell, *Life of Johnson* (1770) (Everyman edition 1960), I, 389.

14. For the Relief Acts of 1771 and 1774, see W. E. H. Lecky, *A History of Ireland in the Eighteenth Century*, 5 vols (London 1892), II, 191–6; text of 1778 Act in *Documents*, 194ff.

15. Text of 1782 Relief Act in *Documents*, 196ff.

16. Texts in *Documents*, 203ff.

17. For Burke's view on Ireland, see T. H. D. Mahoney, *Edmund Burke and Ireland* (London 1960), and Matthew Arnold (ed.), *Burke's Letters, Speeches and Tracts on Irish Affairs* (London 1881).

18. H. Montgomery Hyde, *The Rise of Lord Castlereagh*

(London 1933), 54–65. See also J. H. Whyte, 'Landlord Influence at elections in Ireland, 1760–1885', *English Historical Review*, 80 (1965), and P. Jupp, 'County Down Elections', *Irish Historical Studies*, 18 (1972–3).

19. For the English connection see E. M. Johnston, *Great Britain and Ireland, 1760–1800: a study in political administration* (St Andrews 1963).

20. L. M. Cullen, *An Economic History of Ireland since 1660* (London 1972), 87ff.

21. For Beresford see William Beresford (ed.), ·*The Correspondence of the Rt. Hon. John Beresford, illustrative of the last thirty years of the Irish Parliament*, 2 vols (London 1854).

22. For Grattan, see his son's life, Henry Grattan, *Memoirs of the Life and Times of the Rt. Hon. Henry Grattan*, 5 vols (London 1839–46).

23. Text of 1793 Act in *Documents*, 198ff.

24. Curtis, *op. cit.*, 334–5.

25. Rosamund Jacob, *The Rise of the United Irishmen, 1791–4* (London 1937).

26. Hereward Senior, *Orangeism in Ireland and Britain, 1795–1836* (London 1966).

27. Quoted in Thomas Pakenham, *The Year of Liberty: the Great Irish Rebellion of 1798* (London 1969), 47.

28. *Ibid.*, 98

29. Sir Jonah Barrington, *Historic Memoirs of Ireland* (London 1833).

30. Pakenham, *op. cit.*, 123.

31. *Ibid.*, 144ff.

32. *Ibid.*, 265.

33. Printed in *Faulkner's Dublin Journal*, 12 July 1798.

34. Pakenham, *op. cit.*, 231.

35. *Ibid.*, 289–90.

36. *Ibid.*, 339–46, 350.

37. 3rd Marquess of Londonderry (ed.), *Memoirs and Correspondence of Castlereagh*, 12 vols (London 1848–53), III, 333.

38. C. J. Bartlett, *Castlereagh* (London 1966), 25.

39. S. B. Inglis, *The Freedom of the Press in Ireland, 1784–1841* (London 1954), 52ff. See also R. B. McDowell, *Irish Public Opinon 1750–1800* (London 1944).

40. Sir Jonah Barrington, *The Rise and Fall of the Irish Nation* (London 1833).

41. *Castlereagh Correspondence*, III, 339–40; for the Act itself, see *Documents*, 208ff.

42. Bartlett, *op. cit.*, 6.

43. Quoted in Pakenham, *op. cit.*, 339 (British Museum, Addit. Mss 37844/273).

44. J. C. Beckett, *The Anglo-Irish Tradition* (London 1976).

Chapter Five: Famine and Diaspora

1. For O'Connell, see Angus Macintyre, *The Liberator: Daniel O'Connell and the Irish Party, 1830–1847* (London 1965), and John O'Connell (ed.), *Life and Speeches of Daniel O'Connell MP*, 2 vols (Dublin 1846) and *Select Speeches* (Dublin 1854–5).

2. Elizabeth Longford, *Wellington: Pillar of State* (London 1972), 178–95.

3. See R. B. McDowell, *The Irish Administration, 1801–1914* (London 1964), and Galen Broeker, *Rural Disorder and Police Reform in Ireland, 1812–36* (London 1970).

4. Kevin Barry Nowland, *The Politics of Repeal* (London 1964).

5. Report in *The Nation*, 20 May 1843. Text of speech in *Documents*, 269ff.

6. Sir Charles Gavan Duffy, *Young Ireland: a Fragment of Irish History, 1840–5* (London 1896 edn).

7. Text in W. L. Renwick (ed.), *Complete Works of Spenser* (London 1934), IV.

8. Redcliffe N. Salaman, *The Influence of the Potato on the Course of Irish History* (Dublin 1943).

9. Cullen, *op. cit.*, 118ff.

10. *Ibid.*, 121.

11. Gustave de Beaumont, *L'Irlande, Sociale, Politique et*

Religieuse, 2 vols (Paris 1839); translated by W. C. Taylor (London 1839).

12. Trollope, *Autobiography,* Chapter 4; see James Pope-Hennessy, *Anthony Trollope* (London 1971), 71ff. Trollope was in Ireland in 1841–9.

13. Gordon N. Ray (ed.), *Letters and Private Papers of W. M. Thackeray* (Oxford 1945), II, 78; see also Gordon N. Ray, *Thackeray, the Uses of Adversity, 1811–46* (Oxford 1955), 292ff.

14. W. M. Thackeray, *An Irish Sketch-Book* (1843), Chapter 32.

15. *Ibid.,* Chapter 7.

16. J. T. Ward, *Sir James Graham* (London 1967), 224.

17. *Devon Commission on the Law and Practice in respect to the Occupation of Land in Ireland* (House of Commons 1845).

18. W. F. Moneypenny, *The Life of Benjamin Disraeli* (London 1912), II, 191–2.

19. Cecil Woodham-Smith, *The Great Hunger: Ireland 1845–9* (London 1962), 88–96.

20. James S. Donnelly Jr, *The Land and the People of Nineteenth-Century Cork: the Rural Economy and the Land Question* (London 1975), 73–4.

21. *Ibid.,* 82.

22. Ward, *op. cit.,* 228, 232; A. A. W. Ramsay, *Sir Robert Peel* (London 1971 reissue), 316ff.

23. For Trevelyan's own account, see his *The Irish Crisis, being a narrative of the measures for the relief of the distress caused by the great Irish famine of 1846–7* (2nd edn. London 1880).

24. R. D. Collison Black, *Economic Thought and the Irish Question, 1817–1870* (Cambridge 1960), 113, 115, 116, 117.

25. Charles Greville, *Journal of the Reign of Queen Victoria, 1837–52* (London 1885), II, 434–5.

26. Donnelly, *op. cit.,* 84.

27. *Ibid.,* 85.

28. E. Burritt, *A Journal on a Visit of Three Days to Skibbereen and its Neighbourhood* (London 1847), quoted in Donnelly, *op. cit.*

29. Pope-Hennessy, *op. cit.*, 115.

30. Donnelly, *op. cit.*, 88.

31. Quoted by Beckett, *op. cit.*, 93.

32. *Ibid.*, 101–2.

33. P. M. A. Bourke, 'The agricultural statistics of the 1841 census of Ireland: a critical review', *Economic History Review* (August 1965).

34. *Cork Examiner*, 21 May 1849.

35. Quoted in Donnelly, *op. cit.*, 118.

36. Jasper Ridley, *Lord Palmerston* (London 1970), 322–3.

37. *Census of Ireland 1901* (House of Commons Cmd 1190, 1902), Part II, 109.

38. Arnold Schreier, *Ireland and the American Emigration 1850–1900* (Milwaukee 1958), 3.

39. S. H. Cousebs, 'Regional death-rates in Ireland during the Great Famine from 1846–51', *Population Studies* (July 1960).

40. Cullen, *op. cit.*, 132–3.

41. From *The Untilled Field* (London 1903), republished in Frank O'Connor (ed.), *Modern Irish Short Stories* (Oxford World Classics 1964).

42. Cullen, *op. cit.*, 135.

43. Schreier, *op. cit.*, 172 (notes).

44. *Ibid.*, 6.

45. Desmond Ryan, *The Sword of Light: from the Four Masters to Douglas Hyde 1636–1939* (London 1939).

Chapter Six: Ascendancy Culture

1. Thomas Pakenham, *The Year of Liberty*, 32.

2. Maurice Craig, *Dublin, 1660–1860* (London 1952), 13ff.

3. For Leinster House, see J. P. Mahaffy, etc., *The Georgian Society Records of Eighteenth-century Domestic Architecture and Decoration in Dublin*, 5 vols (Dublin 1909–13), IV.

4. Constantia Maxwell, *A History of Trinity College, Dublin, 1591–1892* (Dublin 1946).

5. Aubrey, *op. cit.*, 139ff.

6. John Forster, *Life and Adventures of Oliver Goldsmith* (London 1848), Book One.

7. James Boswell, *Life of Dr Johnson* (Everyman Edition 1960), I, 619; II, 329.

8. *Ibid.*, I, 468; II, 57–8.

9. Kramnick, *op. cit.*, 191.

10. Harold Nicolson, *Helen's Tower* (London 1937).

11. For Gandon, see the life by his son, James Gandon, *The Life of James Gandon Esq.* (Dublin 1846).

12. *Personal Sketches of His Own Times*, 3 vols (London 1827–32).

13. Beckett, *op. cit.*, 69ff.

14. See M. S. Butler, *Maria Edgeworth, a Literary Biography* (Oxford 1972), and M. C. Hurst, *Maria Edgeworth and the Public Scene: Intellect, fine feeling and landlordism in the age of reform* (Oxford 1971).

15. William Bates, *The Maclise Portrait Gallery* (London 1883), 313ff.

16. For Lady Morgan, see W. H. Dixon (ed.), *Memoirs, Autobiography, Diaries and Correspondence of Lady Morgan*, 2 vols (London 1862).

17. Gordon N. Ray, *Thackeray: the Uses of Adversity*, 293–4.

18. Trollope, *Autobiography*, Chapter 4.

19. *Irish Sketch Book*, Chapter 17.

20. Pope-Hennessy, *op. cit.*, 84–5.

21. Quoted in Beckett, *op. cit.*

22. For Ferguson, see Lady Ferguson, *Sir Samuel Ferguson in the Ireland of his Day*, 2 vols (London 1896).

23. Ellmann, *op. cit.*, 105ff.

24. For the Irish literary movement, see Lennox Robinson, *Ireland's Abbey Theatre: a History, 1899–1951* (London 1951), and R. M. Kain, *Dublin in the Age of William Butler Yeats and James Joyce* (Oklahoma 1962).

25. See a recent study, Philip Edwards, *Threshold of a Nation: A Study of English and Irish Drama* (Cambridge 1979).

26. Ellmann, *op. cit.*, 228

27. See Maurice Collis, *Somerville and Ross: a Biography* (London 1968).

Chapter Seven: Home Rule and the Land

1. MacManus, *op. cit.*, 308–9.

2. A. C. Benson and Lord Esher (eds), *Letters of Queen Victoria* (first series, 1837–61; London 1907), II, 267–8.

3. John Mitchell, *Jail Journal*; quoted in MacManus, *op. cit.*, 314.

4. Cullen, *op. cit.*, 139–40.

5. *Ibid.*, 140; Seamus Brady published a series of articles on Lord Leitrim's diaries in the *Irish Press* (Dublin), 2–7 October 1967.

6. See J. H. Whyte, *The Independent Irish Party 1850–9* (London 1958), and *The Tenant League and Irish Politics in the 1850s* (Irish Historical Association, new edn 1966).

7. Elizabeth R. Hooker, *Readjustments of Agricultural Tenure in Ireland* (Chapel Hill 1938).

8. For Stephens, see Desmond Ryan, *The Fenian Chief: a biography of James Stephens* (Dublin 1967).

9. For the Irish in America and their political influence, see Carl Wittke, *The Irish in America* (Baton Rouge 1956), and T. N. Brown, *Irish-American Nationalism 1870–1890* (Philadelphia 1966).

10. Schreier, *op. cit.*, 125.

11. Leon O'Broin, *Fenian Fever: an Anglo-American Dilemma* (London 1971).

12. *Ibid.*, 47ff.

13. *Ibid.*, 67. See William D'Arcy, *The Fenian Movement in the United States 1858–86* (Washington 1947); for the Canadian incursions, see the *Canadian Historical Review* for 1955 and 1967.

14. O'Broin, *op. cit.*, 8.

15. *Ibid.*, 148.

16. *Ibid.*, 174–210.

17. *Ibid.*, 245–6.

18. W. E. Gladstone, *A Chapter of Autobiography* (London 1868); see Philip Magnus, *Gladstone: A Biography* (London 1954), 196ff.

19. John Brooke and Mary Sorensen (eds), *W. E. Gladstone, Autobiographica* (London, HMSO, 1971), 136.

20. J. J. Auchmuty, *Irish Education: a historical survey* (Dublin 1937).

21. P. M. H. Bell, *Disestablishment in Ireland and Wales* (London 1969); see also J. C. Beckett, 'Gladstone, Queen Victoria and the Disestablishment of the Irish Church, 1868-9', *Irish Historical Studies*, 13 (1962-3).

22. N. St John Stevas (ed.), *Collected Works of Walter Bagehot* (London 1978), XI, 183.

23. For the various land acts, see W. F. Bailey, *The Irish Land Acts: a short sketch of their history and development* (Dublin 1917); and J. E. Pomfret, *The Struggle for Land in Ireland, 1800-1923* (Princeton 1930).

24. Text of resolution of the Home Rule Conference 1873 in *Documents*, 276ff.

25. Cullen, *op. cit.*, 148-9.

26. For Isaac Butt, see David Thornley, *Isaac Butt and Home Rule* (London 1964).

27. *Documents*, 281.

28. N. R. Palmer, *The Irish Land League Crisis* (New Haven 1940).

29. For obstruction, see David Thornley, 'The Irish Home Rule Party and Parliamentary Obstruction, 1874-87', *Irish Historical Studies*, 12 (1960-1).

30. Magnus, *op. cit.*, 297-8.

31. For text of 1881 Act, see *Documents*, 262ff. For a critical analysis, see Barbara Solow, *The Land Question and the Irish Economy, 1870-1903* (Massachusetts 1971).

32. For Parnell and his strategy, see Conor Cruise O'Brien, *Parnell and his Party, 1880-90* (Oxford, rev. edn 1964).

33. Speech at Leeds, 7 October 1881; John Morley, *Life of Gladstone* (London 1903), III, 61.

34. D. A. Hamer, 'The Irish Question and Liberal Politics, 1880–1894', *Historical Journal,* 12 (1969).

35. D. A. Hamer, *John Morley: Liberal Intellectual in Politics* (Oxford 1968), 129–31.

36. For the Kilmainham Treaty, see Richard Hawkins, 'Gladstone, Forster and the Release of Parnell, 1882–8', *Irish Historical Studies,* 16 (1968–9).

37. T. Wemyss Reid, *Life of the Rt. Hon. W. E. Forster* (London, reprint 1970), 442–3.

38. Magnus, *op. cit.,* 304.

39. J. L. Garvin, *Life of Joseph Chamberlain* (London 1932–4), I, 604.

40. John Wilson, *CB: a Life of Sir Henry Campbell-Bannerman* (London 1973), 85–6.

41. Magnus, *op. cit.,* 337.

42. For Gladstone's mental development to Ireland, see J. L. B. Hammond, *Gladstone and the Irish Nation* (London, reprint 1964), and E. D. Steele, 'Gladstone and Ireland', *Irish Historical Studies,* 17 (1970–1).

43. Magnus, *op. cit.,* 341.

44. *Ibid.,* 349.

45. Robert Rhodes James, *Lord Randolph Churchill* (London 1959), 245ff.

46. Speech in Cork, 21 January 1885; text in *Documents,* 282ff.

47. See T. W. Moody, '*The Times* versus Parnell and Co., 1887–90', *Historical Studies,* vi (1965). The judges' report, however, severely implicated the Irish nationalists as a whole: Cmd. 5891, House of Commons 1890.

48. Magnus, *op. cit.,* 387.

49. For Gladstone's conduct, see Morley, *op. cit.,* III, 434ff.

50. For Parnell's fall, see F. S. L. Lyons, *The Fall of Parnell, 1890–1* (London 1960).

51. F. S. L. Lyons, *The Irish Parliamentary Party, 1890–1910* (London 1951), 16–19.

52. Blanche Dugdale, *Arthur James Balfour* (London 1939

edn), I, 93ff.

53. *Ibid.*, 100–101.

54. Conversation with Blanche Dugdale in 1928. *Ibid.*, 113.

55. Elizabeth Longford, *A Pilgrimage of Passion: the Life of Wilfred Scawen Blunt* (London 1979), 247; Blunt subsequently made public a garbled version of this conversation, which Balfour denied; Dugdale, *op. cit.*, 114.

56. Dugdale, *op. cit.*, 121.

57. Robert Rhodes James, *Lord Randolph Churchill* (London 1959), 233.

58. Magnus, *op. cit.*, 354, 397, 412.

59. A. G. Gardiner, *Life of Sir William Harcourt* (New York edn, n.d.), I, 559–60.

60. Hamer, *Morley*, 281.

61. Magnus, *op. cit.*, 414.

62. Brooke and Sorenson, *op. cit.*, 136.

63. J. W. Mackail and Guy Wyndham, *Life and Letters of George Wyndham* (London 1925), II, 454.

64. Text of Wyndham's 1903 Act in *Documents*, 267ff.

65. Figures in Hooker, *op. cit.*

66. Mackail and Wyndham, *op. cit.*, I, 87–105.

Chapter Eight: Ulster Resists, Dublin Rises

1. R. C. K. Ensor, *England 1870–1914* (Oxford 1952 edn), 451. For Redmond, see Denis Rolleston Gwynn, *The Life of John Redmond* (London 1932).

2. Padraic Colum, *Arthur Griffith* (Dublin 1959), 51.

3. For a Marxist account of Connolly, see C. D. Greaves, *The Life and Times of James Connolly* (London 1961); for his writings, Proinsias MacAonghusa and Liam O'Reagain (eds), *The Best of Connolly* (Cork 1967); see also Emmet Larkin, 'Socialism and Catholicism in Ireland', *Church History*, 33 (1964).

4. Text of speech in *Documents*, 310ff. See also Douglas Hyde, *A Literary History of Ireland* (Dublin 1967 edn).

5. Richard Ellmann, *Yeats: the Man and the Masks* (Oxford 1979 edn), 108–10.

6. She herself described her hair as 'gold-brown'; cf. her autobiography, Maud Gonne MacBride, *A Servant of the Queen* (London 1974 edn), 37; there is a portrait of her by Sarah Purser in the Dublin Municipal Gallery of Modern Art.

7. See Denis Donoghue, *Yeats* (London 1971), 38.

8. H. W. Nevinson, *Changes and Chances* (London 1923), 209–10.

9. Ensor, *op. cit.*, 270.

10. For the distribution of population by religion in Northern Ireland, see map printed in appendix of Geoffrey J. Hand (ed.), *Report of the Irish Boundary Commission 1925* (Shannon 1969). See Map 3 below, pp. 160–1.

11. Hereward Senior, *Orangeism in Ireland and Britain, 1795–1836* (London 1966).

12. N. W. Dewar, J. Brown and S. E. Long, *Orangeism: a New Historical Appreciation* (Belfast 1967).

13. For a Marxist-type analysis of the Ulster phenomenon, see Peter Gibbon, *The Origins of Ulster Unionism* (Manchester 1975).

14. Owen Dudley Edwards, *The Sins of Our Fathers: the roots of conflict in Northern Ireland* (Dublin 1970), especially Chapter 4, 'The Breaking of the Irish Working Class'.

15. Ensor, *op. cit.*, 451 fn. 2.

16. For Carson, see H. Montgomery Hyde, *Carson* (London 1953); for Unionism as a whole, see Patrick Buckland, *Irish Unionism*, 2 vols (Dublin 1972–3).

17. Harold Nicolson, *King George V: his Life and Reign* (London 1952), 148ff.

18. Hyde, *op. cit.*, 289–92; see also St John Ervine: *Craigavon, Ulsterman* (London 1949), 191–3.

19. Hyde, *op. cit.*, 298.

20. *Ibid.*, 310–11.

21. Robert Blake, *The Unknown Prime Minister: the life and times of Andrew Bonar Law* (London 1955), 129.

22. The Earl of Birkenhead, *FE: The Life of F. E. Smith* (London 1959 edn), 215.

23. Blake, *op. cit.*, 130-1.

24. Lord Winterton, *Orders of the Day* (London 1953), 38.

25. Printed in A. M. Gollin, *The Observer and J. L. Garvin, 1908-1914* (Oxford 1960), 388-9.

26. Full text of oath in *Documents,* 304.

27. Ervine, *op. cit.*, 234ff.

28. Stanley Salvidge, *Salvidge of Liverpool* (London 1938).

29. Hyde, *op. cit.*, 342-3.

30. Gwynn, *op. cit.*

31. Hyde, *op. cit.*, 352.

32. See A. P. Ryan, *Mutiny at the Curragh* (London 1956), and James Fergusson, *The Curragh Incident* (London 1964). For Gough, see Hyde, *op. cit.*, 357fn.

33. Randolph S. Churchill, *Winston S. Churchill, II: Young Statesman, 1901-14* (London 1967), 491ff, 499.

34. Gollin, *op. cit.*, 421.

35. H. H. Asquith, *Fifty Years in Parliament*, 2 vols (London 1926), II, 140-2, though Carson told Asquith after the war that he would have pleaded guilty: see Hyde, *op. cit.*, 359.

36. For the ICA, see R. M. Fox, *The History of the Irish Citizen Army* (Dublin 1943); for Larkin, see Emmet Larkin, *James Larkin, Irish Labour Leader, 1876-1947* (Cambridge, Mass. 1965).

37. Edgar Holt, *Protest in Arms: the Irish Troubles 1916-23* (London 1960), 53; see also F. X. Martin, *The Irish Volunteers, 1913-15; recollections and documents* (Dublin 1963).

38. For Pearse, see Louis N. LeRoux, *Patrick H. Pearse* (trns. by Desmond Ryan, Dublin 1932), and J. J. Horgan, *Parnell to Pearse* (Dublin 1948). For De Valera, see Lord Longford and T. P. O'Neill, *Eamon de Valera* (London 1970).

39. Brian Inglis, *Roger Casement* (London 1973), 258.

40. For the Buckingham Palace Conference, see Gwynne, *op. cit.*, 336-42, Blake, *op. cit.*, 215-18 and Hyde, *op. cit.*, 270-2.

41. A further proposal was made by Maurice Hankey,

Secretary to the Committee for Imperial Defence, that the boundary dispute be put forward for arbitration; this was rejected by the Ulstermen 'decisively'; see Stephen Roskill, *Hankey: Man of Secrets* (New York 1970), 133–4.

42. Philip Magnus, *Kitchener: Portrait of an Imperialist* (London 1958), 300; Holt, *op. cit.*, 61–2.

43. Holt, *op. cit.*, 63–4.

44. Inglis, *op. cit.*, 266.

45. For Markievicz, see Jacqueline Van Voris, *Constance de Markievicz in the Cause of Ireland* (Amherst, Mass. 1967).

46. For the Easter Rising, see Holt, *op. cit.*, Leon O'Broin, *Dublin Castle and the Easter Rising* (London 1970); and Owen Dudley Edwards and Fergus Pyle, *1916: the Easter Rising* (London 1968).

47. L. G. Redmond-Howard, *Six Days in the Irish Republic* (Dublin 1916), quoted in James Hewitt (ed.), *Eye-witnesses to Ireland in Revolt* (Reading 1974).

48. Mrs Hamilton Norway, *The Sinn Fein Rebellion as I Saw It* (Dublin 1916), quoted in Hewitt, *op. cit.*

49. Nora Connolly O'Brien, *Portrait of a Rebel Father* (London 1936), quoted in Hewitt, *op. cit.*

50. For the controversy over the so-called 'Black Diaries' of Casement, see Inglis, *op. cit.*, 373–88.

51. Arthur Conan Doyle, *The British Campaign in France and Flanders* (London 1918), III, 58–63.

52. Ellmann, *op. cit.*, Preface, XIV, 217–19.

Chapter Nine: Freedom and Partition

1. For Collins, see Rex Taylor, *Michael Collins* (London 1958).

2. For a general survey of the influence of the Church, see Emmet Larkin, *The Roman Catholic Church and the Creation of the Modern Irish State* (London 1975).

3. For a view of the convention, see Beckett, *op. cit.*, 125ff.

4. Text in *Documents*, 318–19.

5. Holt, *op. cit.*, 171.

6. *Ibid.*, 179.

7. David Fitzpatrick, *Politics and Irish Life, 1913–21* (Dublin 1977), 10.

8. For Wilson, see Sir C. E. Callwell, *Field-Marshal Sir Henry Wilson* (London 1927), II, 267ff; and Basil Collier, *Brasshat* (London 1961), both based on the Wilson Papers and diary.

9. Martin Gilbert, *Winston S. Churchill* (London 1975), IV, 447.

10. Government of Ireland Act 1920, 10 and 11 George V, cap 6–7. Extracts in John Magee, *Northern Ireland: Crisis and Conflict* (London 1974), 52ff. Wilson's diary: Callwell, *op. cit.*, II, 237; Gilbert, *op. cit.*, IV, 451.

11. For Greenwood, see *Dictionary of National Biography, 1941–50 Supplement*, article by M. R. D. Foot; for Macready, see Sir Nevil Macready, *Annals of an Active Life* (London 1924), II.

12. Callwell, *op. cit.*, II, 237; Gilbert, *op. cit.*, IV, 451.

13. For the terms of service of Cadets, see Cmd 1618 (HMSO 1922); Richard Bennett, *The Black and Tans* (London, revised edn 1976); for training, see Douglas V. Duff, *Sword for Hire* (London 1934), 58–61; and D. G. Bryce, *Englishmen and Irish Troubles: British Public Opinion and the Making of Irish Policy, 1918–22* (London 1972).

14. Thomas Jones, *Whitehall Diary, Volume III: Ireland 1918–25* (Oxford 1971), 16–23.

15. Bryce, *op. cit.*, 51 and footnote; Bennett, *op. cit.*, 76–7.

16. *House of Commons Debates*, Fifth Series, col. 946, 20 October 1920.

17. Macready, *op. cit.*, II, 497–8.

18. Bryce, *op. cit.*, 52.

19. Quoted in Joyce M. Nankivell and Sydney Loch, *Ireland in Travail* (London 1922), 68; Bryce, *op. cit.*, 43.

20. Macready, *op. cit.*, 497, 485.

21. Hugh Martin, *Ireland in Insurrection* (London 1921), 104–5.

22. Bennett, *op. cit.*

23. *Ibid.*, 94–109, 111–119.

24. Hankey Papers, quoted in Gilbert, *op. cit.*, IV, 453.

25. Gilbert, *op. cit.*, IV, 458ff.

26. Callwell, *op. cit.*, II, 263, 270.

27. Quoted in Gilbert, *op. cit.*, IV, 461.

28. Callwell, *op. cit.*, II, 265.

29. Bryce, *op. cit.*, 55fn.

30. Bennett, *op. cit.*, 222.

31. Middlemass, *op. cit.*, 55–62, 63–70.

32. Nicolson, *op. cit.*, 347; Middlemass, *op. cit.*, 76–7; see also Charles Townshend, *The British Campaign in Ireland 1919–21* (Oxford 1979).

33. Dorothy Macardle, *The Irish Republic* (London 1937); and Bennett, *op. cit.*

34. Text of King George V's speech is given in Middlemass, *op. cit.*, 78–9.

35. *Ibid.*, 89.

36. Frank Pakenham (Earl of Longford), *Peace by Ordeal* (London, 1972 reprint).

37. Middlemass, *op. cit.*, 129–30.

38. *Ibid.*, 156.

39. Pakenham, *op. cit.*, 188.

40. Middlemass, *op. cit.*, 180; for Irish cabinet debate, see Pakenham, *op. cit.*, 255–63.

41. Churchill, *The World Crisis: the Aftermath* (London 1929).

42. Birkenhead, *op. cit.*, 387–8.

43. Colum, *op. cit.* Text of Treaty in *Documents*, 322ff.

44. Hyde, *op. cit.*, 486–7.

45. *Dail Debates*, Session 21 December 1921–2 January 1922; Colum, *op. cit.*, 360.

46. For full text of report, plus maps, see Hand, *op. cit.*, For the political discussion leading to suppression of the Report, see Middlemass, *op. cit.*, 235–43.

47. Articles 6 and 7.

48. Timothy Patrick Coogan, *Ireland Since the Rising* (London 1966), 263.

49. *Ibid.*, 264-5. See also Maurice Manning, *The Blueshirts* (Dublin 1970).

50. See Coogan, *op. cit.*, 273ff, and his *The IRA* (New York 1970); see also Enno Stephan, *Spies in Ireland* (London 1962).

51. V. P. Hogan, *The Neutrality of Ireland in World War II* (Ann Arbor 1953).

52. Magee, *op. cit.*, 19.

53. Coogan, *Ireland since the Rising*, 118ff.

54. T. Ryle Dwyer, *Irish Neutrality and the USA* (New York 1977).

55. For Ulster during World War II, see John W. Blake, *Northern Ireland in World War II* (NI Stationery Office, Belfast 1956).

Chapter Ten: From Revolt to Stalemate

1. 10 and 11 George V, ch. 6, 7; extracts in Magee, *op. cit.*, 52ff.

2. 6 November 1933. Hyde, *op. cit.*, 490-1.

3. Speech at Poyntzpass, *Belfast Newsletter*, 13 July 1932; *House of Commons Debates, Northern Ireland*, XVI, cols 1091-93, 24 April 1934; quoted in John F. Harbinson, *The Ulster Unionist Party, 1882-1973* (Belfast 1974), 137.

4. *Belfast Newsletter*, 14 July 1947.

5. Magee, *op. cit.*, 98-9.

6. Cornelius O'Leary, *Irish Elections, 1918-77: Parties, Voters and Proportional Representation* (Dublin 1979), 113.

7. For election results, 1921-69, see Harbinson, *op. cit.*, Appendix A, 178ff; in 1925, when the official Unionists held 32 seats, there were 4 Independent Unionists.

8. Cornelius O'Leary, 'Northern Ireland, 1945-72', in J. J. Lee (ed.), *Ireland 1945-70* (Dublin 1979).

9. *Disturbances in Northern Ireland: Report of the Cameron Commission 1968* (Belfast, HMSO, Cmd 532, 1969), 69-70.

10. *Violence and Civil Disturbances in Northern Ireland in 1969*

(Belfast, HMSO, Cmd 566, 1972), 71.

11. Ervine, *op. cit.*, 423.

12. Magee, *op. cit.*, 76–7.

13. *Ibid.*, 76–9.

14. Harry Calvert, *Constitutional Law in Northern Ireland* (Belfast 1968); Magee, *op. cit.*, 57ff.

15. *The Future of Northern Ireland: a paper for discussion* (Green Paper; HMSO, London 1972).

16. James Callaghan, *A House Divided: the Dilemma of Northern Ireland* (London 1973), 89.

17. O'Leary, *op. cit.*, 156.

18. R. J. Lawrence, *The Government of Northern Ireland: Public Finance and Public Services, 1921–64* (Oxford 1965).

19. Gearoed O'Tuathaigh, 'Language, literature and culture in Ireland since the War', in J. J. Lee (ed.), *Ireland 1945–70* (Dublin 1979), 112.

20. *Ibid.*; information collected by Deasun Fennell in 1975; see also B. O. Cuiv, *Irish Dialects and Irish Speaking Districts* (Dublin 1971).

21. See L. S. Andrews, *A Black Paper on Irish Education: the Decline of Irish as a School Subject in the Republic of Ireland 1967–77* (Dublin 1978).

22. *Report on Economic Development* (Stationery Office, Dublin 1958); see Brendan M. Walsh, 'Economic Growth and Development 1945–70', in Lee, *op. cit.*, 29.

23. Timothy Patrick Coogan, *The IRA* (New York 1970), 343–4.

24. For Lemass, see B. Farrell, *Chairman or Chief* (Dublin 1971).

25. For the financial background, see Ronan Fanning, *The Irish Department of Finance, 1922–58* (Dublin 1978).

26. J. J. Lee, 'Continuity and Change in Ireland 1945–72', in Lee, *op. cit.*, 174.

27. See A. S. Cohan, *The Irish Political Elite* (Dublin 1972).

28. *Economic Development in Northern Ireland* (Belfast, Cmd 479, 1965).

29. Lee, *op. cit.*, 176.

30. Harbinson, *op. cit.*, 171.

31. Brian Faulkner, *Memoirs of a Statesman*, edited by J. Houston (London 1978), 40-1.

32. For the day-by-day narrative of events in the Ulster crisis, see Richard Deutsch and Vivien Magowan, *Northern Ireland: a Chronology of Events, 1968-74*, 3 vols (Belfast 1973-5).

33. *Cameron Commission*.

34. Magee, *op. cit.*, 25-6.

35. *Ibid.*, 117.

36. James Callaghan, *A House Divided: the Dilemma of Northern Ireland* (London 1973), 26.

37. R. H. S. Crossman, *The Diaries of a Cabinet Minister* (London 1977), III, 450-1, 22 April 1969.

38. *Ibid.*, 619, 15 August 1969.

39. It produced the *Report of the Advisory Committee on Police in Northern Ireland* (The Hunt Report), Cmd 535, October 1969.

40. It produced *Violence and Civil Disturbances in Northern Ireland in 1969* (The Scarman Report), Cmd 566, April 1972 (two volumes).

41. Crossman, *op. cit.*, III, 463-4, 29 April 1969.

42. For O'Neill's views, see *Ulster at the Crossroads* (London 1969) and *The Autobiography of Terence O'Neill* (London 1972).

43. Conor Cruise O'Brien, *States of Ireland* (London 1972).

44. *A Record of Constructive Change*, Cmd 588, August 1971.

45. Faulkner, *op. cit.*

46. *The Future of Northern Ireland: a Paper for Discussion* (London, HMSO, 1972).

47. *Northern Ireland Constitutional Proposals* (London, HMSO, Cmd 5259, 1973).

48. For the aims of the strikers, see *The Ulster General Strike: Strike Bulletins of the Workers Association* (2nd extended edition, Belfast 1974).

49. For army operations, see David Barzilay, *The British Army in Ulster*, 3 vols (Belfast 1973-8).

50. See, for instance, *The Mailed Fist: a Record of Army and Police Brutality* (Portglenoe 1972); Denis Faull and Raymond Murray, *British Army and Special Branch RUC Brutalities* (Cavan 1972); *Torture: The Record of British Brutality in Ireland* (Dublin 1972).

51. Some of the most important are: Edmund Compton, *Report of the Inquiry into Allegations against the Security Forces of Physical Brutality in Northern Ireland Arising Out of Events on 9 August 1971* (London, HMSO, Cmd 4823, 1971); Lord Widgery, *Report of the Tribunal Appointed to Inquire into the Events of Sunday 30 January 1972* (London, HMSO, 1972); Lord Parker, *Report of the Committee of Privy Councillors Appointed to Consider Procedures for the Interrogation of Persons Suspected of Terrorism* (London, HMSO, Cmd 4901, 1972); and Lord Diplock, *Report of the Commission to Consider Legal Procedures to Deal with Terrorist Activities in Northern Ireland* (London, HMSO, Cmd 5158, 1972).

52. See, for instance, Lord Gardiner's Minority Report to the Parker Report; Amnesty International, *Report of an Inquiry into Allegations of Ill-treatment in Northern Ireland* (London 1972); C. Kevin Boyle, *Widgery: a Critique* (Belfast 1972); and Samuel Dash, *Justice Denied: a Challenge to Lord Widgery's Report on 'Bloody Sunday'* (New York 1972).

Index